Backwaters of Global Prosperity

BACKWATERS OF GLOBAL PROSPERITY

*How Forces of Globalization and
GATT/WTO Trade Regimes
Contribute to the Marginalization
of the World's Poorest Nations*

Caf Dowlah

Westport, Connecticut
London

Library of Congress Cataloging-in-Publication Data

Dowlah, C. A. F.
  Backwaters of global prosperity : how forces of globalization and GATT/WTO trade
regimes contribute to the marginalization of the world's poorest nations / Caf
Dowlah.
    p. cm.
  Includes bibliographical references and index.
  ISBN 0–275–98043–X (alk. paper)
  1. Free trade—Developing countries.   2. Developing countries—Economic conditions.
3. Globalization—Economic aspects—Developing countries.   4. Developing countries—
Dependency on foreign countries.   5. World Trade Organization—Developing
countries.   6. General Agreement on Tariffs and Trade (Organization)   I. Title.
  HF2580.9.D68 2004
    382′.09172′4—dc22   2004011890

British Library Cataloguing in Publication Data is available.

Library of Congress Catalog Card Number: 2004011890
ISBN: 0–275–98043–X

First published in 2004

Praeger Publishers, 88 Post Road West, Westport, CT 06881
An imprint of Greenwood Publishing Group, Inc.
www.praeger.com

Printed in the United States of America

The paper used in this book complies with the
Permanent Paper Standard issued by the National
Information Standards Organization (Z39.48–1984).

10 9 8 7 6 5 4 3 2 1

Globalization has brought forth unprecedented prosperity to the contemporary world economy, but it has not raised all boats. By all indications, global prosperity has bypassed more than one-tenth of the world population who live in the poorest countries, which I call backwaters of global prosperity. This book is dedicated to those who find this trend disturbing, and unbecoming of humankind in the New Millennium.

Contents

Tables

Preface

This book is a culmination of my research, publications, and presentations on the GATT/WTO-related issues over the last decade. The work on this manuscript, however, began in earnest in 2000, with a Japan Foundation Fellowship. I am profoundly grateful to the Japan Foundation, and also to the Otaru University of Commerce, for providing me with excellent research and residential facilities. At Otaru, a panoramic seaport of Hokkaido, I also benefited immensely from frequent discussions with Professors Nakamura Hideo and Omori Yoshiaki of OUC, Richard Siddle of Sheffield University (a visiting professor at OUC at that time), and Tomichi Hoshino of Toyoma University, whose intense philosophical insights left indelible marks in my memory. A word of thanks is also due to the Kansai Gaidai University-Osaka, where an outline of the book drew a barrage of questions from enthusiastic audience in March 2001.

My research on this project, however, continued in 2002, when I moved to New York as a visiting scholar with Columbia University. I am grateful to Professor Phillip Oldenburg of the South Asian Institute for granting me unfettered access to the enormous library resources at Columbia. Completion of the project, however, took another full year, when I joined the economics faculty of the City University of New York. I am grateful to Dr. Joseph Culkin, chairman of the Department of Social Sciences, and Dr. Eduwardo Marti, president of the CUNY-Queensborough College, for actively encouraging my research through course release and other supports.

I owe a word of thanks to scores of international organizations, like the World Bank, the US Agency for International Development (USAID), the United Nations Development Program (UNDP), the World Food Program (WFP), German GTZ, and other institutions that supported my research on the GATT/WTO-related issues over the last decade. This book lavishly borrows from those works. I am grateful to my students, especially those who took courses with me on globalization, international economics, development economics, and international business at several colleges and universities in the United States and Japan—interactions with them have profoundly sharpened the arguments and insights in the book.

I am also thankful to scores of officials of government and international organizations, and scholars, who commented on my GATT/WTO-related papers presented at various conferences in Beijing, Dhaka, Kathmandu, New Delhi, San Diego, and Washington, DC. I wish to thank: Peter Drahos of Australian National University, Yu Yongda of Tisnghua University, Paul Dorosh of Cornell University, Patrick Webb of Purdue University, Marlinda D. Ingco, Kapil Kapoor, and Rashid Frauqee of the World Bank, Werner Kiene and Pedro Medrano of the UN-World Food Program, S. S. Meenakshisundaram and Sharad Joshi of the Indian government, Sarfraz Khan Qureshi of the Pakistan Institute of Development Economics, Quazi Sahabuddin of the Bangladesh Institute of Development Studies, Durval de Noronha Goyos Jr. of the Noronha Advogados of Brazil, and Saman Kelegama of the Institute of Policy Studies, Sri Lanka.

I am very grateful to Hillary Claggett and Nicholas Philipson of Greenwood Publishing for their editorial support and guidance for the book—especially for bearing with me for a couple of years as I missed one after another deadline for submitting the final manuscript. Special thanks are also due to production editor Terri M. Jennings of Jennings Publishing Services for her guidance throughout the production process of the book, and to Elaine Grohman for excellent copyediting of the manuscript.

Finally, I owe profound thanks to my two young sons—Jheshan (8) and Dilshan (6)—who painstakingly endured suffering for years because of my preoccupation with the project. Apparently they agree on nothing, but still reached a unanimous conclusion about me—"Dad loves nothing but his computer." Perhaps only compassionate acceptance of this work by the readership will prove one day that their Dad loved millions of people across the world as well.

Abbreviations and Acronyms

AAP	Agreement on Anti-Dumping Procedures
AB	Appellate Body
ACP	African, Caribbean and Pacific countries
ADB	Asian Development Bank
AGOA	Africa Growth and Opportunity Act
AMS	Aggregate Measurement of Support
ASCM	Agreement on Subsidies and Countervailing Measures
ASEAN	Association of Southeast Asian Nations
ATC	Agreement on Textiles and Clothing
BoP	Balance-of-payments
CAP	Common Agricultural Policy
CBD	Convention of Biodiversity
CI	Consumer International
CTE	Committee on Trade and Environment
DSB	Dispute Settlement Body
DSU	Dispute Settlement Understanding
EC	European Communities
ECOSOC	Economic and Social Council
EEC	European Economic Community
ESAF	Enhanced Structural Adjustment Program

EU	European Union
FAO	Food and Agriculture Organization
FDI	Foreign Direct Investment
FTAA	Free Trade Agreement of the Americas
G77	Group of 77
GATS	General Agreement on Trade in Services
GATT	General Agreement on Tariffs and Trade
GDP	Gross Domestic Product
GSP	Generalized System of Preferences
IFFTU	International Federation of Free Trade Unions
ILO	International Labor Organization
IMF	International Monetary Fund
IPR	Intellectual Property Rights
ITC	International Trade Center
ITCB	International Textiles and Clothing Bureau
ITO	International Trade Organization
LDC	Least Developed Countries
MAI	Multilateral Agreement on Investment
MEA	Multilateral Environmental Agreement
MFA	Multifiber Arrangement
MFN	Most-Favored Nation
MTO	Multilateral Trade Organization
NFIDC	Net Food-Importing Developing Country
NTB	Non-Trade Barrier
OECD	Organization for Economic Cooperation and Development
PPMs	Processes and Production methods
PSA	Pre-Shipment Inspection
PSE	Producer Subsidy Equivalent
QRS	Quantitative Restrictions
R&D	Research and Development
SDT	Special and Differential Treatments
SPSS	Sanitary and Phyto-Sanitary Measures
TBT	Technical Barriers to Trade
TBTA	Technical Barriers to Trade Agreement
TED	Turtle Exclusion Device
TNC	Trade Negotiations Committee
TPRB	Trade Policy Review Body
TPRM	Trade Policy Review Mechanism

TRIM	Trade-Related Investment Measures
TRIPS	Trade-Related Aspects of Intellectual Property Rights
TSE	Total Support Estimate
TWN	Third World Network
UNCED	United Nations Conference on Environment and Development
UNCTAD	United Nations Conference for Trade and Development
UNDP	United Nations Development Program
UNEP	United Nations Environment Program
UNIDO	United Nations Industrial Development Organization
UR	Uruguay Round
URAA	Uruguay Round Agreement in Agriculture
WB	World Bank
WFN	Worldwide Fund for Nature
WHO	World Health Organization
WWF	World Wildlife Fund

Introduction

This book is not about globalization and its discontent.[1] It is not a treatise in defense of globalization either.[2] Neither does it provide analytical narratives on economic growth of the countries that achieved prosperity.[3] It is rather about the backwaters of global prosperity—a passionate study about countries and peoples that have largely been bypassed by globalization. It is a narrative on the forces and processes that contribute to marginalization of the poorest nations in the contemporary world economy. It focuses on economic globalization per se—integration of national economies into international economy through trade, direct foreign investment, and flows of capital, labor, and technology (Bhagwati, 2004).[4] More specifically, the book looks into economic integration through international trade, and it does so in the context of multilateral trade regimes instituted by the General Agreement on Tariff and Trade (GATT) and its successor, the World Trade Organization (WTO). A primary objective of the book is to see how multilateral institutions like the GATT and the WTO, and the trade regimes sponsored by them,[5] have been marginalizing the poorest nations, widely branded as the Least Developed Countries (LDCs).

The category of LDCs was established by the United Nations in 1971 on the basis of per capita income and the share of manufacturing sector in a country's gross domestic product (GDP). Initially, 24 countries were placed in this category—16 in Africa, 6 in Asia, and 1 each in the Pacific Islands and the Caribbean. Subsequently, the criteria were revised several times, as the UN mandate requires such revisions every three years. In its triennial review in 2000, the UN used three criteria for determining the LDC status: (a) an income criterion—based on a three-year average estimate of the GDP per capita (under $900 for inclusion and above $1035 for graduation); (b) a human resource criterion—a composite Augmented Physical Quality of Life (APQLI) based on nutrition, health, education and adult literacy indicators; and (c) an income criterion—measured by economic vulnerability index (EVI) based on GDP shares of agriculture, manufacturing, exports and other economic indicators (UNCTAD 2001a, 4–10).[6]

Countries or economies around the world are, however, variously classified by various agencies, such as the World Bank, the International Monetary Fund (IMF), and the United Nations. The UN usually divides countries into two broad categories: (a) developed countries to refer to industrialized countries of the Western Europe, Australia, Canada, Japan, New Zealand, and the United States; and (b) developing countries to signify most of the rest of the world. In 1971, as mentioned above, it has introduced the LDC category to refer to the poorest countries. The World Bank and the IMF normally classify countries into four categories on the basis of gross national product (GNP) per capita. The latest classification of the World Bank, based on 2002 GNI per capita, groups economies into four groups—low income, $735 or less; lower middle income, $736—2,935; upper middle income, $2936—9,075; and high income, $9,076 or more (World Bank 2003a, 299). The LDCs would belong to the World Bank's group of low-income economies, although all low-income countries are not LDCs.

There are other categories of countries, such as newly industrialized economies (NIE), which include the so-called Asian Tigers—Hong Kong, Singapore, South Korea, and Taiwan, and Newly Industrialized Countries (NICs), that include countries like Brazil, Chile, Malaysia, Mexico, and Thailand, as well as the four Asian Tigers (NIEs). We shall be using the concept of developing countries in contradistinction with the LDCs. Here the term "developing countries" would broadly refer to the UN classification of countries that are not grouped as developed or all economies that do not belong to the World Bank's category of "high-income countries."

Mounting evidence suggests that the pace and magnitude of marginalization of the LDCs have been deepening in the rapidly globalizing world economy, especially since the 1980s, while unprecedented levels of benefits, stemming from economic globalization, are being accrued to developed countries, especially the so-called triad—the United States, the European Union (EU), and Japan.[7] While there were 24 LDCs in 1971—16 in Africa, 6 in Asia, and 1 in the Pacific Islands, and I in the Caribbean—the number of LDCs swelled to 50 in 2003–35 in Africa, 9 in Asia, 1 in the Caribbean, and 5 in the Pacific region. In 2003, per capita income in the LDCs, home of more than one-tenth of the world's population, ranged between $90 in the Democratic Republic of Congo to $666 in Angola, while that of the developed (high- income) countries averaged at $26, 310 in 2002 US dollars.[8] In 1997, the LDCs constituted about 10 percent of the world's population, with 0.6 percent share in global imports and 0.4 percent share in global exports, which represented 40 percent decline in their shares since 1980, testifying increasing marginalization of the LDCs in the world economy (UNCTAD 1999a, 12).

In fact, almost all other credible indicators of economic globalization—such as trends in national income growth, global commodity prices, capital flows, and poverty and human development—lead to the unavoidable conclusion that not only have the processes of marginalization of the LDCs been deepening further in recent years, but also the measures undertaken over the years to integrate the LDCs into the global economy or to reverse their marginalization processes have either failed or fallen short of claims or expectations (Dowlah 2003a). The LDCs are, as UNCTAD (2000b) points out, indeed, "structurally handicapped" in development process in many ways—their governments are unstable and inefficient, societies are divided and crisis-prone, economies are undeveloped and inefficient, administrative structures and institutions are archaic and corrupt, their physical and human resource endowments are inadequate, unproductive, and disorganized, and on top of all these unsettling domestic factors, they are prime victims of rapid, large-scale, and across-the-board international trade liberalization processes (Rodrik 2000; TWN 2001).

This book studies this apparently inexorable marginalization process of the LDCs in the context of economic globalization, which, as mentioned above, is viewed as a process of economic integration of trade, migration, technology, and financial flows. Such a process of globalization, however, is not a novel phenomenon occurring in the contemporary world—there have been at least three waves of economic globalization since the 1870s.[9] As articulated by the World Bank (2002), the first wave of such globalization—economic integration—took place between 1970 and 1914, when technological progress, falling transport costs, and reduction in tariff barriers boosted land-intensive commodity exports, raising the share of exports in world income to about 8 percent, facilitating migration of almost 10 percent of the world's population from Europe to North America and Australia as well as from China and India to Sri Lanka, Burma, Thailand, the Philippines, and Vietnam. During this wave, mass migration played a key role in equalizing incomes across globalizing countries.[10]

The second wave of globalization occurred between 1945 and 1980, with a hiatus between the two World Wars when nationalistic phobias plunged the world into protectionist wars, halting migration, pushing back the share of exports in world income to 1870s' levels, and depleting global flow of capital even below that level. The second wave of economic globalization was ushered in mainly by the Bretton Woods Conference of 1944, in which the leading industrial powers of the time, the United States and the United Kingdom, sought to reverse the protectionist policies of the pre-World War II period, mainly in order to ensure "ready supply of cheap raw materials and expanding market for manufactured goods."[11] The Bretton Woods Conference also set binding rules for international economic activities, and paved the way for the establishment of the World Bank—to help reconstruction efforts in war-devastated economies and the International Monetary Fund (IMF)—to monitor global finance and monetary discipline—and laid foundations for the future GATT—to guide international trade as the third pillar of the international economic system. Subsequently, this wave received a shot in the arms in the early 1970s when President Richard Nixon abandoned the gold-based fixed-rate system, removed much control over global capital flows, and neoliberal movements emphasized expansion of the international market.

As a result, during the second wave of globalization, improvements in technology pushed the cost of transport down, global flow of finance and technology increased manifold, and internationalist forces got a new momentum. But, at the same time, the world witnessed a phase of economic globalization bifurcated around the great north-south divide as well as primary and manufactured products. Tariffs and other nontariff barriers (NTBs) went down substantially in developed countries, greatly expanding manufacturing trade among them, while developing countries remained as hinterland for supplying cheap raw materials, as global commodity prices slumped continuously. Moreover, products of export interest to developing countries, in primary commodities, such as agriculture, or primary manufacturing activities, such as textiles and clothing, hardly witnessed any liberalization or came under steeper protection in developed countries. As a result, most of the developing countries were effectively sidetracked during the second wave of globalization, in terms of economic growth, industrialization, or standard of living.

By promoting such a bifurcated mode of economic integration—along the great divides of countries and products—the second wave of globalization effectively played into the so-called center-periphery paradigms of the global production system. Propounded by left thinkers, this paradigm saw continuation of old colonial practices in the postcolonial era—with the division of trading areas into high- and low-value-added activities that perpetuated dependency of the low-value-adding periphery countries on the high-value-adding core countries. The multilateral trading system, which emerged in the post-World War II era, was seen largely as an offshoot of neocolonial designs to secure access to cheap raw materials of former colonies and expansion of manufactured goods in the core countries.[12] Then the famous Prebish-Singer thesis, in the mid-1950s, showed a secular decline of terms of trade for primary commodities relative to manufactures, resulting in a long-term transfer of income from periphery to core countries. These findings were further reinforced in the late 1950s with the Haberler Report, which showed how developing countries faced high tariffs and other nontariff barriers for their exports of primary products in developed country markets.

The second wave of globalization also left some other indubitable marks on global economic development. Putting upside down the principle of comparative advantage based on endowment of factors of production, developed countries specialized in manufacturing depending on gains in productivity from agglomerated clusters. Then, buoyed by the continued reduction of tariffs under successive rounds of the GATT, rapidly growing developed countries concentrated trade largely among themselves, enabling lower-income industrial countries to catch up with high-income industrial countries (Maddison 1995). This convergence among developed countries was further consolidated with unprecedented achievement in income redistribution and social protection in these countries during the second wave of globalization (Clark, Dollar, and Kraay 2001).

Developing countries, on the other hand, missed the boat altogether. Facing ever-increasing tariff and nontariff barriers in developed markets, many of them just emerging from colonial rules and legacies, often torn with nationalistic or ideological proclivity toward autarchic or socialist development, buried under archaic and inefficient rules and regimes, and with overwhelming dependence on primary commodities, they shared next to nothing from the global prosperity ushered in during the second wave of globalization and even ended up worse, especially in terms of per capita income and level of poverty. They were further disadvantaged by the fact that two of the prime forces of the first wave of globalization—migration of labor and flow of foreign capital—were negligible for these countries, and the income gaps between rich and poor countries widened further.

The third wave of globalization, which we are experiencing now, began in the 1980s without a period of reversal as evidenced by the first wave of globalization, when many threads of economic integration were pulled back. The third wave, which further reinforces the momentum toward globalization, can be characterized by several distinctive features. First, a large group of developing countries—such as China, India, Mexico, Singapore, Thailand, Malaysia, Argentina and Brazil—broke into global markets. Many of these developing countries are no longer onlookers to the economic integration processes. Thanks to unprecedented levels of economic liberalization, accompanied by technological breakthroughs—e-commerce, e-economics, and so on—and unprecedented expansion of market economies, as ADB (2001, 29) points out, at present more than half of the world's total output of goods and services is contestable—that is, producers must keep prices competitive to avoid losing market share to competitors. While in 1980 only 25 percent of the exports of developing countries were manufactures, by 1998 that share rose to 80 percent (Martin 2001; World Bank 2002, 32–33). In global exports of manufactures, developing countries increased their share from 10.6 percent to 26.2 percent between 1980 and 1997 (Wiemann, 2002; UNCTAD 2000a).[13]

Second, the third wave of globalization has been witnessing a massive increase in the flows of finance across the world. Global flow of foreign direct investment (FDI) increased from $66 billion in 1966 to $3.2 trillion in 1996. There has been significant capital movement to developing countries, which increased from less than $70 billion in 1970 to $306 billion in 1997 (Schmukler and Zoido-Lobaton 2001).[14] Also, private capital flows to developing countries became more significant than, for example, official flows or aid, and by 1998, foreign capital stock was 22 percent of developing country GDP, almost doubled from the 1970 level (Maddison 2001). Overall volume of transactions on the foreign exchange markets around the world jumped from $100 billion a day in 1979 to $1.5 trillion in 1998 (Martin 1994), and the world currency markets now trade more currencies in six hours than the World Bank lent in its entire history (Clark 1999). At the same time, the bank deposits owned by nonresidents increased from $20 billion in 1964 to $7.9 trillion in 1995 (BIS 1996).[15]

Third, unlike the second wave of globalization, there has been significant increase in migration in the third wave of globalization—in 2000, about 6 percent of the populations of the developed countries were considered to be permanent migrants.[16] Fourth, in contrast with the second wave of globalization when poverty situation worsened in developing countries, available data indicates that the third wave has been contributing to reduction of poverty—between 1993 and 1998, the number of people in absolute poverty declined by 14 percent to 762 million (World Bank 2002, 49). Most important, the third wave of globalization, being staged at the fag end of the twentieth century and at the dawn of the new millennium, has been the most sweeping, the most far-reaching, and the most comprehensive form of globalization that humankind has ever experienced.

Fifth, and finally, from an ideological standpoint, the third wave is driven by neoliberalism—reinventing the classic liberalism of Adam Smith and John Locke that underpins market capitalism as the panacea for economic growth. Neoliberalism calls for restricting governmental intervention or regulations in the rapidly globalizing world economy, and abolition of state control on movements of money, finance, capital, goods, and services. Globally, neoliberalism pushes the frontiers of globalization by pressing for greater liberalization through multilateral institutions, through the Bretton Woods institutions and the GATT trading system since the 1950s, and through the WTO, since its inception in the early 1990s.

But by pushing for globalization and liberalization, under the banner of what is called free market and free trade, neoliberalism has been contributing to further marginalization of the LDCs, which are structurally and institutionally handicapped, and therefore, little equipped to compete in such a competitive world. Evidence clearly shows that so-called free trade has not been equally beneficial for all countries—it failed to deliver universal prosperity for all nations. International trade has, indeed, created "the great divide in the global village."[17] Between 1970 and 1995, real per capita incomes for the richest one-third of the countries rose by 1.9 percent annually, for the middle third the income increased by 0.7 percent, while the bottom third showed no increase at all (World Bank 2000). Scores of these poor countries joined the integration orthodoxy wholeheartedly and liberalized their trade regimes beyond even many developed countries, especially since the 1980s, under the structural adjustment programs of the Bretton Woods institutions.

But, as Rodrik (2001) points out, scores of countries of Latin America and Africa are stagnating, or growing less rapidly than in the heyday of import substitution during the 1960s and 1970s. An earlier study by UNCTAD (2000b) showed that trade liberalization resulted in imports surge in many developing countries, leading to about 3 percent higher average trade deficits in the 1990s, compared with the 1970s. Free trade does make an enormous difference—countries with free trade regimes grow faster than those with restricted trade regimes,[18] and countries dismantle their trade restrictions as they grow richer (Rodrick and Rodriguez, 2000),[19] but the evidence of the 1990s indicates that there is no systematic relationship between a country's average level of tariff and nontariff barriers and its subsequent economic growth rates.

No wonder that instead of prospering, some of LDCs have suffered reversal of incomes in recent decades. The multilateral trade regimes under the GATT, which is essentially an institution of the second wave of globalization, did grant the so-called "GATT waiver" (Article XVIII), which allowed developing countries—especially those in the early stages of development—to use protective measures under certain conditions, to protect "particular industries." But those special and differential rights, under which several programs, such as the Generalized

Systems of Preference (GSP) schemes, popped up in developed countries, especially in the US and the EU, turned out to be less advantageous for developing countries than they were touted to be at their inception. Several studies find that such schemes were advantageous for some products, for some countries, and for some time only, and failed to emerge as a driving force for strengthening integration of developing countries, especially the LDCs, in the world trading system. Therefore, one of the biggest challenges of the third wave of globalization is to devise schemes or programs that can really integrate the LDCs into the global economic system.

The second wave of globalization, despite all its limitations, succeeded in closing gaps among developed countries in terms of growth of income and productivity, and also lifted some of the developing countries in their bid for industrialization and export-led growth. The third wave of globalization faces the challenges of lifting the rest of the nations, especially the LDCs, that missed the boat of prosperity during the second wave of globalization. The challenge before the multilateral institutions, such as the World Bank, the IMF, and the WTO, in the third wave of globalization, is therefore, to reorient themselves to rise up to this challenge. While failing to live up to that challenge, the GATT transformed itself into the WTO, and the World Bank and the IMF have been trying to reinvent themselves without such a major shake-up. The fact that all of them have been looking for hiding places to hold their annual meetings in recent years says it all; that all these institutions suffer from serious legitimacy crises. Much of their success, even viability of their own continued existence, would depend on whether they can help reverse the processes of marginalization of the LDCs, whether they can lift the LDCs from the backwaters of global prosperity, whether they can demonstrate, what John F. Kennedy said long ago, "rising tide raises all boats."

This book is organized as follows. Chapter 1 looks into the pace and magnitude of marginalization of the LDCs in the contemporary world economy. Chapter 2 examines the multilateral trade regimes that evolved under the GATT/WTO over the course of the last five decades to see how they contribute to the marginalization of the LDCs. Chapter 3 looks at the special and differential treatment (SDT) measures that evolved under the GATT/WTO trade regimes, apparently to facilitate integration of developing countries, as well as the LDCs, into the world economic system, in order to see whether they achieved the professed goals. Chapter 4 looks into international trade in textiles and clothing—a manufacturing sector of great exports interest to developing countries, especially to the LDCs, to see how slow liberalization of this sector under the GATT/WTO impeded economic development of the LDCs.

Chapter 5 looks into international trade in agriculture—a primary commodity sector in which developing countries, including the LDCs, traditionally enjoyed comparative advantage, to see how lack of liberalization of this sector under the GATT/WTO impeded economic development of the LDCs. Chapter 6 examines the institutional aspects—structures of multilateral negotiations and implications of various agreements adopted by the WTO—to see how conducive the WTO platform could be for safeguarding and promoting the interests of the LDCs. The final chapter concludes the study with suggestions for a fairer, more humane trading system that could expedite reversal of the marginalization processes of the LDCs through meaningful integration of these countries into the global economic system.

NOTES

1. Title of Nobel laureate economist Professor Joseph Stiglitz's 2002 book, in which he criticizes some aspects of globalization, especially lack of transparency and accountability of the International Monetary Fund.

2. Title of renowned international trade expert Professor Jaghdish Bhagwati's 2004 book—*In Defense of Globalization*—being published by Oxford University Press. As the title indicates, Professor Bhagwati provides a strong defense in favor of globalization.

3. Professor Dani Rodrik's 2003 book is titled—In Search of Prosperity: Analytical Narratives on Economic Growth.

4. A broader interpretation of the concept of globalization would mean increasing global interconnectedness, rapid intensification of worldwide social relations, the compression of time and space, and the swift and relatively unimpeded flow of capital, goods, people, and ideas across national borders. Globalization, therefore, is a multidimensional concept; some scholars defined it as as "distancelessness," "abolition of every possibility of remoteness," and "transworld simultaneity and instantaneity" (Scholte 2000, 41–61). The term "globalization" is, indeed, very complex; it means many things to many people, and it is only fair to say that almost every definition of globalization is incomplete, incorrect, misleading, and either shallow or exaggerating.

5. The concept of trade regime is understood here to mean "sets of implicit or explicit principles, norms, rules, and decision making procedures around which expectations converge in a given area of international relations," as envisaged by Krasner (1983, 2). Obviously, here such international relations refer to trade relations, and we are concerned with multilateral trade regimes, as opposed to international or bilateral ones. Also see Ruggie (1992) for useful discussion on regimes, especially international regimes.

6. In addition, according to the 2000 review of the LDC list, a country can qualify to be added to the list if it meets the above three criteria and does not have a population greater than 75 million. This provision led to inclusion of Senegal to the LDC category in 2003, when the total number of LDCs jumped to 50.

7. It would remind one of the concentration of manufacturing activities before World War 1. In 1913, two-thirds of the world's manufactures were concentrated in another quad: the Great Britain, the United States, Germany, and France, when vast areas of the world strewn across the continents of Asia, Africa, Central America and the Caribbean were reduced into colonies and captive supplier of primary goods. See Bairoch (1982, 296).

8. Based on World Development Report 2004 ((World Bank 2003b).

9. It should, however, be noted that the phases or waves of globalization are viewed in many different ways. In tracing the origins of globalization, some authors take us back even to the medieval periods. Robertson (1992), for example, traces five phases of globalization between the early fifteenth and late twentieth centuries. Scholte (2000), on the other hand, traces three phases of globalization: a gestation period up to the 18th century; incipient globalization between the 1850s and 1950s; and full-scale globalization from the 1960s to the present. Most observers have looked into the variables such as developments in communications, markets, productions, money, finance, social movements, consciousness and similar other factors in discerning different phases of globalization.

10. During the first wave of globalization the world's capital mobility also increased phenomenally. The share of foreign capital stock in the income of developing countries rose from about 9 percent in 1870 to 32 percent in 1914. The World Bank (2002, 21-35) provides an excellent summary of the waves of globalization beginning from 1870. For details on the growth of land-intensive commodity exports during the first wave of globalization, see Maddison (2001), and for migration of population during the period, see Lindert and Williamson (2001, 580-584).

11. According to the TWN (2001), both the United States and the United Kingdom advocated worldwide reduction of tariffs, removal of trade barriers, and "equal access to the markets and raw materials of the world," but their discussions focused on the removal of restrictions to trade by others, and hardly dealt with problems that would be faced by developing countries.

12. Even a World Bank economist believes that decolonization would have been slower in the absence of multilateral trade negotiations in the post–World War II era, as in a protectionist world large nations would have remained more dependent on their colonies for raw materials and markets for their output (Schiff 2000, 4).

13. Of course, most of this share is accounted for by the NIEs, such as Hong Kong, South Korea, and Taiwan. However, countries like Malaysia, China, and Mexico have also moved up in recent decades.

14. The FDI flow, however, was concentrated in only a handful of developing countries, such as so-called Asian Tigers—Singapore, Hong Kong, Taiwan, Malaysia, and China. Also see Table 21 of the *World Development Report* 2000/2001.

15. According to Porter (1993), the share of nonresidents in the deposits with commercial banks around the world rose from 5 percent in 1960 to around 40 percent in 1990 (cited in Scholte [2000, 79]).

16. According to the World Bank (2002, 44-45), currently about 120 million people, or 2 percent of the world population, live in foreign countries, and roughly half of those are in developed countries. Migrants, permanent or temporary, now constitute a major foreign exchange earning sector in many developing countries, including India, Bangladesh, and Mexico.

17. To coin the title of Bruce R. Scott's paper in *Foreign Affairs* (80:1).

18. According to another study, economies that are "open" grew by 2.45 percent points faster annually than closed ones. The report, however, came under criticisms for a major gap between the results actually obtained and the policy conclusions drawn. Often bad performance of some countries was attributed to lack of liberalization, while the actual culprits could be something else (Rodrik 2001).

19. This also explains the phenomenal growth of the East Asian countries, so-called "gang of four," under a mix of outward orientation and unorthodox policies. They hardly followed what is known as the principles of Washington Consensus. Rather, their export-oriented development strategies were blended with high levels of tariff and nontariff barriers, public ownership of large segments of banking and industry, export subsidies, and restrictions on capital flows, including foreign direct investment. It is, however, true that in the 1960s and 1970s, global trade rules were sparse and economists hardly faced today's cost of global integration. At the same time, as many studies point out, it is also true that, the East Asian countries accomplished the phenomenal growth by violating almost every rule of the Bretton Woods institutions.

The State of the LDCs: How Marginalized Are They in the Contemporary World Economy?

INTRODUCTION

This chapter examines the pace and magnitude of marginalization of the poorest countries in the world, which the United Nations categorizes as Least Developed Countries (LDCs). Initially, the UN created this category of countries in 1971 on the basis of per capita income and the share of manufacturing in a country's gross domestic product (GDP). Subsequently, however, the criteria were revised several times. In its latest triennial review in 2000, the UN used three criteria for determining the LDC status of a country: (a) an income criterion—based on a three-year average estimate of the GDP per capita (under $900 for inclusion and above $1035 for graduation); (b) a human resource criterion—a composite Augmented Physical Quality of Life (APQLI)—based on nutrition, health, education, and adult literacy indicators; and (c) an income criterion—measured by economic vulnerability index (EVI)—based on GDP shares of agriculture, manufacturing, exports, and other economic indicators. Currently, as Table 1.1 shows, 50 countries belong to the LDC category, and 35 of them are in Africa, 9 in Asia, 1 in the Caribbean and 5 in the Pacific region.

In 2003, per capita income in the LDCs, home of more than one-tenth of the world's population, ranged between $90 in the Democratic Republic of Congo to $666 in Angola, while that of the developed (high-income) countries averaged at $26,310 in 2002 US dollars (see Table 1.2). In 1997, the LDCs constituted about 10 percent of the world's population, with 0.6 percent share in global imports and 0.4 percent share in global exports, which represented 40 percent decline in their shares since 1980, testifying to increasing globalization of the LDCs in the world economy (UNCTAD 1999a, 12). Most of these LDCs, as UNCTAD (2000b) ob-

Table 1.1
Least Developed Countries, 1971–2003

Year	Number of LDCs	Africa	Asia	Pacific Island	Latin America and the Caribbean
1971	24	16	6	1	1
1975	27	18	7	1	1
1977	29	20	7	1	1
1982	34	25	7	1	1
1985	35	25	7	2	1
1986	38	26	7	4	1
1987	39	26	8	4	1
1988	40	27	8	4	1
1990	41	28	9	4	1
1991	46	31	9	5	1
1994	48	33	9	5	1
2001	49	34	9	5	1
2003	50	35	9	5	1

Source: compiled by the author from various sources.

serves, are "structurally handicapped" in development process—their governments are unstable and inefficient, societies are divided and crisis-prone,
economies are undeveloped and inefficient, administrative structures and institutions are archaic and corrupt, their physical and human resource endowments are
inadequate, unproductive, and disorganized, and on top of all these unsettling domestic factors, they are perhaps the prime victims of rapid, large-scale, and
across-the-board international trade liberalization processes that the contemporary
world has been witnessing (Rodrik 2000; TWN 2001).

There are literally mountains of evidence that suggest that the LDCs have increasingly been marginalized in the rapidly globalizing world economy, and much of this
debacle can be attributed to economic globalization, to the processes of economic integration of trade, migration, technology and financial flows around the world, that
took place during the second wave of globalization (1945–1980). This period not
only witnessed massive improvements in technology that pushed the cost of transportation down and manifold increase in global flows of finance, trade, and technology,
it also saw the establishment of multilateral institutions like the United Nations, the
World Bank, and the International Monetary Fund (IMF). Unfortunately, this period
also witnessed a phase of economic globalization bifurcated around the great
north-south divide as well as primary and manufactured products. As a result, while
great expansions in manufacturing trade brought unprecedented prosperity for industrialized countries, most of the developing countries remained in backwaters, with
products of exports interest to them, such as agriculture and textiles and clothing, facing stiff protection in developed-country markets.

Worse still, marginalization of the LDCs further deepened in the third wave of
globalization that began in the 1980s. While the 1980s were a "lost decade" for

most of the developing countries, including the LDCs, the 1990s came for the LDCs as a decade of "increasing marginalization, inequality, poverty and social exclusion" (UNCTAD 1999a, 2). Even at the dawn of the New Millennium the prospects of economic growth of the LDCs, or reversal of marginalization processes of the LDCs, seem as far-flung as ever. As the next section explains, almost all credible indicators of economic globalization indicate that the processes of marginalization of the LDCs have been deepening further in recent decades.

MAJOR INDICATORS OF MARGINALIZATION OF THE LDCS

This section explains the marginalization processes of the LDCs in terms of the following indicators related to economic globalization: income gaps between rich and poor nations, national income growth trends, trends in global commodity prices, trends in manufacturing value added, global capital flows, and trends in poverty and human development.

Income Disparities between Rich and Poor Nations

None disputes that the income gaps between rich and poor nations, and between developed and developing countries, have been on the rise, since the second wave of globalization in the 1950s, and have further widened since the 1980s, with the third wave of globalization. In fact, the income gaps between developed and developing countries have never been wider than today. The ratio of income of the richest and poorest 20 percent of the world's population increased from 30 to 1 in 1960, to 60 to 1 in 1990, and 74 to 1 in 1997 (UNIDO 2000).[1] The stark reality of the income disparities between the rich and the poor nations, especially in the context of the LDCs, can be gauged from the fact that while the Triad accounted for nearly three-quarters of the world's GNP in the late 1990s, 66 percent of the world trade flows in 1996, 60 percent of the world flows of foreign direct investment (FDI) between 1990 and 1996,[2] the share of the LDCs had been barely 0.5 percent of the world's GNP, less than 0.4 percent of the world's trade flows, and less than 2.2 percent of global FDI flows in the late 1990s.[3]

Globalization seems to have widened intracountry income disparities as well. According to UNCTAD (1997), the income share of the top 20 percent has risen in almost every country since the 1980s, while the bottom 20 percent hardly saw any benefits of globalization. The report traces the roots of these inequalities to: (a) growing wage inequality between skilled and unskilled workers—due mainly to declining industrial employment of unskilled workers and large absolute falls in their real wages; (b) capital gaining in comparison with labor as share of profits rising everywhere; (c) the rise of a new rentier class due to financial liberalization and the rapid rise in debt—with government debt servicing in developing countries also distributing income from the poor to the rich; and (d) the benefits of agricultural price liberalization being reaped mainly by traders rather than farmers.

Table 1.2
Basic Socioeconomic and Political Parameters of the Least Developed Countries, 2002–2004

Country	Population (millions)	Surface area (000 square miles)	Population density (per sq. km of land area)	Actual arable land per caput (hectares)	Gross national income $ billions	Gross national income Per capita $	Human Development Index	Political Freedom Index	Economic Freedom Index
1. Afghanistan	—	—	—	0.47	—	—	—	6	—
2. Angola	14	1247	11	0.33	9.2	660	167	6	—
3. Bangladesh	136	144	1,042	0.08	48.5	360	139	4	131
4. Benin	7	113	60	0.36	2.5	380	159	2	113
5. Bhutan	—	274	—	—	—	—	136	6	—
6. Burkina Faso	12	274	43	0.35	2.6	220	173	4	95
7. Burundi	7	28	275	0.20	0.7	100	171	5	—
8. Cambodia	12	181	71	0.46	3.5	280	130	6	—
9. Cape Verde	—	—	—	—	—	—	103	1	60
10. Central African Rep	4	623	6	0.63	1.0	260	168	7	105
11. Chad	8	1284	6	0.53	1.8	220	165	6	124
12. Comoros	—	—	—	—	—	—	134	5	—
13. Congo, DR	54	2345	24	0.07	5.0	90	167	5	92
14. Djibouti	—	—	—	—	—	—	153	5	130
15. Equatorial Guinea	—	—	—	—	—	—	116	7	—
16. Eritrea	4	118	43	0.15	0.7	160	155	7	104
17. Ethiopia	67	1104	67	0.21	6.4	100	169	5	124
18. Gambia	—	—	—	0.12	—	—	151	4	93
19. Guinea	8	246	32	0.26	3.1	410	157	6	139
20. Guinea-Bissau	—	—	—	0.10	—	—	166	6	137
21. Haiti	8	28	301	0.13	3.7	440	150	6	—
22. Kiribati	—	—	—	—	—	—	—	—	—
23. Lao PDR	6	237	24	0.20	1.7	310	135	1	118
24. Lesotho	2	30	69	0.17	1.0	470	137	2	—
25. Liberia	—	—	—	0.16	—	—	—	6	86
26. Madagascar	16	587	28	0.18	3.9	240	149	3	114
27. Malawi	11	118	114	0.22	1.7	160	162	3	—
28. Maldives	—	—	—	—	—	—	86	6	—
29. Mali	11	1240	9	0.18	2.8	240	172	2	102
30. Mauritania	3	1026	3	0.24	1.0	340	154	6	67
31. Mozambique	18	802	24	0.09	3.9	210	170	3	95

No.	Country									
32.	Myanmar	49	677	74	0.22	—	—	131	7	151
33.	Nepal	24	147	169	0.11	5.6	230	143	5	121
34.	Niger	12	1267	9	—	2.0	170	174	4	111
35.	Rwanda	8	26	331	0.30	1.9	230	158	6	103
36.	Samoa	—	—	—	—	—	—	—	2	—
37.	Sao Tome and Principe	10	197	52	—	—	—	122	2	72
38.	Senegal	5	72	73	0.29	4.7	470	156	4	134
39.	Sierra Leon	—	—	—	—	0.7	140	175	3	—
40.	Solomon Islands	—	—	—	0.36	—	—	—	6	—
41.	Somalia	—	—	—	0.32	—	—	138	7	98
42.	Sudan	35	945	40	0.23	9.6	280	160	4	134
43.	Tanzania	5	57	88	0.61	1.3	270	141	—	48
44.	Timor-Leste	—	—	—	—	—	—	—	6	—
45.	Togo	23	241	119	0.36	5.9	250	147	1	131
46.	Tuvalu	—	—	—	—	—	—	128	5	—
47.	Uganda	19	528	35	0.10	9.4	490	148	2	118
48.	Vanuatu	10	753	14	0.67	3.5	330	—	5	—
49.	Yemen									
50.	Zambia									

Sources: Population, surface area, population density, and gross national income data for the year 2002 are obtained from the World Bank/Oxford University Press (2003b), *World Development Report, 2004.* Economic Freedom Index data relates taken from Heritage Foundation and the Wall Street Journal (2004), *Index of Economic Freedom 2004.* Human Development Index taken from UNDP(2003), *Human Development Report 2004.* Arable land per caput taken from FAO (2001); the data represent actual arable land use per caput for 1994.

Notes: Economic Freedom Index ranking is based on 161 countries—the higher the ranking, the lower the economic freedom. For political ranking—highest score is 7.0 and lowest is 1.0—in which 1.0—2.5 is free, 3.0—5.0 partly free, and 5.5—7.0 is not free. UNDP's Human Development Index (HDI) of 2004 ranked 175 countries, the higher the number the lower is the ranking. Ranks 1—55 refer to countries with high human development, ranks 56—141 refer to countries with medium human development, and ranks 142—175 refer to countries with lower human development.

Trends in National Income Growth

During the 1990–1998 period, the LDCs, excluding Bangladesh, grew by 2.4 percent per annum, compared to 3.4 percent and 2.5 percent per annum growth rates in the low- and middle-income countries and the world, respectively.[4] During the same period, population growth in the LDCs was almost double that of the world average, because of which per capita GDP growth in the LDCs, again excluding Bangladesh, stood at 0.4 percent, while per capita of the world grew by 1.1 percent, that for the low- and middle income countries grew by 5.4 percent, and the developing countries, excluding LDCs, grew by 3.6 percent. As Table 1.3 indicates, the performance of the LDCs has been disappointing even in respect to developing countries—during the 1980s the mean per capita growth rate in the developing countries was double the mean per capita growth of the LDCs, but during 1990–1998, the mean per capita growth in developing countries was four times higher than that of the LDCs.

Growth of the LDCs had been unstable and diverse as well during the 1990–1998 period, when 15 LDCs, 7 in Asia, had per capita growth exceeding 2 percent, while 22 LDCs faced stagnation or economic regress, half of which were civil strife-torn countries with serious armed conflicts, which experienced a 3 percent per annum decline in per capita GDP growth.[5] Overall, there were 32 LDCs, which either fell behind the per capita income of other developing countries in relative terms, or experienced an absolute decline in living standards during 1990–1998 period. Per capita GDP in the LDCs grew at 0.4 percent (with –0.4 percent in African LDCs) during the period, compared with 1.1 percent worldwide, 5.4 percent in low- and middle income countries, and 3.6 percent in developing countries (UNCTAD 2000a, 1–14).[6]

Trends in Global Commodity Prices

The LDCs have also experienced a precipitous decline in commodity prices in the 1990s. As Table 1.4 indicates, annual average growth of primary commodity prices, in which stakes of the LDCs are very high, declined by 3.8 percent during 1989–1993, and then with the exception of the 1994–1997 period when commodity prices rose by 6 percent, commodity prices dipped again in 1998 and 1999, to –13 percent and –14.2 percent, respectively. Worsening terms-of-trade hit hard almost all LDCs[7] that faced low primary commodity prices and rising oil import bills simultaneously (UNCTAD 2000a, 7).[8] Between 1997 and 2001, international price indices of food fell by more than 30 percent and that of agricultural raw materials, minerals, ores, and metals fell by 20 percent. As a result, the value of merchandise exports of commodity exporting LDCs, mostly in Africa, dropped by 7.5 percent, and 19 of the 26 non-oil-exporting LDCs experienced a fall in their export income (UNCTAD 2002, 5–6).[9]

Trends in Manufacturing

The overall share of developing countries, viewed as a group, in manufacturing value added (MVA) increased form 14.4 percent in 1980 to 23.6 percent in 2000 (UNIDO 2000), but much of this industrialization occurred in the East Asian

Table 1.3
Real GDP and per Capita GDP Growth Rate of Least Developed Countries, 1980–1990 versus 1990–1998

	GDP growth rates		Per capita GDP growth rates	
	1980–1990	1990–1998	1980–1990	1990–1998
Least Developed Countries	2.5	3.2	-0.1	0.9
LDCs excluding Bangladesh	1.9	2.4	-0.9	0.4
African LDCs	1.6	2.1	-1.1	-0.4
Asian LDCs	4.3	4.7	1.7	2.9
Island LDCs	4.8	3.5	2.2	0.9
Developing Countries, excluding LDCs	3.9	5.2	1.9	3.6
World	3.1	2.5	1.4	1.1

Source: Based on Table 1 in UNCTAD (2000a, 2).

newly industrialized economies (NIEs), with small shares of other developing countries, and a marginal role of the LDCs. As Table 1.5 indicates, the share of sub-Saharan Africa in world MVA fell from 2.6 percent in 1980 to 1.6 percent in 2000, and the manufacturing exporter LDCs—Bangladesh, Cambodia, Lao People's Democratic Republic, Lesotho, Madagascar, Myanmar, Nepal and Haiti—experienced volatile growth rates during the period. Their exports—primarily composed of clothing and other labor-intensive products—grew by 7 percent in 1999, 24 percent in 2000, and 9 percent in 2001 (WTO 2003b, 7). In the 1997–2000 period, however, manufacturing exporter LDCs fared better—as their manufacturing merchandise exports increased by 36 percent, with a hefty 30 percent increase between 1999 and 2000, when exports of these countries constituted almost one-third of total LDC exports (UNCTAD 2002, 6). Much of these exports are textiles and garments—indicating rudimentary stage of industrialization of these countries. The slow pace of industrialization of the LDCs, even the so-called manufacturing LDCs, can be gauged from the fact that no discernible trend is noticeable to narrow down technological gaps of the LDCs with developed countries or to raise the level of total factor productivity in the LDCs.[10]

Table 1.4
Merchandise Exports of Least Developed Countries by Selected
Country Groups, 1990–2001

Country group	Value (US$ billion) 2001	Annual percentage change			
		1990–00	1999	2000	2001
Total LDC	37	7	11	28	1
Oil exporters*	14	12	51	65	-10
Exporters of manufactures**	13	15	7	24	9
Commodity exporters†	9	2	-5	-3	12
LDC with civil strife‡	1	-9	-19	-12	-7
World	5984	6	4	13	-4

Source: WTO (2002, 7).
Notes: *Includes Angola, Equatorial Guinea, Sudan, and Yemen. **Includes Bangladesh, Cambodia, Lao People's Democratic Republic, Lesotho, Madagascar, Myanmar, Nepal, and Haiti. †31 LDCs not included in other categories. ‡Includes Afghanistan, Burundi, Congo Dem. Republic, Rwanda, Sierra Leone, and Somalia.

Trends in the Flow of External Finance

Flow of development assistance. A sharp decline in official development assistance (ODA) in recent years has further contributed to the processes of marginalization of LDCs.[11] The ODA flow from the Organization for Economic Co-operation and Development/Development Assistance Committee (OECD/DAC) countries to LDCs declined from roughly 37 percent of the donor's total aid in 1989–1990 to 30 percent of the assistance in 1999–2000. As Table 1.6 indicates, the decline was specially pronounced in respect to the EU and the US—the aid/GNI (gross national income) ratios of these donors fell to 0.32 percent and 0.10 percent in 1999–2000, from 0.45 percent, and 0.20 percent in 1985–1989, respectively (ECOSOC 2003).[12] Also, distribution of aid flow has been quite erratic—while sub-Saharan countries like Nigeria and Ethiopia, with very low per capita income (US$250 and US$100 respectively in 1999), had ODA/GNI ratios of 0.50 percent and 2.3 percent, respectively, countries like Cape Verde and Mozambique (with per capita incomes of US$1330 and US$220, respectively) had ODA/GNI ratios of 25.7 percent and 22 percent, respectively. Moreover, while the share of ODA commitments designated to social infrastructures and services in the LDCs increased to 33 percent in 1995–1998, from 14 percent in 1985–1989, commitments to economic in-

Table 1.5
Structure and Performance of World Industry, Selected Indicators, 1980–2000

Economic Groups	Distribution of world MVA (%)*		Distribution of MVA among developing countries (%)		Share of MVA in GDP (%)		Average annual growth (%)			
							MVA		GDP	
	1980	2000**	1980	2000**	1980	2000**	1980–1990	1990–1999	1980–1990	1990–1999
World	100.0	100.0	—	—	22.7	22.2	3.2	2.6	3.0	2.5
Developed market economies	77.9	72.7	—	—	22.8	21.4	2.8	2.2	2.9	2.3
Transition economies	7.7	3.5	—	—	29.7	27.6	2.5	-5.9	2.1	-4.8
Developing economies	14.4	23.8	100.0	100.0	19.8	24.6	5.1	6.5	3.8	4.8
—Sub-Saharan Africa			2.6	1.5	9.8	9.5	3.7	1.1	2.5	2.6
—North Africa			3.5	2.6	12.1	14.6	4.7	2.8	2.5	2.7
—South & East Asia			19.0	29.5	16.2	23.7	8.7	6.8	5.5	5.5

Source: UNIDO (2000).

Notes: *Distribution of world MVA at constant 1990 prices. **Projected figures.

Table 1.6

Flow of Official Development Assistance and the LDCs

A. ODA as a share of gross national income (GNI) of selected donors			
(Period average; percentage)			
Donors	1985–1989	1990–1994	1999–2000
EU	0.45	0.44	0.32
Japan	0.31	0.29	0.31
US	0.20	0.18	0.10
B. ODA by major purpose, 2000 (percentage)			
Social/administrative infrastructure	31.7	Program assistance	7.1
		Debt relief	7.8
Economic infrastructure	16.5	Emergency assistance	7.7
Production	7.0	Administrative/ unspecified	13.9
Multisectorial	8.2		

Source: Compiled from *The DAC Journal*. Vol. 3, No. 1 (2002).

frastructure and services and other multisectorial projects fell to 39 percent from 59 percent during the same period. The 1990s also saw a significant increase in emergency aid and debt forgiveness. All these indicate how political considerations of donors, instead of long-term effect on productivity and growth in LDCs, shaped the ODA flows in recent years and decades.[13]

Foreign Direct Investment Inflow. Between 1990 and 2000, global FDI flows increased from $209 billion to more than $1.3 trillion, of which only 0.5 percent was invested in the LDCs. During the 1998–2000 period, 86 percent of all FDI flows to LDCs ended up in 10 countries—Angola, Bangladesh, Cambodia, Lesotho, Mozambique, Myanmar, Sudan, Uganda, Tanzania, and Zambia.[14] As Table 1.7 indicates, the share of the rest of the LDCs in global FDI flow declined from 29 percent in 1997 to 14 percent in 1998, then 13.2 percent in 1999, and rose slightly to 14.7 percent in 2000. For African countries in particular, FDI inflows declined from $19 billion in 2000 to $11 billion in 2002. In 23 of the continent's 53 countries FDI inflow declined, while FDI flows to oil industries of Angola, Algeria, Chad, Nigeria, and Tunisia accounted for more than half of the continent's total FDI inflow. In the Asia-Pacific region, FDI inflows to 31 of the region's 57 countries declined in 2002, fell to $95 billion from $107 billion in 2001, mainly because of the electronics industry losing momentum. In Latin America and the Caribbean, FDI inflow declined in 24 of the region's 40 countries—in 2002 the region received $56 billion, compared to $84 billion in 2001. The fall is attributed

Table 1.7

FDI Inflows into LDCs by Group of LDCs, 1997–2000 (US$ Millions, Percentages Share in Parentheses)

	1997	1998	1999	2000
Total LDCs	2976.3	3678.7	5176.3	4414.3
Oil-exporting LDCs	391.1	1242.5	2633.1	2046.0
	(13.1)	(33.8)	(50.9)	(46.3)
Top ten LDCs	2115.0	3165.2	4495.1	3764.4
	(71.1)	(86.0)	(86.8)	(85.3)
Rest of LDCs	861.3	513.5	681.2	649.8
	(28.9)	(14.0)	(13.2)	(14.7)

Source: Based on Table 9, UNCTAD (2002, 11).
Notes: Based on top ten LDC recipients of 1999—Angola, Sudan, Uganda, Myanmar, Lesotho, Zambia, Tanzania, Bangladesh, Cambodia, and Mozambique.

to a decline in the service sector and political and economic uncertainties in the region (UNCTAD 2003, 9).

External Debt. High levels of external debt remain an important predicament for the LDCs, although in recent years the levels of debt stocks are lower in relation to GDP and exports as well as in absolute terms. As UNCTAD (2000a) points out, the nominal value of the total external debt stock rose from $121.2 billion in 1990 to $150.4 billion in 1998, and during the period total debt service paid by the LDCs rose from $4 billion to $4.4 billion. In 1998, total debt stock corresponded to more than 100 percent of the combined GDP of the LDCs, compared with 92 percent in 1990.[15] For 27 of the LDCs, out of 42 LDCs for which data were available, the external debt was unsustainable.

By the end of 2000, as (UNCTAD 2002, 14–15) indicates, the total debt stock with the LDCs rose to $143.2 billion, which was about $14 billion less than the previous year, reflecting debt forgiveness and changes in cross-currency valuations that counterbalanced newly issued loans. The total debt stocks of LDCs also fell to 78 percent of their combined GDP. Also, a substantial part of the LDC loans are official loans, mainly multilateral loans. In 2000, multilateral loans, excluding IMF credits, were equivalent to 115 percent of net official debt of the LDCs. The debt-service payment situation, however, improved just a little in recent years. The LDCs made debt service payments of $4.7 billion in 1999 and $4.6 billion in 2000. As a ratio of exports, debt service payments dropped to 9.6 percent in 2000, compared to 11.8 percent in 1999. But the ratio of debt stocks declined in 18 LDCs in 2000, total arrears on long-term debt declined only in 8 LDCs, 29 LDCs had unsustainable debt between 1999 and 2000, and in 14 of 20 HIPC-LDCs, debt service payments were the equivalent of 40 percent or more of government social expenditures.[16]

Trends in Poverty

The Least Developed Countries Report 2002: Escaping the Poverty Trap of
UNCTAD describes the poverty situation in the LDCs as "generalized poverty,"
meaning that a major part of the population lives at or below income levels sufficient for meeting basic needs, and the available resources of the country are insufficient to meet the basic needs of the population on a sustainable basis, even if the
resources are equally distributed. The Report (UNCTAD 2002, 51–67) points out
that poverty in the LDCs as a group has been persistent and even growing over
time. Focusing on average per capita income, private consumption, and the average incidence and depth of poverty weighted by population, the Report gives the
following sobering assessment of the state of poverty in the LDCs during the
1995–1999 period:

- Over 80 percent of the LDC population lived on less than $2 a day; the percentage is 88
  percent in the African LDCs and 68 percent in the Asian LDCs. Average private consumption per capita of the LDC population with less than $2 a day income was $1.03 a
  day (in 1985 PPP dollars).

- Over 50 percent of the LDC population lived on less than $1 a day; the percentage is 65
  percent for African LDCs and 23 percent for Asian LDCs. Average private consumption
  per capita of the LDC population with less than $1 a day income was 64 cents a day (in
  1985 PPP dollars).

- Per capita GDP in high-income OECD countries (in current dollars and in official exchange rate) is on average more than 100 times higher than in the African and Asian
  LDCs. A similar ratio applies to the differences between the average per capita consumption of the LDCs and the high-income OECD countries. The poorest 10 percent of
  the population in industrialized countries have an average per capita consumption of
  about $13 a day.

- The incidence of poverty in the LDCs has increased from 48 percent during 1965–1969
  to 50 percent during 1995–1999 for the $1 poverty line. For the $2 poverty line, the incidence of poverty has been fluctuating around 80 percent over the past few decades.

- While in Asian LDCs the incidence of poverty ($1 a day) fell from 35.5 percent in the
  late 1990s, to about 23 percent in the late 1990s, in African LDCs the incidence of poverty increased over the last few decades—from 56 percent in the late 1960s to 65 percent
  in the late 1990s.

- In terms of alleviating poverty, the LDCs are worse off even compared to the developing
  countries, where the incidence of poverty ($1 a day) declined from 45 percent in the late
  1960s to about 8 percent in the late 1990s. With poverty line of $2 a day, incidence of
  poverty in developing countries declined from 83 percent to 35 percent during the same
  period.

- Only three LDCs—Cape Verde, Lao, and Sudan—managed to reduce the incidence of
  poverty with respect to the $1 poverty line by more than 20 percent during the 1980s
  through the 1990s, all others remained in generalized and persistent poverty. Seven
  other LDCs—Burundi, Guinea-Bissau, Mali, Niger, Rwanda, Senegal, and Togo—witnessed improvements in the 1980s, but faced worsening poverty in the 1990s. Table 1.8
  summarizes these findings.

Table 1.8
Poverty Trends in LDCs, 1965–1999 (1985 PPP US$1)

	1965–1969	1975–1979	1985–1989	1995–1999
Population living on less than $1 a day (%)				
39 LDCs*	48.0	48.5	49.0	50.1
African LDCs	55.8	56.4	61.9	64.9
Asian LDCs	35.8	35.9	27.6	23.0
Developing countries**	44.8	32.5	15.0	7.5
Population living on less than $2 a day (%)				
39 LDCs	80.8	82.1	81.9	80.7
African LDCs	82.0	83.7	87.0	87.5
Asian LDCs	78.8	79.6	73.4	68.2
Developing countries	82.8	76.5	61.6	35.3

Source: Compiled from UNCTAD (2002, 59).
Notes: *UNCTAD (2002, 55) shows poverty map of the 39 LDCs for which data could be compiled by the UNCTAD. **Developing countries include 22 countries: Algeria, Cameron, China, Congo, Cote d'Ivoire, Dominican Republic, Egypt, Ghana, India, Indonesia, Jamaica, Kenya, Morocco, Namibia, Nigeria, Pakistan, Philippines, Sri Lanka, Thailand, Tunisia, Turkey and Zimbabwe.

Trends in Human Development

In addition to the poverty trap, the LDCs are also caught in a vicious trap of lower human development, high morbidity and illiteracy rates, lower life expectancies and wide gender disparities.[17] While per capita health expenditure was $1700 in the OECD countries and $100 in the developing countries in the early 1990s, the LDCs spent on average only $11 per capita. What is worse is that in the 1990s, 11 LDCs actually experienced reversals in life expectancy trends.[18] In 2000, the Human Development Index (HDI) of UNDP put 32 LDCs in its lowest category of 35 countries. In 2002, the HDI had all but 11 LDCs in its low human development category, the same trend continued in 2003 (see Table 1.2). According to UNCTAD (2000a, 6) projections, by 2015, net primary enrollment rate in the LDCs would be on average about 76 percent for the males, compared to 65 percent in 1997, and female enrollment rate would be 60 percent, compared to 1997 levels.

Over the years, a plethora of global summits have set seven so-called "International Development Goals" for improving the human resources in developing

.....ies, especially in the LDCs. They include: (a) the proportion of people living in extreme poverty should be cut by half by 2015 (World Summit, Copenhagen 1996); (b) universal primary education in all countries by 2015 (Jomitien, Beijing, Copenhagen); (c) elimination of gender disparity in primary and secondary education by 2005 (Cairo, Beijing, Copenhagen); (d) reduction of death rates of infant and children by two-thirds by 2015 (Cairo); (e) reduction of the rate of maternal mortality by three-quarters by 2015 (Cairo, Beijing); (f) ensuring access to primary healthcare for all by 2015 (Cairo); and (g) reversing loss of environmental resources by 2015 (Rio).[19]

A January 2004 review of the Millennium Development Goals, by a distinguished group of experts, commissioned by the World Economic Forum (WEF), found the signatories to the goals last year did barely one-third of the work needed to meet the goals set for fighting poverty, hunger, and disease by 2015. The Global Governance Initiative, compiled by more than 40 experts—including former U.N. High Commissioner for Refugees Sadako Ogata and ex-Irish president Mary Robinson—assessed the progress in respect to seven of the challenges, giving the world a mark from zero to 10 for each goal, with 10 indicating an excellent performance. The score was 3 for hunger, but the experts noted that China had already halved the proportion of hungry people in line with its Millennium challenge, while East Asia and Latin America were on target to do so by 2015. The experts, however, predicted the level of hunger in the Middle East, sub-Saharan Africa, and South Asia was likely to rise. China and India, in particular, were highlighted among at least 96 countries that have failed to provide primary education for over 100 million children. Unless the current pace of and magnitude of marginalization of LDCs are not reversed, swiftly and decisively, achievement of most of these international development goals will remain a far cry.

CONCLUDING REMARKS

Objective conditions in the contemporary world economy clearly demonstrate that benefits of globalization are increasingly being accruing to industrialized countries, especially in the so-called triad—the United States, the European Union, and Japan. Except for a few newly industrialized economies, most of the developing countries, and almost all the LDCs, are increasingly being marginalized. The momentum toward globalization seems to be pursued at the expense of the LDCs, home for more than one-tenth of the world population. The LDCs are not only losing ground in terms of economic growth, raising export income, increasing standard of living, reducing poverty, and gaining in human development, they are also literally caught in a vicious circle—they face disappointing prospects in mobilizing domestic resources, harnessing domestic or external resources for investment, and attaining any meaningful gains in factor productivity. As Table 1.9 shows, almost all credible indicators of economic globalization—such as economic growth, income gaps between rich and poor nations, flows of foreign aid and foreign direct investment (FDI), manufacturing value added (MVA), trade balances, technology transfer, and debt burdens—lead to an unavoidable conclu-

Table 1.9
Ten Indicators of Marginalization of the LDCs

Indicators	
1. Number of LDCs	Increased from 24 in 1973 to 50 in 2003
2. LDCs share in global GDP	Roughly 0.5% in the 1990s
3. LDC share in global trade flows	Less than 0.4% between 1990 and 1996
4. Per capita GDP growth in LDCs	0.4% during 1990–1998 period
5. Share in global flows of foreign direct investment	2.2% in the late 1990s
6. Share in manufacturing value added (sub-Saharan Africa only)	Fell from 2.6% in 1980 to 1.6% in 2000
7. Trend in primary commodity prices	Dipped to –13% in 1998 and –14.2% in 1999
8. Technology transfer	Specialized technology imports declined and general purpose technology imports increased
9. Income gaps between rich and poor nations	Ratio increased from 30 to 1 in 1960 to 60 to 1 in 1990, and 74 to 1 in 1997
10. Official Development Assistance (ODA)	ODA declined from 37% of OECD/DAC countries' total aid in 1989/90 to 30% in 1999/2000

Source: Complied from Dowlah (2004).

sion that the processes of marginalization of the LDCs have been deepening further in recent years and decades. Then a look at Table 1.10 would indicate how willing the global community is to write-off one-tenth of the humanity that lives in the LDCs at the altar of globalization.

NOTES

1. See Khor (2000) for other dimensions of rising inequality between rich and poor countries, such as polarization of economic benefits of globalization in a few countries, and their implications on different income groups, investment flows, and job and income securities.

2. The Triad, along with ten other most favored destinations of FDI—including Argentina, China, Mexico, Poland, and Singapore—accounted for 84 percent of the world's FDI flows during the same period. See Hirst and Thompson (1999); Kozul-Wright and Rowthorn (1998); and Held (2000, 110).

3. See Draft Zanzibar Declaration of the LDC Trade Ministers (2001); ADB (2001); and Chapter 1 in David, Nordstorm, and Winters (2001).

4. Inclusion of Bangladesh, which accounts for a quarter of the economic size of the LDC group and which maintained a steady and sustained growth rate during the period, gives a 3.2 percent per annum growth rate for the LDCs.

Table 1.10

Structure and Protection in Quad Countries Facing LDC Exports, 1999 (in Percentages)

	Japan	US	Canada	EU
A. LDC share of competitive imports	0.81	1.32	0.27	1.55
B. LDC share of total imports	0.33	0.69	0.11	1.26
C. Share of LDC exports facing protection	51.1	48.3	54.6	3.1
D. Share of LDC exports facing tariff > 5%	22.2	47.0	54.4	3.1
E. Share of duty free LDCs in nonoil and nonarm imports into Quad countries in 2000*	63.1	13.6	30.6	97.3

Source: UNCTAD (2002).
Note: *Bora (2002).

5. The LDCs that are considered civil-strife-torn include: Afghanistan, Burundi, Congo Democratic Republic, Rwanda, Sierra Leone, and Somalia.

6. Even those LDCs that are growing, warned UNCTAD Secretary General, "there will be an ever present danger that external shocks, natural disasters, or negative spillover effects from neighboring LDCs, will disrupt economic activity and throw them off their fragile growth trajectories" (UNCTAD 2000b).

7. Except, of course, the oil-exporting LDCs—Angola, Equatorial Guinea, Sudan, and Yemen.

8. A negative growth trend in LDC merchandise exports continued in 2000, when 31 LDCs, those the WTO categorizes as merchandise exporters, registered a negative growth of 3 percent. But those LDCs that experienced prolong periods of conflict and civil strife in the 1990s (Afghanistan, Burundi, Congo, Rwanda, Sierra Leone, and Somalia) experienced a precipitous 12 percent decline in merchandise exports in the same year. In 2001, however, merchandise exports of LDCs bounced back—commodity exporting 31 LDCs grew at a hefty rate of 12 percent, while negative growth rates of 6 LDCs with civil strife fell to 7 percent (WTO 2002, 6–7).

9. UNCTAD (2000b, 15) sees a rather strong correlation between the commodity terms of trade and LDC economic performance. It observes that if the current trend in commodity price persists, "there is a danger that growth rates in many LDCs will return to the weak performance of the early 1990s, a period when the commodity terms of trade also fell sharply."

10. Mayer (2000), on the basis of a study on 46 low-income countries, suggests that although trade integration as well as technology imports of low-income countries as a group have increased over the past two decades, specialized technology imports have been smaller compared to general-purpose technology. The GDP ratio of specialized technology imports was generally about half of general-purpose technology imports; it fell to about one third in the 1990s.

11. As Kofi Anan, the UN Secretary-General, pointed out at the Third UN LDC Conference in Brussels in May 2001, "During the 1990s—a decade of unprecedented prosperity

for most industrialised countries—official development aid declined and LDCs suffered disproportionately."

12. Japan, however, maintained its aid flow at a stable aid/GNI ratio of around 0.30 percent during the same period. By 1998, only five Scandinavian countries—Denmark, Luxemburg, the Netherlands, Norway, and Sweden—had met the special targets for the ODA as set forth in the UN Program of Action for the LDCs for the 1990s (ECOSOC 2003).

13. For details see the Report on the Fourth Session (8–12 April 2002) of the UN Committee for Development Policy (ECOSOC 2003) and the *DAC Journal—Development Cooperation: 2001 Report*, Vol. 3, No. 1 (2002).

14. In the same period, four oil-exporting LDCs received over 50 percent of the FDI flows.

15. It is, however, notable that about half of this debt stock was concentrated in six countries—Angola, Bangladesh, Democratic Republic of Congo, Ethiopia, Mozambique, and Sudan.

16. Unsustainable external debt is measured by a ratio of the net present value of debt stocks to exports.

17. Fifteen percent of children born in the LDCs do not survive their fifth birthday, double the rate in the developed world, and life expectancy in LDCs is 51 years, compared to 65 years in the developed world.

18. These countries are: Burkina Faso, Burundi; Central African Republic; Congo, Ethiopia, Lesotho, Malawi, Togo, Uganda, Tanzania, and Zambia. However, the AIDS epidemic is considered to be the main cause for this debacle.

19. See for details, IMF/OECD/UN/World Bank Group (2000). A Better World for All—Progress Towards the International Development Goals.

Multilateral Trade Regimes under the GATT/WTO: How Do They Contribute to Marginalization of the LDCs?

INTRODUCTION

This chapter examines multilateral trade negotiations held, and agreements reached, under the auspices of the General Agreement on Tariff and Trade (GATT)—and its successor, the World Trade Organization (WTO)—in order to ascertain how these trade regimes—negotiation processes and agreements—contributed to the marginalization of the LDCs in the contemporary world economy.[1] It is, indeed, interesting that when it comes to international trade policies and regimes—rules and regulations that govern interrelationships between and among trading nations—John Maynard Keynes' (1936, 383) famous statement that all practical men "who believe themselves exempt from any intellectual influence, are usually the slaves of some defunct economist" does not seem to hold much ground. In the realm of international trade and trade regimes, the statement that rather fits the reality the best perhaps comes from Robert Baldwin, who asserts that international trade is "a subject where the advice of economists is routinely disregarded" (cited in Appleyard and Field 2001, 231).

Despite the fact that most economists are for free trade, ever since the emergence of powerful liberal thinkers like Adam Smith, David Hume, John Stuart Mill, and David Ricardo, trade policies and regimes around the world have emerged almost entirely in the opposite direction over the course of last two centuries.[2] Ironically, the actual trade regimes did not make protectionist theorists happy either, as prosperity of the so-called core countries surged and with the exception of a handful of countries most of the so-called periphery countries remained in the periphery. Moreover, neither did the GATT nor does the WTO promote free trade—they rather provide platforms for negotiated trade, and such negotiations never hinged on economic and business interests alone, never demonstrated unreserved commitment to the principle and practice of free trade, and they, indeed, always demonstrate an exercise in political economy.

Historically international trade policies and regimes were conditioned by economic as well as political and social factors—whereby interactions of individuals and institutions, interest groups and business interests, domestic and international issues came to interplay in the ultimate policy outcomes. While multilateral trade regimes provide platforms for "exchange of liberalization commitments," where bargaining and negotiation power is largely based on a member country's "market power" in influencing prices on world market (Hoekman and Kostecki 2001, 25–26), a member country's response to international trade rules and regulations is shaped by "how the institutions, values and ideologies, and distribution of international economic and political power" (Baldwin 1996, 156), that is, individual citizens, common-interest groups, the domestic government, and foreign governments/international organizations, react to such international trade shocks.

This chapter is organized as follows. The next section sheds light on the evolution of multilateral trade institutions of the GATT and the WTO. The section following that one looks into the multilateral trade negotiations and agreements that took place under the auspices of the GATT, and the section following that one explains the negotiations and outcomes of the WTO ministerials held so far. The following section evaluates the GATT/WTO trade regimes from the perspectives of the LDCs, followed by the conclusion.

FROM GATT TO WTO—INSTITUTIONAL EVOLUTION

The General Agreement on Tariffs and Trade

The GATT was essentially an institution of what we called the second wave of globalization. The original GATT agreement was signed by 23 countries, known as contracting parties, on October 30, 1947. Eleven of the signatories were developing countries—Brazil, Burma (Myanmar), Ceylon (Sri Lanka), Chile, China, Cuba, India, Lebanon, Pakistan, Rhodesia, and Syria. The developed country signatories to the agreement were: Australia, Belgium, Luxembourg, Netherlands, New Zealand, Norway, the United Kingdom, the United States, France, Canada, and Czechoslovakia.[3] The GATT was established with the objective to raise the standard of living across the world, by ensuring full utilization of global resources, increasing volume of real income and effective demand, and expanding production and exchange of goods and services globally (GATT 1972). Moreover, the GATT emphasized the twin principles of reciprocity and uniform rights and obligations for all contracting parties—it contained no special provision for developing countries, although almost half of the contracting parties that signed the original agreement were developing countries.

Soon, however, the GATT would change its grandiose design and vision, befitting the character of the second wave of globalization, transforming itself into an exclusive club of the rich and industrialized countries. Responding to the "'hanging power equations" in the immediate aftermath of World War II (Shukla 2000), the GATT effectively turned itself at the mercy of global corporate interests, and instead of promoting trade liberalization or rule-based trade across the world, its agenda and actions came to be conditioned more by the pursuit of corporate capitalist interests (Jackson 1992). Although the GATT had no official obligation to promote free trade, as the original GATT agreement never accompanied such a political rhetoric, it was obliged to administer rule-based international trade and commerce, as opposed to results-based trade policies. The major differences between the two approaches of international trade are that while the former adheres to commonly accepted international rules, such as most-favored-nation (MFN) treatment, and prefers tariffs rather than import quotas restrictions or voluntary export restraints (VERs), multilateral negotiations, and so on, the latter, which is more sort of managed trade, is more geared at unilateral and discriminatory actions for achieving specific targets with specific trading partners.

Also, the GATT's life and time was further conditioned by the fact that it emerged as an interim body with the limited objectives of reversing the protectionist policies of the pre–World War II period, in order to pave the way to the establishment of a permanent body to be called the International Trade Organization (ITO), with similar authority as the Bretton Woods institutions—the International Monetary Fund (IMF) and the World Bank. Although 53 countries, at the United Nations-sponsored Havana Conference agreed to create such an institution on March 24, 1948, the idea never materialized, thanks to resistance from the US Congress.[4] Eventually, the temporary GATT turned into a permanent organization, although it lacked the kind of authority envisaged for the ITO under the Havana Charter. The existence of the GATT largely depended on the mercy of the contracting parties. But thanks to the commitment of most of the contracting parties to the spirit, if not the letter, of the GATT Agreement, the GATT not only survived for decades, but also eventually could be transformed into the World Trade Organization in 1994 (Shutt 1985, 12–17). Throughout its existence, the Interim Commission for the International Trade Organization (ICITO), created by the Havana Charter for the proposed ITO, served as the secretariat of the GATT.[5]

Over the course of its five-decade-long life span, the GATT provided a global platform for rule-based trade regimes and settled scores of international trade disputes. According to Hudec (1993), the GATT succeeded in settling nine out of ten disputes among GATT trading partners. The GATT, however, met irregularly; often there were no meeting for a decade. In all, there were eight multilateral trade negotiations (henceforth MTNs) under the GATT, and in most of those MTNs developing countries largely remained "onlookers" up to the end, except the last round—the Uruguay Round (1986–1993)—that replaced the GATT with the WTO (more on this later).

The World Trade Organization

The WTO, the successor of the GATT, emerged in the midst of what we called the third wave of globalization. At the fag end of the last round of the GATT—the Uruguay Round—commerce and trade ministers from around the world signed what is called the Marrakech Ministerial Declaration, which not only ratified one of the most comprehensive and sweeping trade agreements ever reached in the entire history of human civilization, it also dismantled the GATT itself, and paved the way for the establishment of the WTO from January 1, 2005.[6] The WTO Agreement embodied the GATT (1994)—the results of seven years of UR negotiations that significantly expanded jurisdiction of the multilateral trade watchdog into the areas of services, intellectual property rights, investment measures, and so on, and also further strengthened its dispute settlement and enforcement mechanisms. The WTO is also equipped with the mandate to play a greater role in global economic policy making in cooperation with the Bretton Woods institutions—the World Bank and the IMF.[7]

The Final Act Embodying the Results of the Uruguay Round—the WTO Agreement—consists of a preamble, 16 Articles, and four Annexes. The expanded GATT system under the WTO included 12 agreements in the goods area, in addition to the General Agreement on Trade in Services (GATS), the Trade-Related Intellectual Property Rights (TRIPs), the Trade-Related Investment Measures (TRIMs), and the Dispute Settlement Understanding (DSU). The WTO agreement not only empowered the institution with stronger monitoring and enforcement authorities, compared with its predecessor GATT, it also founded the WTO on a very different foundation. While the GATT was an intergovernmental treaty, in which signatories were designated as "contracting parties," the WTO came as an international organization, in which signatories were designated as members, and the organization is mandated to serve as a "regulator of regulatory actions taken by governments [member countries] that affect trade and the conditions of competition facing imported products on domestic markets" (Hoekman and Kostecki 2001, 37).

Moreover, unlike the Bretton Woods Institutions, in which voting rights of member countries depend on the principle of financial contribution they make to these institutions, and thus, the institutions are dominated by rich countries, the WTO agreement grants equal voting rights to each member country, and thereby eliminates lawful opportunity for rich countries to wield disproportionate power on the decision-making processes in the WTO.[8] Also, unlike the United Nations, the World Bank, and the IMF, the decisions of the WTO are binding for the members—thanks to the so-called "single- undertaking" approach that underpins the WTO agreement. Although the WTO continues the member-driven and consensus-based decision making approach, following the GATT tradition, many loopholes that blocked multilateral decisions, especially dispute settlement mechanisms in good old GATT days, have been eliminated. So far, five ministerial conferences took place under the WTO, and all were overwhelmingly participated in by developing country members, in sharp contrast to the GATT days when they were mere onlookers to MTNs.

MULTILATERAL NEGOTIATIONS AND AGREEMENTS UNDER THE GATT

The First Seven Rounds

As the following list shows, there had been eight rounds of MTNs under the GATT: the first round, held in Geneva in 1947 and participated in by 23 countries, established the GATT; the second round, held in Annecy (France) in 1948, was participated in by 29 countries; the third round, held in Torquay (England) in 1950, was participated in by 32 countries; the fourth round, held in Geneva in 1955–1956, was participated in by 33 countries; the fifth round, called the Dillion Round, held in 1960–1961, was participated in by 39 countries; the sixth round, called the Kennedy Round, held in 1964–1967, was participated in by 74 countries; the seventh round, called the Tokyo Round, held in 1973–1979, was participated in by 99 countries; and the eighth and final round, called the Uruguay Round, held in 1986–1994, was participated in by 117 countries.

- October 30, 1947—The first Round of contracting Parties, held in Geneva, established the General Agreement on Tariff and Trade (GATT)—23 countries signed the agreement. The GATT, however, came into force on January 1, 1948.
- March 24, 1948—53 countries agree sign the Havana Charter to create the International Trade Organization (ITO) with similar authority as the Bretton Woods institutions—the World Bank and the International Monetary Fund (IMF).
- 1949—The second round of the GATT negotiations—known as the Annecy Round—took place at Annecy, France—13 contracting parties agreed to 5000 tariff concessions.
- 1950—1951—the third round of GATT negotiations—known as the Torquay Round—took place in Torquay, England. A total of 38 contracting parties exchanged 8700 tariff concessions.
- 1956—The fourth round of GATT negotiations—known as the Geneva Round—took place in Geneva; with participation by 26 countries.
- 1960–1962—the fifth round of the GATT negotiations—known as Dillion Round—took place in Geneva, contracting parties agreed to 4400 tariff concessions.
- 1964–1967—the sixth round of the GATT negotiations—known as the Kennedy Round—took place in Geneva—62 contracting parties exchanged trade concessions, representing 75 percent of total world trade.
- 1973–1979—the seventh round of GATT negotiations—known as the Tokyo Round—took place mostly in Geneva. It was joined by 102 countries. GATT negotiations cover nontariff issues as well—as subsidies, government procurement, dairy products, and civil aircraft were brought under the GATT negotiations.
- 1986–1993—The eighth round—known as the Uruaguay Round—took place mostly in Geneva. This round succeeded in reaching one of the most comprehensive trade agreements in world history.
- April 15, 1994—Ministers from some 120 countries signed the Final Act of Uruguay Round in Marrakech, replacing the GATT with the World Trade Organization.

The first GATT round, which established the GATT itself, envisaged reciprocal and mutually advantageous arrangements of international trade, elimination of discriminatory treatment in international commerce, and the granting of most-favored-nation (MFN) status to all contracting parties on a reciprocal basis. The participants also agreed on concessions to some 45,000 tariff lines, besides setting up some specific rules to prevent restrictive trade regimes. The next four rounds of GATT negotiations concentrated primarily on tariff reductions, often on a cumbersome product-by-product basis. The second round negotiated some 5000 tariff concessions, the third round negotiated a further 8700 tariff concessions, and the fourth round negotiated a further 44,00o tariff lines. Estimated benefits of such tariff concessions ran into billions of dollars per year—the tariff cuts of the Dillion Round alone were estimated at $5 billion.

But a real breakthrough in tariff cuts came at the Kennedy Round, when participating countries agreed to an average tariff cut by 35 percent, in addition to binding tariffs on 33,000 tariff lines. The round also addressed some nontariff trade barriers (NTBs), especially by reaching agreements on customs valuation and antidumping issues.[9] Then, the Tokyo Round succeeded in further tariff reductions; it alone was responsible for bringing down weighted average tariff on manufactured goods in the OECD countries from 7 percent to 4.7 percent (Das 2000, 183–84). The Tokyo Round also further widened the GATT coverage on NTBs—it reached agreements on scores of trade-related issues, including subsidies and countervailing measures, technical barriers to trade (TBT), import licensing procedures, antidumping laws, and government procurement.

The first seven rounds of MTNs under the GATT were specifically devoted to reduction of manufacturing tariffs, and they all were actively participated in by developed countries, while developing countries were passive onlookers to the negotiations. Several factors were responsible for this situation. First, many developing countries were not members of the GATT, and only a handful of them maintained official representation in Geneva. Most of the developing countries—37 of them—joined the GATT in 1987, after the seventh round of the GATT, and when the eighth round, the Uruguay Round, was well underway. Moreover, developing country members of the GATT, prior to the UR, were swimming against trade liberalization—kept themselves busy in seeking legitimacies for sheltering domestic production under import substitution, infant industry protection, and other protectionist agendas.[10]

Second, as TWN (2001) points out, until the Kennedy Round (1964–1967), all GATT tariff negotiations were bilateral, based on reciprocal, product-by-product exchange of concessions of manufactures. Developing countries, being primarily commodity exporters, had little to gain or lose from such negotiations. The first seven rounds of GATT MTNs did bring down tariff rates significantly, but that affected products of export interest to industrialized countries, not much so for products of export interest to developing countries. The Kennedy Round, for example, brought down tariffs by 50 percent for many manufacturing goods, but that affected 26 percent of goods of export interest to developing countries, compared to 36 percent of goods of export interest of developed countries. Similarly, the tariff reduction of the Tokyo Round affected 26 percent of goods of export interests to developing countries, compared with 33 percent for developed countries (Hudec 1987). Third, as Tussie and Lengyel (2002) point out, up until the Uruguay Round, developed countries saw the minimal size of developing countries' markets "as not being worth the effort of pressing for greater access."

Fourth, while manufacturing tariffs, in which developed countries had export interests, crumbled down with successive rounds of GATT, trade in primary products, such as agriculture, in which developing countries had export interests, remained almost absolutely outside the GATT discipline. On the other hand, trade in some manufacturing products, in which developing countries had export interests, such as textiles and clothing, was left to scores of arbitrary and bilateral agreements.[11]

Of course, the GATT followed the path of tariff reduction in manufacturing, but it did so adhering to the twin principles of reciprocity and MFN agreements, while carefully avoiding the textiles and clothing sector in which developing countries had great export interest. As Dowlah (1999) points out, the trade regimes in textiles and clothing were ruled by a complex mosaic of bilateral quotas and quantitative restrictions (QRS) throughout the GATT period. As discussed in Chapter 4, while each of the GATT rounds led to further trade liberalization in manufacturing products of export interest to the developed world, trade in textile and clothing evolved in the opposite direction. International trade in this sector came under multiple forms of restrictive measures negotiated bilaterally under the Multifiber Arrangements (MFA), which began in early 1970s, survived more than two decades in full sweep, until the UR called for its elimination by 2005. The GATT also allowed developed countries to impose voluntary export restraints (VER) on emerging developing country suppliers in many products, such as shoes and iron and steel, restraining developing country entry into the processed goods markets. Similarly, under the GATT waiver, known as the Special and Differential Treatment (SDT) measures, various schemes of tariff quotas and escalations often discouraged product processing, in agriculture as well as manufacturing, in developing countries (discussed in Chapter 3).

As agricultural trade remained almost completely outside the GATT discipline, up until the launching of the UR in 1986, the GATT had no qualms with the highly subsidized and protected US agricultural trade regime, ushered in by the Agricultural Adjustment Act of 1933, way before the establishment of the GATT itself. Then, in the 1960s, the European Community emulated the US example, by creating the Common Agricultural Policy (CAP), which perhaps set one of the most glaring examples of heavily subsidized agricultural production as well as exports in the history of international trade, but the GATT had no face to oppose it.

The pursuance of such economically costly and highly inefficient agricultural trade policies, although they often served deeply entrenched and vested interests in developed countries, gravely impacted global welfare, especially in developing countries, which enjoyed natural comparative advantage in agriculture (discussed in Chapter 5). One of the most serious consequences of this trend had been that declining prices of primary commodities relative to manufactured goods led to worsening of terms of trade for developing countries relative to manufacturing exporters. According to Bleaney and Greenaway (1993), during the 1950s through the 1980s (1955–1989, to be precise), a 1 percent deterioration in the terms of trade of primary products translated into a 0.3 percent deterioration in the terms of trade for developing countries as a whole.[12] Deterioration in commodity terms of trade resulted in developing countries' loss of around $300 billion of foreign exchange in the 1980s, which is more than twice the net inflow of resources into these countries during the decade (UNCTAD cited in Thirlwall 2003, 666).[13]

The Uruguay Round (1986–1993)

The Uruguay Round, the eighth and last round of multilateral trade negotiations under the GATT, came as a watershed event in the entire history of global governance in international trade. Many of the contentious issues, mentioned above, received greater attention, even led to prolonged and acrimonious negotiations in this round. The UR produced the most comprehensive trade agreement in the history of international trade, if not in the entire history of humankind. It also paved the way for replacement of the GATT—which, by design or default, consciously or subconsciously, served the purposes of rich industrialized countries, often at the expense of poor countries—by the WTO, a multilateral trade watchdog bent on a grandiose promise to liberalize trade across the world, across the sectors—no matter in manufacturing, agriculture, or service, no matter in developed, developing, or least developed countries.

The UR agreements were reached by the end of 1994, in the immediate aftermath of the Cold War that heralded a unipolar world, symbolizing, politically, universal triumph of capitalism over its archrival socialism/communism, and economically, a knockout victory of free market and free trade over autarchic, nationalistic, or protectionist policies. They also came in the midst of the more inclusive third wave of globalization, as many as 123 countries, most of them from developing parts of the world, took active part in seven years of protracted negotiations under the UR. Also, by mid-1980s, scores of developing countries developed a stake in global trade—not only did they graduate from primary commodities to manufactures, but they also began to swim with the current, as multilateral trade negotiations and rule-based trading system became more relevant to their export interests. Facing increasing competition in manufactures from developing countries, industrialized countries also found it worthwhile to involve developing countries more actively in MTNs. The rest of the developing countries, including LDCs, also embraced a more participatory attitude, "either out of conviction or because of fears of closing markets and the implications of conditional most-favored-nation (MFN) principle" (Tussie and Lengyel 2002, 486).

The UR agreements, which, unlike the previous GATT rounds, professed commitment to free-market and free-trade principles, succeeded in correcting some of the long-standing aberrations in international trade and commerce under the GATT system. First, in sharp departure from the previous GATT rounds, the UR called for phasing out of the Multi-fiber Arrangement (MFA) that kept the textile and clothing sector under protective shields in the developed world, and a gradual but complete integration of agricultural trade into the GATT discipline. Second, as discussed in Chapter 4, the UR Agreement in Agriculture (URAA) called for "strengthened and more operationally effective" rules in agricultural market access, export subsidies, and domestic supports for liberalizing this sector from protectionist measures. At the same time, the UR left out much of the reforms necessary for liberalizing agricultural trade to diverse interpretations, country discretions and future negotiations, breeding considerable controversy and mixed outcomes of the agreement ever since the agreement was signed (Valdes and McCalla 1996; Dowlah 2003b; Ingco and Kandiero 2001). Similarly, discontent of developing countries continued with the UR Agreement on Textiles and Clothing (ATC) as the end-loaded agreement allows developed countries to maintain significant tariff walls and protection until early 1995 (Martin and Winters 1996; Dowlah 1999).

Third, prolonged negotiations under the UR also brought in scores of new areas under the rule-based trade system envisaged under the WTO. As mentioned above, the final document of the UR agreements included scores of agreements covering wide-ranging issues, such as international trade in services, intellectual property rights, sanitary and phytosanitary measures, safeguard measures, technical barriers, dispute settlement, customs valuation, antidumping, import licensing, and subsidies. Most of these agreements are still highly controversial, indicating that many of the member countries might have signed these agreements, being carried away with the euphoria of the collapse of communism and the triumph of capitalism, without proper understanding of their implications on their economies or international trade.

Some of these new issues, such as labor issues, eco-labeling, and phytosanitary measures, may not strictly fall into trade agenda, and are rather widely believed to be new forms of NTBs. The UR, however, grants either exemption or transition periods to developing countries and the LDCs in respects to many of these agreements. The UR also continued the so-called GATT waiver,[14] the STD measures of the GATT, albeit in a diluted form than under the GATT, although the benefits of SDTs to developing countries and LDCs are also questionable (Dowlah 2003a).

Finally, there are still concerns with the sweeping character of the UR agreements, and the way developing countries were herded into signing these agreement in Marrakech in 1994. Many argue that the organizers exploited the paranoia that persisted at the end of the Cold War. Most developing countries and LDCs, which took little part in the prolonged negotiations under the UR, were least prepared to face the onslaught of global competition and still, suffering from the paranoia in the immediate aftermath of the sudden death of communism, found it difficult not to jump on the bandwagon of free trade and economic globalization. With the setting in of greater understanding of the implications of the agreements that they might have signed in 1994 without much understanding, many developing countries, their governments as well as civil societies, are now even trying to reverse some of those agreements, instead of moving forward with the developed countries' agenda of widening and deepening the WTO.

WTO MINISTERIAL CONFERENCES

The post-UR period, although brief, just about a decade, has already witnessed transfixing developments, thanks to sweeping momentum in the third wave of globalization, in which information revolution, especially the Internet, has literally wiped out geographical distance, and made it possible for millions of people from across the world to watch events and developments simultaneously anywhere in the world, and more important, to communicate and interact right away. Then, there are e-commerce and e-economics, and about half of goods and services produced in the world are facing competition; almost every production and trade everywhere in the world is somehow affected by the rules and regulations, disputes and decrees, debates and deliberations of the WTO. No wonder, the world community, in the strictest sense of the term, has been watching the WTO activities more closely than any other multilateral organization that ever existed before.[15]

The WTO has come to global limelight for several reasons. First, the WTO agreement mandates it to hold a biannual meeting of its top decision-making body, known as the WTO Ministerial. Its predecessor—the GATT—had no such obligation. In fact, the GATT decision-making body often did not meet for years. Second, the WTO agreements commit the institution to greater transparency and accountability in all its deliberations and multilateral trade negotiations, and this transparency requirement applies to both the WTO and its members.[16] Third, as mentioned above, unlike the World Bank, the IMF, or the United Nations, the WTO entitles equal voting rights to each of its member countries, and all decisions are to be reached through consensus.[17] Finally, the WTO agreements are enshrined in what is called "the single undertaking approach," which requires all member countries to the WTO—no matter developed or developing—to enforce almost the same set of trade rules and obligations.[18]

The WTO, as a global watchdog of international trade and trading policies, as Hoekman (2002) has enumerated, has five distinct areas of responsibilities: (a) providing an institutional framework for implementation of multinational trade agreements (MTAs)—that is, monitoring and surveillance of implementation of agreements to which member countries committed themselves; (b) providing a forum for MTNs—that is, providing a global platform for exchange of information and communication on national trade policies and regimes, conducting negotiations and bargains on multilateral trading agreements; (c) administering dispute settlement mechanisms—that is, adjudicating trade disputes as well as noncompliance of WTO rules on a multilateral basis, through panels of impartial experts; (d) monitoring trade policies of member countries—that is, making sure that member countries reform their trade rules, laws, and regulations conforming their WTO obligations; and finally, (e) cooperating with sister organizations, such as the World Bank and the IMF, in order to "achieve greater coherence in global economic policy making." Unlike the GATT, the WTO is obliged by its own mandate, as well as by the agreements signed with the Bretton Woods institutions, to strengthen interagency cooperation and collaboration through periodic joint meetings at top policy levels as well as official levels.

The WTO is also responsible for maintaining the principles of nondiscrimination, reciprocity, and enforceability. The principles of nondiscrimination refer to the MFN principle—treating same or similar products of every member country with the same levels of tariff—and the principle of national treatment—which refers to treating goods imported from another country to the same set of rules—taxes and other charges—that apply to identical goods of domestic origin. The principle of reciprocity basically refers to trade liberalization on a quid pro quo basis, reducing domestic barriers on a reciprocal and mutually advantageous basis. But the concept often draws controversy as "neither the GATT nor the WTO provides further specification of what is 'reciprocal' or of what is 'mutually advantageous'" (Finger and Winters 2002, 51). The principle of enforceability refers to ensuring that liberalization commitments and agreements are implemented and maintained.[19]

Since the Marrakech Ministerial in 1994, which founded the WTO, so far there have been five ministerial conferences. As the following list shows, those where held in Singapore (1996), Geneva (1998), Seattle (1999), Doha (2001), and Cancun (2003). Major accomplishments of these ministerials are discussed later.

- January 1, 1995—The WTO came into force.
- December 1996—The first Ministerial Conference of the WTO was held in Singapore. Participated in by more than 120 member countries, the ministerial established working groups on so-called Singapore Issues, such as trade and investment, trade and competition policy, and transparency in government procurement.
- May 18–20, 1998—The second Ministerial Conference of the WTO was held in Geneva.
- November–December 1999—The third Ministerial Conference of the WTO was held in Seattle. Attended by 135 member countries, the ministerial ended up in fiasco, mainly over farm subsidies and labor standards, and also because of massive anti-WTO demonstrations.
- November 2001—The fourth Ministerial Conference of the WTO was held in Doha, Qatar. More than 140 member countries launched a new round call "the Doha Round," to cut farm subsidies, cut industrial tariffs, and resolve Singapore issues.
- September 2003—The fifth Ministerial Conference of the WTO took place in Cancun, Mexico. Participated in by 150 member countries, the conference collapsed mainly over farm subsidies and the Singapore issues.

Singapore Ministerial (1996)

The Singapore Ministerial, the first since the WTO came into existence, expressed the WTO's commitment to "a fair, equitable and more open rule-based" global trading system, and found global and regional trade liberalization as "mutually supportive processes" that could assist the LDCs and transition economies in integrating into the international trading system. For "faithful implementation" of the provisions of the UR Agreement on Textiles and Clothing, it asked members to use safeguard measures "as sparingly as possible." The Ministerial also reviewed progress made in fulfillment of the Marrakech objectives in financial services,

movement of natural persons, maritime transport services, and basic telecommunications, and called for concluding negotiations on basic telecommunications and
maritime transport services and resumption of negotiations on financial services
by 1997. The directives were followed through. By 1997, negotiations on the
Agreement on Telecommunications, the Financial Services Agreement, and the
Information Technology Agreement were successfully concluded.[20]

The Ministerial also emphasized greater efforts for implementing Marrakech
commitments made to the agricultural sector, in respect to market access concessions, domestic subsidy, and export subsidy, expressing concerns for possible negative effects of agricultural reform program on LDCs and net food-importing
developing countries. There were, however, no concrete goals to achieve by any
specific deadline. In regard to the concerns of the LDCs, the Singapore Ministerial
agreed to: (a) a Plan of Action for expanding duty-free access; (b) enhance conditions for predictable and favorable market access conditions for LDCs' products;
and (c) involve aid agencies and multilateral financial institutions to foster an integrated approach to assist the LDCs in enhancing their trading opportunities.
Finally, the Ministerial agreed to establish four working groups—on trade and investment, trade and competition policy, transparency in government procurement,
and trade facilitation—which subsequently came down as the "Singapore Issues."
The Ministerial, however, opposed an EU proposal to launch a new round on the
Singapore Issues. Developing countries rather called for proper implementation of
already-agreed-upon issues during the Uruguay Round.

Geneva Ministerial (1998)

The second WTO Ministerial, held in Geneva, was more modest compared to
the Singapore Ministerial. It coincided with two contrasting developments—a
cause of celebration for the multilateral trading system as the GATT turned fifty,
and a great cause of concern, as a rapidly-brewing-up financial crisis in the East
Asian countries put the IMF under fire. The Ministerial welcomed the successful
conclusion of the negotiations on basic telecommunications, financial services,
and the implementation of the Information Technology Agreement. It also expressed concern at the marginalization of the LDCs and certain small economies,
called for redressing the chronic foreign debt problem that many of these countries
faced. The Ministerial also asked the WTO General Council to ensure full and
timely implementation of existing agreements and decisions taken in Marrakech
and Singapore.

Seattle Ministerial (1999)

In contrast to the Geneva Ministerial, the Seattle Ministerial in 1999 came with
great expectations—as thousands of people from all over the world—academics
and observers, policy makers and civil society activists—flocked together in Seattle.[21] With the famous V-shaped recovery of the East Asian economies along with
US and other major economies growing robustly,[22] organizers kept their fingers

crossed to launch the first-ever round of multilateral trade negotiations under the WTO. The Seattle Ministerial, however, ended in fiasco, without launching a new round and without even deciding where to meet the next time. There had been divergent explanations of the debacle—from all kinds of viewpoints and platforms. A careful look into the evolving literature on this issue would lead one to at least three major strands of thought: (a) backlash from antiglobalization forces, (b) a serious deadlock at the negotiating table, and (c) problems with the structure and process of multilateral negotiations.

The Backlash Theory. Globalization has, indeed, produced losers and gainers, and has increased income and social disparities between and within countries. There is no dearth of people, forums, and institutions who are disgruntled with the processes of globalization, or the nations and institutions that are at the forefront of the globalizing forces. As the world witnessed in Seattle, several thousand protesters, representing more than 1000 nongovernmental organizations (NGOs) of environmentalists, labor unions, human rights activists, and others demonstrated on the streets. To them the WTO was the scapegoat for all global ills—such as deforestation, child labor, overfishing, and pollution. And then, as Bhagwati (2004) points out, although they come from different intellectual and ideological directions and do not share the same set of ideas or sentiments, they are linked by a "trilogy of discontents"—composed of anticapitalist, antiglobalization, and an acute anticorporation mind-set. Many of them, especially those who want to broaden their targets to the Bretton Woods institutions as well, are also critical of imposing policy prescriptions of unelected and unaccountable international bureaucracies on the sovereign national governments (Lindsay 2000). Ironically, most of the protesters—people as well as institutions—that gathered in Seattle were from developed countries, while ordinarily one would hope that the resistance would come from the poorer parts of the world (Bhagwati 2004, 21–27).

The Deadlock Theory. Those who ascribe the Seattle debacle to a deadlock at the negotiating table make the following arguments. First, the US Congress denied "fast-track" negotiating authority to the Clinton Administration for negotiations at the WTO; therefore, US Trade Representative Charlene Barshefsky did not have legal backing to push for any specific agenda. Second, while industrial economies in Seattle pressed for "broadening and deepening" of the WTO with the inclusion of the so-called Singapore Issues—investment, competition, government procurement, labor and environment—developing countries not only rebuffed the effort, but also sought relief from some of the previously agreed upon obligations. But neither the United States, nor other developed country members of the Cairns Group were willing to consider any exemptions from the obligations negotiated under the UR. Moreover, the United States declared that acceleration of its textile commitments and discussion of its antidumping mechanism were off the table, and the EU sought to defer negotiations on implementation issues to a comprehensive new round.

Finally, the Seattle Ministerial had no previously agreed-upon agenda—thanks to significant disagreements among member countries over a number of basic issues. Especially, acrimonious debates between two major parties—the United

States and the European Union—involving two major issues–agriculture and labor—continued. The EU, in order to protect its highly protectionist Common Agricultural Policy (CAP), was pushing for a broader negotiating agenda focusing on
investment and competition policy. The United States, on the other hand, opposed
the EU position of "anything but agriculture," and insisted on links between trade
and labor rights. Also, while leading agricultural exporters like Argentina, Australia, Brazil, and the US wanted an all-out assault on agricultural trade, the EU, Japan, and Korea together with their allies fought to keep a more modest agenda in
agriculture. The developing countries also played a role, as they opposed talks on
further liberalizations under the WTO, until they were granted leeway in implementing previous commitments.[23]

The Faulty Structure Theory. This theory puts the blame for the Seattle fiasco
squarely on lack of transparency and accountability in the WTO, and with the
faulty structure of the so-called Green Room processes of negotiations. As mentioned above, theoretically, the WTO decisions are made by consensus. In reality,
however, the members of the so-called Quad–Canada, the EU, Japan and the
United States–act as an informal steering committee for the system. This so-called
Green Room process worked well during the GATT period. Normally the Quad
members and some active members such as Australia, New Zealand, Switzerland,
Norway, and some members of the transition economies and some developing
countries like Argentina, Brazil, Hong Kong, India, and Mexico took part in the
Green Room meetings or negotiations. The Green Room process worked well under the GATT as there were fewer members, developing countries hardly participated actively, and the GATT consensus worked negatively–a consensus was
achieved when none of the members present in the negotiation disagreed with a decision. Also, as Schott and Watal (2000) point out, the participants were less political in GATT negotiations—the delegations left political rhetoric to other
international forums, such as the United Nations, and developing countries remained passive as trade accords inflicted no new demands on them, while they
gained from trade accords that gradually opened MFN status to them.

But the Green Room process fell apart at the Seattle Ministerial—it literally back-
fired when the US Trade Representative Charlene Barshefsky and WTO Director
General Mike Moore attempted to pull together a declaration to launch a new Round.
The attempt infuriated many developing country members, as they were insisting on
implementation of the earlier agreements, while the Quad were trying to launch a new
round with the support of a handful of powerful developing-country members. On the
concluding day of the meeting, many developing country members from Africa, the
Caribbean basin, and Latin America voiced concern over transparency of the Green
Room process and the discontent was so strong that the ministerial had to be suspended without even presenting any declaration. As discussed in Chapter 6, the Seattle debacle raised serious questions about the efficiency of the age-old Green Room
process mainly because, unlike the good old days of GATT, now many developing
countries have developed a stake with WTO negotiations and their outcomes, their
number swelled to more than 100, and, in the post-UR period, developing countries

have increased the size and activities of their diplomatic missions in Geneva. They can no longer be taken for granted.

Doha Ministerial (2001)

The Doha Ministerial, although held in Qatar, an unlikely place for transparency or accountability or anything else that the WTO supposedly stands for, sought to bring the trade issue at the center of development and poverty alleviation, underscoring the need for benefiting all people "from the increased opportunities and welfare gains that the multilateral trading system generates." The Ministerial promised to "make positive efforts" to ensure that developing countries, and especially the LDCs, secure "a share in the growth of world trade commensurate with the needs of their economic development." The Ministerial underlined that special and differential treatments (SDTs) to developing countries "shall be an integral part of all negotiations" so that schedules of concessions, commitments, rules, and disciplines can be negotiated by taking into account the development needs of these countries. Also, responding to the Zanzibar Declaration of the LDCs,[24] the Doha Ministerial committed itself to the objective of "duty-free, quota-free market access for products originating from LDCs," and recognized that integration of the LDCs into the multilateral trading system would require "meaningful market access, support for the diversification of their production and export base, and trade-related technical assistance and capacity building." It also made a commitment to a significant increase in the contributions to the Integrated Framework (IF) trust fund[25] and the WTO extrabudgetary trust funds in favor of LDCs. The Ministerial also resolved to review all SDT measures "with a view to strengthening them and making them more precise, effective and operational."[26]

Cancun Ministerial (2003)

The Cancun (Mexico) Ministerial, held in September 2003, collapsed mainly because of deadlocks in negotiations on the issues advanced at the Doha ministerial and the Singapore Ministerial. At the center of the storm was the farm reforms—the issues of reduction of domestic support, increasing market access, and elimination of export subsidies, areas in which the Doha Ministerial promised to bring about substantial improvements. At the Ministerial, the Cairns Group joined Australia, Canada, and Brazil, which accounted for one-third of world farm exports, pushed for market openings and for the EU, Japan, and United States to cut subsidies and reduce import tariffs. Also Cancun saw a formidable developing country group, called the G-21— which included Argentina, Brazil, China, Egypt, India, Indonesia, Mexico, Nigeria, Pakistan, Philippines, Thailand, South Africa, and Venezuela—countries from three continents—Africa and Asia and Latin America, that could claim representation of over 60 percent of the world's farmers. The G-21 demanded that the EU and the United States slash their agricultural supports and subsidies. Most other developing countries also made it clear that without progress in agriculture, there could be no real movement on lowering barriers to trade in industrial goods or services.

The Cancun Ministerial, however, failed to reach any agreement in farm issues. It considered the so-called Harbinson draft, which the EU rejected as "too ambitious," and developing countries, as well as Australia and the United States, found to be "too tentative."[27] Another proposal by Uruguay ambassador Carlos Perez del Castillo, proposing a compromise between the EU and the US positions, was also watered down. The eventual collapse of the Cancun, however, centered around the so-called Singapore issues—WTO rules for investment and competition policies, government contracts or procurement, and customs duties. While developed countries pressed for greater liberalization in these issues, developing countries, mainly led by India, Brazil, China, and Malaysia, rejected any deal on these issues arguing that not enough preparatory work was done for such negotiations and such agreements would infringe on government's discretion on economic decisions.

Thanks to the assertive role of developing countries in Cancun trade talks, and earlier in the Seattle Round, it has been amply demonstrated that any future negotiations have to be fairer and more participatory than ever before—gone are the good old days when the positions of developing countries could be taken for granted. One can guess the handwriting on the wall by looking at the press statements of delegates at the Cancun Conference. For example, Malaysian minister for international trade and industry Rafidah Aziz said, "Our boys have come around. We proved that the developing countries were not to be taken for granted." An African delegate said, "When our priorities are ignored and the conference refuses to discuss them, they call it a collapse. I won't call this a collapse. It is better to have no deal than to have a bad deal." Martin Khor, of the Third World Network , said, "As long as they [developed countries] insist on putting these things [Singapore issues], they will always have these types of debates and conflicts. For example, TRIPs should not belong to the WTO. These rich countries should not be looking toward exploiting us all the time." Indian Trade Minsiter Arun Jaitley said, "It seems that the much-hyped development round is meant to be development of the developed countries."[28]

But the LDCs, as a group, however, were marginalized even further—as amid acrimonious debates on protectionist agricultural policies and Singapore issues, they had little chance to push their agenda, agreed in Dhaka Declaration in July 2003, that called for greater areas of duty-free and quota-free market access, greater special and differential treatments, more assistance for capacity building, and free movement of semiskilled labor forces.[29]

CONCLUDING REMARKS: THE GATT/WTO TRADE REGIMES AND THE INTERESTS OF THE LDCS

Adverse and discriminatory effects of various GATT rounds on the interests and concerns of developing countries and the LDCs have been discussed above. A careful look at the WTO ministerial negotiations and outcomes would indicate that developed country members have been pushing for widening and deepening of the

WTO, without taking seriously the commitments they made in earlier rounds, agreements, or negotiations. The so-called widening and deepening agenda troubles developing countries because it puts them in double jeopardy—they are asked to swallow even bigger bites while they cannot chew the bites they have already taken by signing the UR agreements, knowingly or unknowingly. Many developing countries smell rat in this rat race. Second, developing countries are now required to participate actively, as the agreements reached would be binding to all, but most of them lack human or physical resources to withstand negotiation challenges, as they can hardly face the well-prepared, well-paid and well-equipped developed country delegates.

And there are some operational problems—many developing countries, especially LDCs, can hardly afford the legal expenses to challenge antidumping measures or other trade disputes, although their rights are otherwise guaranteed well in the statutes of the WTO. Moreover, as TWN/UNDP 2001 points out, "a strong enforcement system for flawed rules cannot be said to be serving a good function" when they do not promote "balance and fairness in outcome." At the same time, many developing countries, especially LDCs, lack institutional arrangements and legal infrastructures to effectively deal with WTO matters. Commitments of the multilateral bodies and the developed countries to help in capacity building in the developing countries and LDCs, as discussed in the next chapter, so far fell flat at implementation levels.

Moreover, developing countries also have problems with their parliaments, civil societies and NGOs, communist leftovers and hangovers, and so on. The agreements they sign at the WTO rounds or ministerials have to be sold to the domestic audience. Developing country delegations do not come to the WTO ministerial meetings equipped with "first track authority;" they go back to their parliaments to rubber-stamp the agreements that they have already agreed to or committed to. Many developing countries, including LDCs, burnt their fingers by signing the Marrakech Declaration without prior approval of their parliaments. Eventually, legislatures in those countries rubber-stamped the agreement without having much of a choice. Given growing consciousness of the WTO activities and agreements around the world, and global momentum toward democratic governance, these governments will find it increasingly difficult to obtain approval from their parliaments, or their electorate.

Most important, developing countries expected that in return for their joining the Uruguay Round, and subsequently the WTO, they would have greater market access to developed country markets, nontariff barriers to their trade would decline, and they would reap greater benefits from expanding international trade. The LDCs also expected a reversal of marginalization processes in the post-UR period, especially counting on liberalization of textiles and the clothing sector and agriculture, in which they have greater comparative advantage. But the post-UR experience has dashed that hope—thanks to end-loaded implementation strategies of developed countries, the textiles and clothing sector, even at the ninth year of the transition period, still remains quota-ridden and discriminatory. Agriculture, remains a highly subsidized and protected "sacred cow" in the United States and the EU, the two biggest subsidized exporters of agricultural goods in the world. The next three chapters explain in greater details how the GATT-WTO trade regimes contributed to marginalization of the LDCs, focusing on: (a) the dysfunctional consequences of the special and differential treatment measures (Chapter 3); (b) the discriminatory trade regimes in the textile and clothing sector (Chapter 4); and (c) the exclusion of the agricultural sector from the GATT discipline (Chapter 5).

NOTES

1. The concept of trade regime here is understood as the "sets of implicit or explicit principles, norms, rules, and decision making procedures around which expectations converge" in multilateral trade relations, as defined by Krasner (1983, 2). It is also notable that of the 50 countries currently classified as LDCs, 30 were members of the GATT, and became original members of the WTO. Nine more LDCs are currently negotiating for membership with the WTO: Bhutan, Cambodia, Cape Verde, Laos, Nepal, Samoa, Sudan, Vanuatu and Yemen.

2. Prior to the advent of liberal thinkers, the world was a fertile ground for the mercantilists, who preached the doctrines of nationalism and self-sufficiency, and promoted foreign trade principally through acquisition of colonies and blocking imports. The mercantilist policies brought unprecedented prosperity for many European states throughout the sixteenth and seventeenth centuries, as overseas trade expanded and colonization spread across continents. The "beggar thy neighbor policy" of the mercantilist era, however, pauperized the rest of the world. Two principal exponents of the mercantilist school; Phillip von Hornick (1638–1712) warned that "gold and silver once in the country are under no circumstances to be taken out for any purpose," and Thomas Munn (1571–1641) argued for government intervention in the economy to stimulate trade, encourage exports, and promote favorable balance of trade by importing gold. While the mercantilist era showed how feverishly the Western countries pursued trade protectionist policies when their domestic industries needed shelter, the liberal trade era showed how the same set of countries pursued the doctrine of free trade when their own industrialization bids were completed.

3. It is noticeable that Germany and Japan were not among the signatories to the original GATT agreement. Germany became a member of the GATT in 1951, Japan followed suit in 1955, and in the meantime, by 1950, three original signatories to the GATT agreement—China, Lebanon, and Syria—withdrew their membership from the organization.

4. Apparently, the US Congress' threat not to ratify the Havana Charter had to do with the comprehensive character of the institution of ITO as envisaged by the Charter. The Charter included wide ranging provisions, such as employment and economic activity, economic development and reconstruction, commercial policy, restrictive business practices (of private parties), and intergovernmental commodity agreements. Apparently, the US Congress was unwilling to give up so much to a multilateral body, and President Harry Truman preferred to withdraw it from the consideration of the Congress rather than having it voted down (see TWN 2001).

5. It is notable that although the GATT emerged from the UN-sponsored ITO negotiations, its preparatory work was done by the UN Economic and Social Council (ECOSOC), and it enjoyed "special agency" status with the UN system, "the formal relationship between the GATT and the UN was always tenuous" (Hoekman and Kostecki 2001, 38). The

WTO, successor of the GATT, does not even have such a "special agency" status with the UN. This has far-reaching implications for the operations of the WTO.

6. It is notable that a total of 125 member countries formally participated at the Marrakech Ministerial Meeting in April 1994 that ratified the Final Act Embodying the Results of the Uruguay Round of the Multilateral Trade Negotiations. But only 104 participants/countries signed the WTO Agreement. Seven countries—Australia, Botswana, Burundi, India, Japan, Republic of Korea, and the United States—did not sign the WTO Agreement in Marrakech because of legislative procedures back home.

7. The idea to establish a global trade watchdog, endowed with a permanent and solid institutional status to play a greater role in global economic policy making in cooperation with the Bretton Woods institutions, however, surfaced in 1990 with a Canadian proposal, subsequently backed by the EU. The Canadian proposal sought to call it Multilateral Trade Organization (MTO). Eventually, however, the acronym WTO was chosen, although there is another UN organization with the same acronym—the World Tourism Organization, based in Madrid.

8. All member countries are, however, responsible for contributing to the WTO budget. The budgetary share of each member country is based on each member's share in total trade of all WTO members. Share of a member country in such trade is based on a three-year average of most recent trade figures. If a member country has less than 0.12 percent share in such trade, a minimum contribution is assessed. In 1999, as Hoekman and Kostecki (2001, 19-25) point out, the nine largest trading nations contributed about two-thirds of WTO budgetary expenditures. As the largest trading nations bear a substantial burden of the WTO budget, their influence on its functioning, although not officially sanctioned, can hardly be ruled out.

9. The Kennedy Round also adopted the so-called "Enabling Clause," allowing GATT contracting parties to grant favorable tariff and nontariff treatment in favor of developing countries and among developing countries, which came down as Special and Differential Treatment measures. For details on this see next chapter.

10. See Dowlah (2003a) and Michalopoulos (1999) to see how protectionist policies might have led to dysfunctional consequences in many developing countries. Also see Sutherland and Sewell (2000) and World Bank (2003a).

11. The roots of such a bifurcated trade policy of the GATT can be traced to the US legislations in manufacturing and agricultural sectors of the 1930s, way before the formation of the GATT. As Goldstein (1993) points out, while the 1934 Trade Act set the United States down a path of reduction of barriers to manufacturing trade, the 1933 Agricultural Adjustment Act helped the United States to erect protectionist walls around its agricultural trade.

12. The author also found that the deterioration in terms of trade would be higher for commodity-dependent countries in Africa and Latin America than in Asia.

13. Declining commodity terms of trade, however, has been a controversial area for decades, perhaps beginning with the famous Prebisch-Singer thesis of the 1950s. Prebisch (1950) showed a secular decline of terms of trade of primary commodities by 0.9 percent per annum during the period of 1876–1938, and then Singer (1950) also showed 0.64 percent per annum decline during the same period, both suggesting that such a historical trend of declining terms of commodity trade resulted in a long-term transfer of income from poor to rich countries. Later, in the 1980s, Spraos (1980) confirmed the historical trend, but at a lower rate of 0.5 percent per annum.

14. The so-called "GATT-waiver," as mentioned above and to be discussed in greater details in the next chapter, stems from the Enabling Clause of the GATT, which provides for: (a) preferential market access of developing countries to developed markets on a nonreciprocal, nondiscriminatory basis; (b) preferential tariff treatment for developing countries; (c) more favorable treatment for developing countries in other GATT rules dealing with nontariff barriers (such as technical barriers to trade, subsidies, and countervailing duties); and finally, (d) special treatment to the LDCs, as a group, distinguished by their special economic situation, development, financial and other needs. See (Dowlah 2003a).

15. For example, during the Seattle Ministerial, which ended in fiasco, the number of WTO Internet users broke the 200,000 barrier as early as October 1999, when 201,101 users accessed the site from 61 countries, and the number of documents and data downloaded reached a world record of 88,000 megabytes, equivalent of about 88 million pages (Das 2001, 189). The "world community" is a widely misused term. For example, many decisions are made at the United Nations at the behest of a handful of powerful members, then routinely passed on to the world claiming that those are opinions of the world community.

16. All WTO decisions and actions, as well as rules and regulations, have to be made public, and at the same time, the member countries are required to keep the WTO informed of all changes in their trade-related rules, laws, and regulations, even judicial decisions, on an annual basis.

17. The consensus, however, means absence of a negative consensus, that is, all must oppose a decision in order to turn down a decision. Then again, only the opinions of the deliberating participants are counted, while opinions of non-participating members are ignored. Again, negative opinion of participating member countries will be counted depending on the concerned member country's share in global trade as well as how fundamental the objection is.

18. As explained earlier, and also in Chapter 3, the WTO grants exemptions to its rules and transition periods to developing countries and the LDCs within the context of reciprocal and multilateral commitments—on a multilateral basis—unlike the GATT exemptions that were aimed at waiving or ignoring reciprocity. It is, however, notable that the Punta de Este Declaration, which launched the Uruguay Round negotiations, treated negotiations on goods as a "single undertaking" and put negotiations on services on a separate track, stipulating that negotiations on both tracks should begin and end at the same time, and at the end of negotiations the Ministerial Conference would decide on implementation of the results. By the end of the Round, however, the two tracks were merged, and treated as a single undertaking (see TWN 2001).

19. See Hoekman (2002), Hoekman and Kostecki (2001, 28–37), and GATT (1994) for further details.

20. In February 1997, 69 governments agreed to a wide range of liberalization measures under the telecommunications agreement, which came into force in February 1998. The agreement on financial services, signed by 70 governments, came into force in March 1999. It covered more than 95 percent of global trade in banking, insurance, securities, and financial information. The agreement on information technology (IT) products, reached in March 1997, was signed by 40 countries agreeing to eliminate all tariffs on IT products by 2000.

21. As mentioned earlier, the number of WTO Internet users broke the 200,000 barrier as early as October 1999, when 201,101 users accessed the site from 61 countries.

22. The world GDP grew by 3.3 percent in 1999, compared to 2.5 percent in the previous year. In 1999, global merchandise exports grew by 3.5 percent and exports of commercial

services grew by 1.5 percent. On top of all that, the US economy continued to provide major stimulus to international trade, as its domestic demand increased by 5.5 percent.

23. According to Das (2000), the fate of the Seattle ministerial was sealed well before the members met. He argues that seeds of discord were sown by several pre-Seattle developments, such as: (a) the Free Trade Agreement of the Americas (FTAA) was stalled; (b) the enlargement of the EU was slowed down; (c) the Early Voluntary Sectoral Liberalization proposals in the Asia-Pacific Economic Cooperation (APEC) at the Kuala Lumpur meeting in November 1998 were defeated; (d) the Multilateral Agreement on Investment (MAI) was killed in December 1998; and (e) the US Congress stalled a twin vote on NAFTA parity for the Caribbean Basin countries and the Africa Growth and Opportunity Act (AGOA).

24. The Zanzibar Declaration of the LDC Trade Ministers, held in Zanzibar, Tanzania, in July 2001, called upon "all development partners" for recognition of "special structural difficulties faced by LDCs" in global economy, and demanded "full implementation" of the commitments undertaken at the Brussels Conference of LDCs. It pointed out that despite repeated commitments from the international community for "beneficial and meaningful integration of LDCs" at the ministerials in Marrakech, Singapore, and Geneva and at the UNCTAD Conference of LDCs in Brussels (2000), marginalization of the LDCs continued. The Zanzibar Declaration sought binding commitment on duty-free and quota-free market access for products from LDCs on a "secure, long-term and predictable basis" and for making the rules of origin more realistic and flexible to match the industrial capacities of the LDCs.

25. The so-called Integrated Framework for Trade-Related Technical Assistance for the LDCs emerged in 1997 as a follow-up of the Plan of Action for LDCs, adopted at the Singapore Ministerial. The framework brought relevant multilateral agencies—such as the International Trade Center (ITC), the IMF, UNDP, the World Bank, and the WTO—together to assume joint responsibility for delivering coordinated trade-related technical assistance to the LDCs, to help them overcome shortcomings in technical and institutional capacity, particularly in the areas of trade policy, human resources, and export supply, so that they could meet their WTO commitments and obligations. The framework also called for greater coordination of technical assistance from bilateral, regional, and other multilateral sources.

26. For details on Doha Ministerial Conference and the Doha Declaration see World Trade Center (WT/MIN(01)/DEC/1, 20 November 2001; and Annual Report of WTO, 2003.

27. Stuart Harbinson, chief negotiator of the WTO Committee on Agriculture, in his first draft on agricultural negotiation, released in February 2003 in Japan, suggested full elimination of export subsidies within nine years, but demanded that this would be flanked by deeper cuts in tariffs as well as in Amber Box (trade-distorting domestic support) and Blue Box (only partly decoupled support under production-limiting programs) subsidization. While the United States and the Cairn Group expressed disappointment with the draft, for lack of ambition regarding the proposed cuts in tariffs and trade-distorting support, the EU complained that the draft was biased toward agricultural-exporting countries such as the United States and those of the Cairns Group. The EU also criticized the report for insufficient attention to agricultural nontrade concerns (NTCs), such as environment and food safety. Developing countries such as India, Kenya, and Nigeria, however, welcomed the Harbinson proposal, noting that it would provide poorer countries with the flexibility they needed to address their developmental needs. (See *Bridges,* February 19, 2003).

28. Cited in Dowlah (2003a) from press reports on the ongoing Cancun Ministerial.

29. The Dhaka Declaration (2003) was adopted by representatives from 39 LDCs, including 24 ministers, on June 2 in the capital city of Bangladesh, which is also the largest LDC and the leader of LDCs in the WTO. The declaration, adopted as a platform for the LDCs at the upcoming Cancun Ministerial in September 2003, emphasized a thirteen-point negotiating position that included: (a) duty-free, restriction-free market access to developed country markets with relaxed rules of origin; (b) resolving all special and differential treatment and implementation of commitments; free movement of natural persons, especially unskilled and semiskilled labor; (c) flexible undertaking of LDC commitments and obligations consistent with capacity; (d) substantial technical and financial assistance to strengthen LDC export base; (e) strengthened integrated framework for overcoming LDC supply side constraints; (f) exemption of antidumping and similar measures; (g) mechanism to protect genetic resources, traditional knowledge, and farmers' rights as well as no patents on life; (h) effective compulsory licensing of medicine for providing sound solution for LDCs if applicable, and (i) expeditious LDC accession to the WTO.

3

Special and Differential Treatment Measures under the GATT/WTO: How Advantageous Are They for the Development of the LDCs?

INTRODUCTION

This chapter examines the Special and Differential Treatment (SDT) measures granted to developing countries, including the LDCs, under various GATT/WTO trade regimes to see how they helped or hindered economic growth and development in these countries, especially in the LDCs, over the course of last five decades. The SDT measures refer to trade restrictive measures, such as infant industry protection, import substitution, export subsidies, and balance-of-payments protection, and such other restrictive measures that the developing countries and LDCs were allowed to pursue while being members of the GATT and its successor, the WTO. This chapter looks into the processes and developments that led to the establishment of those flexibilities, the consequent trade protectionist strategies, and their outcomes, in the context of an increasingly globalized world in which barriers to trade and commerce fell apart in the rest of the world as it swept through the second to the third wave of globalization.

Historical evidence suggests that some doses of protectionism did play an important role in the industrialization processes and economic growth of many nations that are now highly industrialized. For example, the United States, the United Kingdom, and Germany used protectionist trade agendas throughout the nineteenth century as well as in the early part of the twentieth century, Japan followed suit in the mid-twentieth century, while the newly industrialized economies (NIEs)—Singapore, Hong Kong, Taiwan, and South Korea—did the same in the 1970s through the early 1980s. The argument that countries in the early stages of economic development need protectionist policies to build infrastructures of industrialization or to catch up with industrialization, therefore, has much to do with the history of industrialization and economic development itself. In fact, history of economic development provides not a single example of industrialization without some forms of protection.[1] The UK protected its industries up until the nineteenth century, the United States did not call for free trade up until the 1930s, and even the most recent industrializers—Japan and the so-called Asian Tigers—had experienced maximalist, not minimalist, state intervention, although some studies tend to suggest otherwise.[2]

Also, historical evidence clearly suggests that industrialization, whether pursued with protectionist strategies or not, served as an engine of economic growth in almost every industrialized country in the world.[3] Industrialization led to higher levels of labor productivity, which, in turn, led to higher economic growth, putting the industrializing countries on the track of a virtuous circle of growth, as Kaldor's Growth Laws stipulate,[4] through three interlinkages: between the growth of manufacturing and the growth of GD, between the growth of manufacturing and the growth of manufacturing productivity, and finally, between the growth of manufacturing output and the growth of productivity outside of manufacturing.

From a theoretical standpoint, protectionist trade policies draw their intellectual inspirations primarily from two major theorists—Frederick List, a nineteenth-century German economist to whom the theory of infant industry protection (IIP) is attributed, and Raul Prebisch, a twentieth-century Latin American political economist, to whom the theory of import substitution strategy (ISS) is often attributed.[5] Frederick List saw trade as an instrument of development, but prescribed that IIP should be used as an instrument for industrialization by countries in the early stage of development. Such a strategy, he postulated, will eventually result in massive exports of manufactured goods from the less developed countries. List (1856), however, did not consider IIP as a strategy for protection of all sectors, and rather emphasized selective and temporary protection. He identified four phases in the development of international trade and industrialization: (a) the expansion of imports of manufactured goods; (b) the starting up of domestic production with the help of protection; (c) satisfaction of domestic market; and finally, (d) massive expansion of the exports. After attainment of a certain stage of development, each country will join the "universal association" for trade among all nations, and need for protection will cease.[6]

Raul Prebisch, a powerful exponent of import substitution strategy, argued that import substitution, although costly, was inevitable in the developing countries in the early 1950s, because these countries were primary commodity exporters, they lacked industrial infrastructure and faced unfavorable external market conditions for exports of manufactured goods. Prebisch's theory was based on what is called the Prebisch-Singer thesis, which showed how a historical trend of declining terms of commodity trade resulted in a long-term transfer of income from poor to rich countries. Prebisch (1950) showed a decline in terms of trade for primary commodities by 0.9 percent per annum during the period of 1876–1938, while Singer showed 0.64 percent per annum decline during the same period.[7]

Based on these findings, the Prebisch-Singer thesis argued that many primary commodities have intrinsically low income elasticities of demand because they are necessities, and many primary commodities also face competition from synthetic substitutes.[8] They argued that by adopting protectionist strategies, developing countries could diversify their productions and produce goods with much higher income elasticity of demand in world markets, and arrest deterioration of terms of trade, and also better control the balance-of-payment problems. At a later point, however, Prebisch (1959) called for such strategies for a specific time and sector, maintaining that inward-looking industrialization strategies or infant industry protection should be viewed as "a step towards export expansion" and not a permanent feature of industrial strategy. In his later works, he also criticized inward-looking industrialization strategies, as practiced by many developing countries, and discouraged any blanket measure of import substitution or uniform incentives to imports.[9]

Obviously, these theories came as a formidable challenge to mainstream economics that underpins global prosperity from free trade without counting for differential levels of economic, industrial, and technological capabilities and other structural characteristics of individual economies, assuming that commodity as well as factor markets operate freely and perfectly everywhere—irrespective of exporting or importing country. In reality, neither commodities market nor factors market is perfect anywhere in the world. None of the conditions of perfect competition—such as perfect information and rational decision by atomistic operators of market, free entry and exit of firms, consumer sovereignty, and constant return to scale—works in the real world. And then, it gets worse with the international trade, which is essentially dominated by transnational corporations (TNCs), which are neither atomistic or passive, nor competitive or price-taker, as stipulated by mainstream economics.[10]

Also, factors of production are neither homogeneous nor perfectly mobile in domestic markets. Many developing countries have surplus labor; it is possible to expand exports without adversely affecting existing allocation of resources.[11] Moreover, neither transaction costs nor transfer of technology is cost-less—in the actual world neither transports nor technology moves freely across countries. Similarly, the real world trade relations do not reflect the Ricardian principle of comparative advantage—they are rather ruled by economic distortions, subsidies and protections, tariff and nontariff barriers, trade-related, even trade-unrelated, noneconomic, and political considerations.[12] Therefore, developing country contracting parties of the GATT, those who sought to pursue protectionist policies, had an arsenal of both empirical and theoretical ammunition in their hands, to push for what came down as the special and differential treatment (SDT) measures under the multilateral trading system.

SPECIAL AND DIFFERENTIAL TREATMENT MEASURES UNDER THE GATT

The demand for protectionist trade policies began to surface in the arena of multilateral trade negotiations (MTNs) under the GATT in the early 1950s. Obviously, besides their economic backwardness as well as overwhelming dependence on primary commodities, scores of newly independent former colonies drew their intellectual inspirations mainly from the so-called Prebisch-Singer thesis discussed above. Developing countries argued that liberal trade policies, as envisaged by the GATT, could impair their prospects for industrialization or sustainable growth, as they faced low and unstable price and high elasticity of demand for primary commodities that they exported, while they paid significantly higher and stable prices for manufactures, capital goods, and machineries that they imported. Following the arguments put forward by the Prebisch-Singer thesis, many developing countries saw the roots of their deteriorating terms-of-trade and worsening balance-of-payment problems in the existing international trade regime that favored industrialized countries at the expense of developing countries.

As noted before, although almost half of the original contracting parties to the GATT were developing countries, still the GATT emphasized principles of reciprocity and uniform rights and obligations for all contracting parties, without containing any special provision for developing countries. But facing growing pressures from developing countries, as well as the need to broaden membership of these countries in the just-emerging multilateral trading system,[13] a GATT Review Session in 1954–1955 modified the GATT Article XVIII to grant contracting parties in "an early stage of development" flexibilities to impose both tariff and nontariff trade restrictions to support their infant industries and balance-of-payments problems.[14]

In the latter part of the 1950s, declining terms of trade in commodities led the developing countries to demand stabilization in the global commodity market, which eventually resulted in the establishment of an expert committee with international trade experts, such as Professors Haberler, Meade, Tinbergen, and Campos. The Haberler Report of 1958 found "substance in the feeling of disquiet among primary producing countries" as many commodities of export interest to developing countries, such as vegetable oils, coffee, tea, cocoa, jute and cotton products, leather, and some other manufacturing products were subjected to high levels of tariffs in developed countries. The Haberler Report recommended stabilization programs to address commodity price fluctuations through buffer stocks and also called for reduction in developed countries' internal taxes on primary products, such as coffee, tea, and tobacco, which restrained consumption and import demand in developed countries (GATT 1958).

Throughout the 1960s through the 1980s, developing countries continued to emphasize their "uniqueness" in international trade by pursuing a two-prong strategy—they pressed for preferential access to developed country markets, while insisting on SDT measures for themselves so that liberalization of their own trade could be avoided. In sharp contrast to the original GATT principles, they emphasized nonreciprocity or less-than-full reciprocity in trade relations between them and developed countries, so that they could adopt trade protectionist measures to promote their own economic development.

The 1960s witnessed several important developments toward preferential treatment for developing countries. In 1961 came the so-called GATT declaration—Promotion of Trade of Less Developed Countries—that called for preferential market access for developing countries. In 1964, GATT adopted a specific legal framework allowing member countries to provide "more favorable and acceptable market access" to products of export interest to developing countries, especially primary products and processed or manufactured products. Developing countries were also granted less-than-full reciprocity, creating scopes for them to avoid contributions that might be inconsistent with their level of development in the process of trade negotiations.[15]

The year 1964 also saw the emergence of the United Nations Conference on Trade and Development (UNCTAD), primarily to address the concerns of developing countries. The same year a common platform of developing countries known as Group 77 also emerged. Both institutions emerged as distinctive forums through which the developing countries could pursue their own trade agenda. Finally, in 1968, came the so-called Generalized Systems of Preferences (GSP) through which developing countries could be granted "GATT-waiver" by developed as well as other developing countries.

Then, the Enabling Clause, adopted by the Tokyo Round (1973–1979), granted: (a) preferential market access of developing countries to developed country markets on a nonreciprocal, nondiscriminatory basis; (b) preferential tariff treatment for developing countries, as provided by the GSP and similar other schemes, such as the Lome Convention, granted by the European Commission to the ACP countries; (c) more favorable treatment for developing countries in other GATT rules dealing with nontariff barriers (such as technical barriers to trade, subsidies, and countervailing duties); and finally, (d) special treatment to the LDCs, as a group, distinguished by their special economic situation, development, financial, and other needs. The Enabling Clause, however, allowed discretionary, rather than legally binding, differential treatment. Finally, in 1980, came the Common Fund for Commodities (actually materialized in 1989), with the objectives of financing international buffer stocks and commodity development measures.

Thus, as Michalopoulos (2000) points out, by the 1980s an impressive array of SDT measures helped the developing countries to attain most of their trade objectives under the GATT, as they could: (a) protect their infant industries on balance-of-payment grounds; (b) follow the principle of nonreciprocity—not to liberalize their economies fully; (c) resort to export subsidies without risking countervailing duties; (d) demand greater access to developed country markets; and finally, (e) use a fund to support their commodity stabilization schemes. The actual development, however, might look less rosy. For example, the tariff cuts in successive rounds of GATT during 1950–1970—that brought down the average import weighted tariff on manufactured products in the industrialized countries to about 6 percent—were less beneficial for the developing countries (Hoekman and Kostecki 1995).[16]

Second, while declining tariff rates brought unprecedented prosperity to developed countries during the 1950s through the 1970s, developing countries, except a few, missed that wave of prosperity almost completely. Tariff cuts under successive rounds of GATT not only excluded two major sectors of export interest to developing countries—agriculture and textiles and clothing—but also subjected these sectors to very high levels of tariff escalation and nontariff barriers. While a plethora of bilateral agreements, quotas, and other import restrictions, such as the Multi-Fiber Arrangement (MFA), besieged the textiles and clothing sector, the agricultural sector remained almost absolutely outside the GATT discipline, allowing developed countries, especially the United States and the EU, to continue with wide-ranging trade-distorting agricultural support and protections (Dowlah 2001).

SPECIAL AND DIFFERENTIAL TREATMENT MEASURES UNDER THE URUGUAY ROUND

Despite mixed outcome of the SDT provisions under the GATT, the Uruguay Round, which brought forth sweeping transformation in the global trading system, especially by integrating the textiles and clothing sector and bringing the agricultural sector into the expanded GATT discipline, also continued such provisions. But it did so under what is called the "single undertaking approach" that required all contracting parties to WTO to enforce almost the same set of trade rules and obligations. The WTO granted exemptions to its rules and transition periods to developing countries within the context of reciprocal and multilateral commitments—on a multilateral basis—unlike the GATT exemptions, which were aimed at waiving or ignoring reciprocity. The SDT provisions, granted under the UR were based on three major considerations: (a) that developing countries are intrinsically disadvantaged in their participation in international trade—therefore, this intrinsic weakness must be considered in defining their rights and responsibilities with the international trading system; (b) that trade policies that work in the developed world may not work in the developing countries—therefore, there should be some exceptions; and (c) that, it is in the interest of the developed countries to assist developing countries in their fuller integration and participation in the international trading system (Michalopoulos 2000).

The UR, therefore, urged developing countries, including LDCs, to move gradually to WTO rules, while granting them freedom to limit access to their markets, or provide support to domestic producers or exporters, and a greater time frame to meet their obligations and commitments. The UR granted transition periods of ten years for agriculture, five years for TRIMs (trade-related investment measures) and TRIPs (trade-related intellectual property rights), and extendable transition periods for TBT (technical barriers to trade), Dispute Settlement, SPS (Sanitary and Phytosanitary Measures), Import Licensing, and ASCM (Agreement on Subsidies and Countervailing Measures), in addition to differential and more favorable treatment in respect to the textiles and clothing sector (Fukasaku 2000). Also, the ASCM permits low-income countries and LDCs to maintain certain kinds of export subsidies, which are otherwise prohibited; GATS allows developing countries to liberalize fewer sectors or fewer types of transactions. At the same time, GATT Article XVIII continued, which gave developing countries greater flexibility in providing protection to domestic industry, to set up a particular industry or apply QRS for balance-of-payment purposes.

The extension in time frame is given with the stipulation that with additional time developing countries and LDCs will be able to strengthen their institutional capacities to implement the agreements. At the same time, the UR urged developed countries and international institutions to take positive actions, such as providing developing countries with preferential market access to their markets—developed countries promised to provide tariff preferences to exports of manufacturers from developing countries, and to grant special treatment to LDCs, in addition to or expansion of GSP facilities that the developing countries enjoyed at that time. The UR also identified several areas for technical assistance, such as TBT, SPS measures, customs valuation, preshipment inspection, dispute settlement, and TRIPS, while asking developed countries and multilateral institutions to provide technical and other assistance to developing countries to help improve their institutional capabilities to meet their WTO obligations. The World Bank (2003a, 206) rightly argues that the SDT measures that the developing countries demand concentrate around three core areas: (a) preferential access to developed country markets (as under the GATT); (b) exemptions (as in the GATT) and deferrals (new under WTO); and (c) technical assistance to implement WTO mandates (new under WTO).

SPECIAL AND DIFFERENTIAL TREATMENTS UNDER THE WTO

Over the years, since the 1994 Marrakech Declaration adopted the WTO, SDT measures continued, with occasional attempts to fine-tune them with an apparent acknowledgment–in both donor and beneficiary countries—that some of the SDT measures worked, while others did not. In all WTO Ministerials held so far—Singapore (1996), Geneva (1998), Seattle (1999), Doha (2001), and Cancun (2003)—developing countries, including the LDCs, continued to insist on more favorable SDTs, especially for greater market access and technical and financial assistance. Numerous gatherings of governments, businesses, and civil societies that took place across the world since the Marrakech Declaration sought to put development and poverty reduction at the center of all economic policies, in order to overcome the deepening processes of marginalization of developing countries in general, and the LDCs in particular. Some of the important developments since 1994 include the following.

The G15 Symposium

Held in New Delhi in 1998, the Symposium of 15 developing countries expressed reservations about the "single-undertaking approach" of the WTO, pointing out that this approach was guided more by some "ideological baggage," rather than clear understanding of the SDT measures and their impact on competitiveness of developing countries. The Symposium identified twofold challenges for developing countries in the post-UR world: (a) to maintain existing SDTs where these are crucial to the success of development programs; and (b) to adapt the concept of

SDTs to the realities of globalization and liberalization. It maintained that GSP and other unilateral schemes could ensure access to markets and reduce marginalization if they were directed to agricultural and the textile and clothing sectors, in which developing countries enjoy comparative advantage. The Symposium also envisaged greater access to technology, information networks, and distribution systems, objectives that may not coincide with global strategies of transnational organizations, for deriving benefits from and to successfully confront the challenges of globalization. The Symposium also called for extensions and revisions of several UR agreements, including TRIMs, TRIPs, and GATS (Gibbs and Mashayekhi 1998).

The UN Conference on LDCs (2001)

Then, the Third UN Conference on the LDCs, held in Brussels in May 2001, adopted what is called the Millennium Declaration, emphasizing "a transparent, non-discriminatory and rules-based multilateral trading system," which could help the LDCs reap benefits from globalization.[17] It called for continuation of SDTs for "beneficial integration" of the LDCs into the global economy through "sustained economic growth and sustainable development," so that the processes of their marginalization could be reversed. The Conference reached substantial agreements on measures aimed at improving LDC position in terms of aid, trade, debt relief, and investment, and called for duty-free, quota-free access of LDC goods to developed country markets. It also sought greater technical and financial assistance from the developed world as well as multilateral institutions.

The Zanzibar Declaration (2001)

Subsequently, the LDC Trade Ministers Meeting, held in Zanzibar, Tanzania, in July 2001, called upon "all development partners" for recognition of "special structural difficulties faced by LDCs" in global economy, and demanded "full implementation" of the commitments undertaken at the Brussels Conference of LDCs. It pointed out that despite repeated commitments from the international community for "beneficial and meaningful integration of LDCs" in Marrakech, Singapore, Geneva, and Brussels, marginalization of the LDCs continued. The Zanzibar Declaration sought binding commitment on duty-free and quota-free market access for products from LDCs on a "secure, long-term and predictable basis" and for making the rules of origin more realistic and flexible to match the industrial capacities of the LDCs (Zanzibar Declaration 2001).

The Doha Ministerial (2001)

The Doha Ministerial in 2001 sought to bring the trade issue at the center of development and alleviation of poverty, underscoring the need for benefiting all people "from the increased opportunities and welfare gains that the multilateral trading system generates." The ministerial promised to "make positive efforts" to ensure that developing countries, and especially the LDCs, secure "a share in the growth of world trade commensurate with the needs of their economic development." The Ministerial underlined that SDTs to developing countries "shall be an integral part of all negotiations" so that schedules of concessions, commitments, rules, and disciplines can be negotiated by taking into account the development needs of these countries. It called for reviewing the SDT provisions with a view to "strengthening them and making them more precise, effective, and operational."

Also, acknowledging the seriousness of the concerns expressed by the LDCs in the Zanzibar Declaration, the Doha Ministerial committed to the objective of "duty-free, quota-free market access for products originating from LDCs," and recognized that integration of the LDCs into the multilateral trading system would require "meaningful market access, support for the diversification of their production and export base, and trade-related technical assistance and capacity building." It also made a commitment to "significantly increase contributions" to the Integrated Framework (IF) trust fund and WTO extrabudgetary trust funds in favor of LDCs and resolved to review all SDT measures "with a view to strengthening them and making them more precise, effective and operational."[18]

The Dhaka Declaration (2003)

The Dhaka Declaration was adopted by representatives from 39 LDCs, including 24 ministers, on June 2, 2003 in the capital city of Bangladesh, which is also the largest LDC and the leader of LDCs in the WTO. The declaration worked out a thirteen-point negotiating position for the LDCs at the Cancun Ministerial, scheduled for September 2003. Major points of the declaration include: (a) duty-free, restriction-free market access to developed country markets with relaxed rules of origin; (b) resolving all special and differential treatment and implementation of commitments; free movement of natural persons, especially unskilled and semi-skilled labor; (c) flexible undertaking of LDC commitments and obligations consistent with capacity; (d) substantial technical and financial assistance to strengthen LDC export base; (e) strengthened integrated framework for overcoming LDC supply side constraints; (f) exemption of antidumping and similar measures; (g) mechanism to protect genetic resources, traditional knowledge, and farmers' rights as well as no patents on life; (h) effective compulsory licensing of medicine for providing sound solution for LDCs if applicable, and (i) expeditious accession of LDCs into the WTO.

The Cancun Ministerial (2003)

The collapse of the Cancun Ministerial in September 2003 centered around deadlocks in negotiations of Doha Ministerial issues as well as Singapore Ministerial issues, and largely demonstrated the fact that developed country members of the 146-member WTO can no longer take the positions of developing countries as granted. At center stage were the farm reforms—the issues of domestic support, market access, and export subsidies, as a follow-up of the Doha Ministerial, which agreed to substantial improvements in lowering tariffs, reductions of all forms of export subsidies with a view to phasing them out, and significant reductions in trade-distorting domestic support.

The eventual collapse of the Cancun, however, centered around the so-called Singapore Issues—WTO rules for investment and competition policies, government contracts or procurement, and customs duties. While developed countries pressed for greater liberalization in these issues, developing countries, mainly led by India, Brazil, China, and Malaysia, rejected any deal on these issues, arguing that not enough preparatory work has been done for such negotiations. Thanks to the assertive role of developing countries in trade talks, developed countries' continued effort to exploit the poorer nations under the banners of MTNs met failure—leaving fingerprints all over—any future negotiations have to be fairer and more participatory than ever before.[19] The LDCs, as a group, however, were marginalized even further—as amid acrimonious debates on protectionist agricultural policies and Singapore Issues, they had little chance to push their agenda, agreed to in the Dhaka Declaration in June 2003, that called for greater areas of duty-free and quota-free market access, greater special and differential treatments, more assistance for capacity building, and free movement of semiskilled labor forces.

DYSFUNCTIONAL CONSEQUENCES OF THE SDT MEASURES

Given such an impressive buildup of SDT measures over the last five decades, under the GATT as well as the WTO, it is not surprising that this area has attracted considerable scholarly attention over the decades. Scholars and observers raised questions whether: (a) by allowing flexibilities in the implementation of the GATT/WTO rules and commitments, the SDT measures might have introduced a bias in favor of protection and against exports in the developing countries (Michalopoulos 2000, World Bank 2003a); (b) strategies of infant industry protection, import substitution or other protective measures aimed at trade restrictions were actually advantageous for the developing countries (Bhagwati 1988; Krueger 1978). In this section we look into the ongoing debate by asking an overarching question—if the SDT provisions as well as other flexibilities in international trade regimes granted to the LDCs were trade-boosting and growth-enhancing, why then are the LDCs increasingly being marginalized in the contemporary world economy? What follows is a stock checking on some of the most enduring questions about marginalization of the LDCs.

How Advantageous Are the GSP Schemes for the LDCs?

The Generalized System of Preferences (GSP) emerged in the early 1970s with sweeping promises of increasing export earnings, promoting industrialization, and accelerating economic growth of less developed countries (GATT 1972). It has, however, accomplished nothing of this sort in the last three decades. There is, however, no denying that GSP has been a significant vehicle for promoting exports of primary and manufacturing goods to developed countries, under special GATT-waiver provisions that allowed tariff reductions in developed countries requiring less-than-full reciprocity from GSP-recipient countries.[20] Obviously, GSP schemes compromised two of the most basic principles of the GATT—reciprocity and nondiscrimination—by allowing industrialized countries (as well as developing countries) to grant better-than-MFN (most-favored nation) treatment to less developed countries. The EU was the first to implement its own version of GSP in 1971, followed by the United States with its own version in 1976, with the professed objective to support industrialization of developing countries by providing lower-than-normal duty rates for manufactured goods and processed agricultural products from less developed countries.

GSP Schemes of the United States. The first US GSP schemes, introduced for the first time in 1976, grant complete duty and quota free access to eligible products from eligible countries. Eligibility of countries depends on not aiding international terrorists and complying with international environmental, labor, and intellectual property rights. Also, eligibility of products excludes textiles and apparel, footwear, and many agricultural products. On top of those eligibilities, there were "competitive need limits'" on exports as well as rules-of-origin requirements.[21]

Other preferential schemes of the United States include the Caribbean Basin Initiative (CBI), the Andean Community Preferences (ACP), and, most recently, the African Growth and Opportunity Act (AGOA). The CBI was introduced under the Caribbean Basin Economic Recovery Act, 1984, which provided duty-free access to American markets for goods from 24 countries of the region. But many products are not eligible for duty-free access, such as textiles and apparel, luggage, certain footwear, certain leather products, canned tuna. The ACP was introduced with the Andean Trade Preference Act, 1991 to grant market access to products from Bolivia, Columbia, Ecuador, and Peru. Directed to reduce narcotic production and trafficking, this scheme makes rum and sugar, syrup, and molasses ineligible for duty-free access to the US market, in addition to the products made ineligible for the ACP countries. The AGOA was passed in 2000, to grant preferential market access to 36 countries in sub-Saharan African. AGOA provides duty-free market and quota-free access to most products, including textiles, provided they are made of US yarn and fabrics.

GSP Schemes of the European Union. The EU GSP schemes provide preferential market access to products from all developing countries, but the market access is administered through a more complex mechanism than is the case with the United States. Tariff lines are divided into several categories—36 percent tariff lines are eligible for reduced tariffs, 32 percent are eligible for duty-free access, and 12 percent of tariff lines are not eligible for preferential access. Many agricultural products, meat and diary products, cereals, sugar, and wine are among the products not eligible for preferential market access. In addition, 36 percent of tariff lines are designated as "sensitive products," subject to higher tariffs, which include almost all agricultural and food products, and all textiles, apparel, and leather goods.[22]

The EU's preferential scheme for Africa, the Caribbean and the Pacific (ACP), maintained under the Lome Convention, however, provides duty-free and quota-free access to most industrial products made in these countries, but agricultural products face higher tariffs. The most recent EU preferential scheme—Everything-but-Arms (EBA) initiative—introduced in 2001—allows the world's poorest countries—the LDCs—duty-free, quota-free, without any quantity restrictions, market access to the EU for all products except arms and munitions. The initiative, however, restricts three sensitive products—sugar and rice are to be liberalized by 2009 and bananas by 2006.

Outcome of the GSP Schemes. The experience with the GSP schemes has not been quite exemplary. Available literature rather points to an almost undisputed conclusion that the GSP turned out to be less advantageous for developing countries than it was touted to be at its inception. The main reason for its failure to emerge as a driving force for strengthening integration of developing countries in the world trading system lies with the fact that even at its best, GSP has been advantageous for some products, for some countries, and for some times only. Some major factors responsible for the less-than-reassuring outcome of GSP schemes can be enumerated as follows.

First, GSP is a voluntary scheme—the importing countries could design it "as they see fit," and developing country suppliers had no certainty of market conditions (Hudec 1987; Jackson 1997). Being outside the purview of binding GATT-WTO legal system, nonreciprocal preferences like GSP could be unilaterally modified or cancelled by GSP-granting country at any time (Ozden and Reinhardt 2002a). Also, it was directed more at advanced developing countries, which needed it the least, than to the LDCs, which needed it the most. As World Bank (2003a, 211) remarks, "A relatively small number of mostly middle-income countries are the main beneficiaries of preference (GSP) schemes."

In 1996, as Table 3.1 shows, the top ten beneficiaries of the EU GSP were China (32 percent), India (12 percent), Indonesia (9 percent), Thailand (8 percent), Malaysia (7 percent), Brazil (5 percent), Pakistan (4 percent), Colombia (2 percent), Mexico (2 percent), and South Korea (2 percent).[23] Similarly, in 2001, the top nine beneficiaries of the US GSP were Thailand (20 percent), Indonesia (13 percent), India (11 percent), Philippines (7 percent), Venezuela (6 percent), South Africa (5 percent), Russia (4 percent), Chile (4 percent), and Turkey (4 percent). These countries accounted for 77 percent of US nonoil imports under the GSP schemes in 2001.

Second, in general, GSP coverage of developing country exports has not been robust. Most of the GSP schemes exclude most of the goods in which developing countries have export interests or comparative advantage—textiles, agricultural, and some other products are almost routinely, almost exclusively, excluded from GSP coverage. As Table 3.2 shows, in dairy products, textiles and yarn, apparel and clothing, leather products, footwear, and ceramics and glassware, average tariff rates faced by the GSP recipients are much higher than average tariff on these products in both the US and the EU. As a result, the shares of the LDCs in most of

Table 3.1
Top Ten Beneficiaries of the EU GSP, 1986–1995

Rank	Country	Share in GSP benefiting EU imports in 1996 (in percent)	Degree of utilization of GSP preferences in 1995 (in percent))
1	China	32	77.9
2	India	11.6	83.8
3	Indonesia	8.9	76.8
4	Thailand	7.7	63.2
5	Malaysia	6.8	40.5
6	Brazil	4.7	73.3
7	Pakistan	3.6	86.9
8	Colombia	2.3	89.9
9	Mexico	2.2	48.7
10	South Korea	1.9	62.4

Source: European Commission, cited in Cuyvers (1998).

Table 3.2
Applied Average Tariffs (Tariff Escalation Rates) on Some Selected Products of Exports Interest to Developing Countries (in Percentages)

Import markets	Live, fresh, chilled, or frozen crustaceans (0306)	Leather, leather clothing accessories (4203) and footwear (6403)	Textiles and clothing products		
			6210	5906	6113
EU	60.1	52.5	12.6	6.5	10.3
Japan	110.9	17.7	12.4	5.5	10.6
US	109.6	319.5	6.2	3.5	6.1
Canada	18.3	500.0	12.5	8.3	10.2

Source: Based on Bacchetta and Bora (2003).

these products in both the EU and the United States markets are next to nothing. Despite the recent GSP programs, like the EBA in the EU and the AGOA in the United States, which remove barriers to some of these products of export interest to the LDCs, the total imports of the EU or the United States have not increased significantly from the LDCs.

In fact, the share of the LDCs in the imports of the EU has declined—the LDCs had 0.8% share in the EU imports in 1986, which fell to 0.5 percent in 1991, and remained at that level up to 2000, but then it dropped below 0.4 percent in 2002.[24] The main reason for this, as Brenton (2003) points out, is that most of the LDCs products were eligible for duty-free access to the EU market even before the EBA was enacted, and the EU still restricts the products that matter the most to many LDCs—bananas, rice, and sugar.[25] In the United States, preferential schemes have helped the LDCs to maintain a share of around 0.8 percent in US imports since 2000, while the share hovered between 0.6 to 0.8 percent during the period of 1986—2002. Recent modifications in the CBI and the Andean and the introduction of the AGOA have contributed to a rise in the share of these regions in US imports, but that has not led to increase in the overall share of the LDCs in US imports, as the gain of these regions came from "exemptions of quotas and tariffs imposed on other exporters" (World Bank 2003a, 213–214).

Third, the actual utilization rate of the GSP schemes has been significantly smaller than potentials. As Inama (2003) shows, the rate of use of preferences in the imports of Quad countries—the United States, the EU, Canada and Japan—fell from 51 percent in 1994 to 39 percent in 2001. The LDCs, however, scored better here—their combined share in preference utilization was 60 percent in 2001. The same year, of the $588 billions of imports from the GSP beneficiaries, only $71 billions received benefits from preferences, while $184 billions were eligible for GSP benefits. Similarly, in 2000, 47 percent of the $175.6 billions of US imports from GSP beneficiaries were eligible for GSP benefits, but the actual utilization rate was far below (USITC cited in Ozden and Reinhardt, 2002a). In 1995, 72 percent of all dutiable imports from beneficiary countries were covered by the EU GSP system, but 60 percent of the imports could benefit from the preferences.[26]

Why Have the GSP Schemes Failed? As the previous discussion indicates, coverage of GSP preferences has been narrow—often they exclude goods of major export interest to developing countries, the actual utilization rate by the GSP beneficiaries was much lower than what was available for GSP benefits, and the prime beneficiaries of the GSP schemes have not been those who needed such benefits the most. Here are some of the factors responsible for such a lopsided outcome of the GSP schemes.

First, often GSP schemes come with stringent economic and noneconomic conditionalities, such as rules-of-origin requirements, workers' rights, environmental standards, and even a country's position in respect to terrorism or guarantee of private-property rights. For example, the 1974 US Trade Act makes a country ineligible for GSP benefits if it harbors international terrorists, violates workers' rights or human rights, or a country is either communist or it nationalizes American property without compensation. Then rules-of-origin requirements can often be excruciating. As mentioned above, even the most recently enacted AGOA of the United States provides duty-free market and quota-free access to almost all products, including textiles, provided they are made of US yarn and fabrics. In case the textile products are not made of regionally acquired raw materials, they are subject to a cap of 1.5 percent of US imports, which could be increased to 3.5 percent of US imports in eight years.

The value addition requirements and other conditions of derogation make the EU GSP even more stringent. The recent EU GSP regulations 2001–2004, which grant 30 percent duty reduction for sensitive and 100 percent duty reduction for nonsensitive products, subject textile and clothing products to 30 percent duties as they are classified as sensitive products (see Table 3.3). The EU GSP rules of origin also require two manufacturing processes in the country of export to make it eligible for duty reduction. Although in some cases they allow regional accumulation of derogation, the procedural requirements remain onerous, often quite prohibiting the recipient countries from deriving full advantage of the GSP schemes.

Second, often technical requirements have been highly stringent and rigorous, which prohibited many developing countries, especially LDCs, to take full advantage of GSP schemes. For example, the EU GSP regulations for 2001–2004 continue to envisage enhanced social, labor, drug trafficking, and ecological conditions. Recipient countries are eligible for additional five-percentage-points reduction for respecting freedom of association, collective bargaining, and minimum age of children for employment as stipulated in the ILO Conventions, and for strict upholding of international environmental standards, especially in respect to the ozone layer and climatic conditions. Similarly, the EU continues to insist on conditions of drug production and trafficking for a host of South and Central American countries, and most recently added Pakistan in the list. But "to date, most countries have been unwilling to apply for the additional tariff reductions, as they are suspicious of linking these sensitive issues" (*Bridges*, 12 December 2001). And there is what is called "competitive needs limit" of $100 million, and the clauses such as damage to domestic industries and sensitive products, which also restrict GSP benefits to recipient countries.

Third, GSP-granting countries often severely restrict GSP benefits yielding to domestic protectionist forces. This has been manifested time and again in a number of products in which developing countries had greater export interests, but it has been most pronounced in textiles and agricultural products. Evidence suggests that GSP preferences are typically revoked when they actually start to boost the recipients' exports (Ozden and Reinhardt 2002b). Under the US GSP, out of 154 eligible countries, 36 have "graduated" so far, and the most recent EU GSP graduated Hong Kong (China), North Korea, and South Korea and excluded India and Pakistan from GSP benefits with respect to textile products and China, Malaysia, and Thailand for clothing products. Through the processes, often labeled as country graduation or product graduation, the GSP-granting countries unilaterally can exclude some countries or some products from GSP benefits.[27]

Finally, the margin of GSP has been eroding as a consequence of the sustained reduction of MFN tariffs over the decades, and because of other preferential systems as well as thoroughgoing liberalizations in the developing countries. As Sutherland and Sewell (2000) point out, in the five decades since the establishment of the GATT, average manufacturing tariffs in industrialized countries declined from around 40 percent to less than four percent. Also, preferential treatments themselves contributed to the erosion of benefits from such schemes—for example, the Lome Convention granted deeper than GSP preferences to ACP countries

Table 3.3
The EU GSP—Comparison of Pre-2002 Scheme with Post-2002 Scheme

Commodities	GSP scheme in 2001		GSP scheme in 2002–2004	
	Normal Pre-Uruguay Round Tariff (percent)	GSP Tariff* (percent)	Normal Pre-Uruguay Round Tariff (percent)	GSP Tariff** (percent)
Yarn	6	5.1	4	2.81
Fabric	10	8.5	8	5.6
Made-up articles	13	11.05	12	8.4
Clothing	14	11.9	12	8.4

Source: ITCB (2002).
Notes: *On the basis of 15 percent reduction in normal tariff (in 2001 textile and clothing products were allowed reduction of 15 percent in the normal tariff because these were classified as "very sensitive." **On the basis of 30 percent reduction in normal tariff (in 2002, under the new GSP scheme, textile and clothing products were classified as "sensitive," eligible for 30 percent reduction in the normal tariff.

in the EU markets, the US AGOA granted more flexible conditions to SSA countries. And then, over the years trade liberalization had been so thorough that special preferences like GSP or Lome preferences appeared to be substitutes for liberalization of trade (Leutwiller 1985). Overall, it can be argued that GSP schemes have at best underperformed, yielded modest increase in imports from beneficiary states, and largely failed in their mission to promote industrialization and accelerated economic growth of the less developed countries.

Have the Commodity Terms-of-Trade Actually Improved for the LDCs?

Falling commodity terms-of-trade, as epitomized by the famous Prebisch-Singer thesis, had been a prime reason for developing countries to demand special and differential treatment measures to begin with. But have the terms-of-trade for commodities improved over the last five decades for the LDCs?[28] Available literature indicates that it has not—instability of demand for and declining terms of commodity trade still remain a matter of great concern for the developing countries, income losses resulting from failing terms of trade still constitute a formidable mechanism of resource transfer from poor to the rich countries. According to UNCTAD (2000a), the LDCs experienced declining growth rates in the early 1990s, then a rise in the 1995–1998 period, when real per capita growth had been above that of the 1980s and early 1990s, demonstrating a strong correlation with the terms of commodity trade.[29] The terms-of-trade of nonfuel commodities vis-à-vis manufactures fell from 147 in 1980 to 100 in 1985 to 80 in 1990, and to 71 in 1992—resulting in a 52 percent decline in terms-of-trade between 1980 and 1992 with catastrophic effect on the LDCs. A 28 percent fall in terms-of-trade for sub-Saharan Africa between 1980 and 1989 led to an income loss of $16 billion in 1989 alone. Between 1987 and 1989, these countries lost 15–16 percent of their GDPs owing to falls in terms of trade. Middle-income countries lost 5–6 percent of their GDPs during the 1986–1989 period owing to falls in terms of trade, causing in average $45 billion loss per year.

The general level of commodity prices fell even more in relation to manufactures in the 1990s, causing serious setbacks in many commodity-dependent developing countries. According to UNCTAD (1999a), oil and nonoil primary commodity prices fell by 16.4 percent and 33.8 percent, respectively, between end-1996 and February 1999, resulting in a cumulative terms-of-trade loss of more than 4.5 percent of income for developing countries. Then, income losses were greater in the 1990s than the 1980s, because larger terms-of-trade losses were associated with higher share of trade in developing countries' GDP. For example, Third World merchandise trade balances steadily worsened during the 1980s and early 1990s—falling from 55.8 billion in 1981 to -42.3 billion in 1993—declining by $2.5 billion per year. On the other hand, merchandise trade balances during the 1994–1997 period showed a significant rise, 6 percent annually, but then again dipped in 1998 to -13 percent and in 1999 to -14.2 percent, reflecting a precipitous decline in the commodity prices of major exports of the LDCs in these years (UNCTAD 1999a).[30]

Have the Strategies of Trade Protection Helped the LDCs?

The strategies of the infant industry protection as well as import substitution were adopted by many developing countries, under the shelters of special and differential treatment measures, to accelerate their industrialization, without liberalizing their economies or adhering to the principle of reciprocity as envisaged by the GATT discipline. Have these strategies helped developing countries over the period of last five decades to achieve their goals? Here again, the answer is categorically negative—overwhelming evidence indicates that none of the trade protectionist policies–neither the IIP nor the ISS nor any other packages of that sort—served as a credible vehicle for industrialization, sustainable development, or economic growth in developing countries.

Originally such protectionist policies were stipulated to be temporary measures aimed at facilitation of industrialization of developing countries; unfortunately they took a kind of permanent shape, and emerged as widely practiced protectionist strategies in many developing countries. Most of them, perhaps with the exception of East Asian countries, used ISS/IIP as across-the-board import restriction measures to overcome balance-of-payment crises—to withstand booms and busts of world economy that caused widespread fluctuations in the prices of primary commodities and to protect domestic industries from international competition. GATT Article XVIII also contributed to the sustenance of such protectionist strategies by allowing less developed countries—those in early stages of development—to use protective measures, under certain conditions, to protect "particular industries."

But many studies indicate that trade openness is associated with more rapid growth.[31] Dollar and Kraay (2001), for example, show that recent globalizers (developing countries that cut tariffs significantly, 22 points on average, compared to 11 points for nonglobalizers, in the post-1980 period) have experienced an increase of their growth rates, from 2.9 percent per year in the 1970s to 3.5 percent in the 1980s, and 5.0 percent in the 1990s, while nonglobalizers had a decline in the average growth rate from 3.3 percent per annum in the 1970s to 0.8 percent in the 1980s, and recovered to only 1.4 percent in the 1990s. The same authors also found high correlation between growth rates and trade volumes in their decade-over-decade study of 100 countries—the top one-third of developing countries had seen increase of their trade from 16 percent of GDP in 1970s to 33 percent of GDP in the 1990s. They also found validity of their proposition in pairwise comparison of globalizers and nonglobalizers, such as Vietnam versus Burma (Myanmar), Bangladesh versus Pakistan, Costa Rica versus Honduras—in each case the economy that has opened up more has had better economic performance.[32]

In addition, thanks to the blanket protection provided under IIP strategies, many infant industries in many developing countries remained infant for decades, hardly breeding efficiency and competitiveness needed for achieving export competitiveness.[33] Some developing countries that used selective incentives faced too complex administrative problems and protective measures, such as quantitative restrictions (QRS) and exchange rate controls, which often resulted in increased bureaucratic rent-seeking (Krueger 1974). Also, IIP strategies typically discriminated against the agricultural sector, and thus contributed to deterioration of rural poverty (Krueger et al. 1988). Also, fiscal and monetary instruments are found to be far superior to trade and exchange control measures, which, in turn, erode any justification for resorting to trade restrictions to address balance-of-payments difficulties (Bhagwati 1988). In this context, the UR took a step in the right direction—it denied subsidies for export expansion or export supply capabilities.[34]

Has Market Access Widened for the LDCs in the Post-UR World?

A greater market access has been a long-standing demand of developing countries, and such demands were raised by developing countries, under the banners of the special and differential treatment measures especially since the early 1960s.[35] Over the decades, scores of MTNs under the GATT as well as the WTO repeated those commitments, and in the meantime, developed countries reaped massive benefits from freer international trade, but improved market access for developing countries remains as elusive as ever. One main reason for this debacle is that while tariff cuts on manufacturing products achieved under the GATT rounds hardly benefited developing countries, products of export interest to developing countries—no matter whether primary or processed—faced formidable tariff and nontariff barriers (NTBs) in industrialized countries.

Perhaps the most protracted and prolonged sufferings of developing countries stemmed from the fact that agriculture and textiles and clothing—two sectors that account for two-thirds of the world economy and in which developing countries have great export interest—faced systematic and deliberate trade protection in industrialized countries. While tariff and nontariff barriers were reduced for products of export interest to industrialized countries, the textile and clothing sector, in which developing countries enjoy comparative advantage, remained largely outside the GATT negotiations, and was subjected to ever- increasing protectionist measures in developed countries. At the same time, the agricultural sector, in which developing countries enjoy natural comparative advantage, was systematically kept outside the GATT discipline, permitting the developed countries to constrain imports and subsidize exports. Given the overwhelming importance of these two sectors to the LDCs, the market access for the LDCs in these sectors are discussed in greater detail in the next two chapters.

How Helpful Are the So-Called Capacity-Building Initiatives for the LDCs?

As mentioned earlier, developing countries added another demand under the baggage for special and differential treatment rights under the WTO—technical assistance from developed countries and multilateral institutions to strengthen their capacity to implement their WTO commitments. Accordingly, under the so-called Plan of Action, adopted at the Singapore Ministerial in 1996, a so-called Integrated Framework for Trade-Related Technical Assistance for the LDCs emerged in 1997. The framework brought together relevant multilateral agencies—the International Trade Center (ITC), the IMF, UNDP, the World Bank, and the WTO—to assume joint responsibility for delivering coordinated trade-related technical assistance to the LDCs, to help them overcome shortcomings in technical and institutional capacity, particularly in the areas of trade policy, human resources, and export supply, so that they can meet their WTO commitments and obligations.[36]

The LDCs have long been demanding such assistance—technical and financial—largely because many of the preamblar statements of the UR agreements, to which they committed themselves in droves in the early 1990s, made such commitments,[37] and also a wide range of WTO agreements and activities now incorporate provisions for technical assistance, mainly because many development thinkers as well as practitioners, both within and outside multilateral agencies, tend to stipulate that enhanced technical assistance from industrialized countries and multilateral agencies could help in achieving better outcome out of the flexibilities granted by the UR to the LDCs in terms of commitments as well as transition periods.

A review of the activities of the interagency framework in July 2000, however, envisaged that the capacity-building needs of the LDCs should be articulated in a broad development context, so that the trade-related assistance could be assessed alongside a country's other priorities. Such an all-inclusive approach most certainly has further widened powers and jurisdictions of multilateral donor agencies on both domestic and international issues of recipient countries (not only on WTO-related matters), but whether benefits are actually accruing to the recipient countries is not so clear. If growing complaints from the LDCs, as manifested in scores of forums since the emergence of the WTO in 1994, are any guide, much of the promised technical assistance is yet to be delivered.[38]

Besides, the capacity of the multilateral institutions responsible for providing capacity-building assistance seems to be quite inadequate. Most of these institutions lack adequate budgetary allocations to meet their obligations or assigned roles under the integrated framework. The WTO, for example, allocates less than one percent of its total annual budget for technical cooperation, and the WTO secretariat seems to be unable to meet the growing demand for technical assistance.[39] The World Bank's assistance to technical cooperation for trade-related matters has most certainly increased in recent years, compared with the early 1990s, but it is still less than in the 1980s.[40] Moreover, evidence also suggests that some developed countries demonstrated serious difficulties in including trade assistance measures as a part of the overall measures of assistance to developing countries, consistent with the basic premise of the SDT provisions of the WTO.

Also, the structure and delivery of technical assistance seem to be problematic as well. Most of the so-called technical assistance for capacity building is ending up with seminars and workshops aimed at raising awareness—not with enhancing skills and expertise necessary for meeting WTO obligations or strengthening negotiating capacity of the LDCs. The so-called capacity-building programs also lack financial assistance, which is needed for implementing WTO agreements in the LDCs (Finger and Schuler 1999). The capacity-building initiatives also undermine the fact that slow development of developing countries, or inability of LDCs to meet WTO obligations and commitments, is often the result of exogenous factors, such as terms-of-trade, trade barriers, and dependency on aid and technology from the developed world. After all, dependence on aid from the developed world has not resulted in desired economic development in all parts of the world.[41] The experience with the structural adjustment programs carried out by the Bretton Woods Institutions reveals that lack of coordination and integration in aid programs leads to fragmentation of the aid-delivery system, which, in turn, negatively affects resource allocation and growth in recipient countries. Also, there had been proliferations of inappropriate "off-the-shelf" programs/blueprints that eventually harm the recipient economies, as they do not wholly own foreign-aided programs with donors in the driving seat, a problem a former chief economist of the World Bank pointed out (Stiglitz 2002).

CONCLUDING REMARKS

There is little dispute that the magnitude of marginalization of the LDCs in the world economy has been deepening, rather than softening. The SDT measures granted to developing countries, including the LDCs, under the GATT/WTO trade regimes, as an effort to promote economic growth and industrialization in the developing countries, have so far failed to halt this processes of marginalization, and in many sectors and areas, indeed, such measures have led to dysfunctional consequences. Serious questions have been raised whether such measures contributed to growth and development of recipient countries, whether preferential treatments led to trade retardation rather than trade creation, whether SDT measures created a safety net for inefficient developing-country exporters, whether prolonged dependency on preferential treatment helped or hindered liberalization, and above all, whether such preferences are guided more by the interests of developed countries rather than the real concern for eradicating poverty and reducing marginalization of LDCs.

At the same time, the LDCs are caught in a unique dilemma—while fifty years of SDT measures hardly helped them to move to a track of sustainable growth, and further continuation of the same measures looks less reassuring than ever before, they are also least ready to compete in a liberal global trading system in which all contracting parties must adhere to the same or almost the same set of rules. The seemingly inexorable process of marginalization of LDCs in the post-UR world also indicates how flawed is the mainstream economic theory that postulates that free trade will benefit all countries irrespective of their level of development, industrial and technological capabilities, and other structural characteristics. At the same time, although all WTO rounds since the Marrakech Declaration reiterated commitments to reverse the processes of marginalization and mainstreaming the LDCs in the global economy by ensuring "a share in the growth of world trade commensurate with the needs of their economic development," in reality such commitments bordered around political rhetoric, widening the credibility gap between promises and actual actions.

NOTES

1. This, however, does not mean that protection always leads to or results in industrialization or economic growth. As discussed below, history is rather full of examples in which protectionist strategies retarded industrialization and economic growth prospects in many countries.

2. The growth stories of Asian Tigers—Singapore, Hong Kong, Taiwan, and South Korea—have been interpreted by many as miracles (World Bank 1993), as examples of growth without much protection, but as many others have pointed out, those miracles had heavy doses of state intervention and trade protection (see Bairoch 1993; Hobsbawm 1994). Even Japan, the best story of economic growth in the twentieth century, has experienced maximalist state intervention. Japan's remarkable economic expansion in the post-war period was based on what Thurow (1992) calls a "communitarian" approach or what Zysman (1983) calls "guided capitalism," which sharply differed from Western capitalism that emphasizes market-based economic policies and minimal government intervention in the economy.

3. Except perhaps a few countries, such as Australia, New Zealand, and Canada, in which agriculture had been instrumental for economic growth.

4. Kaldor's Growth Laws, named after its founder, Lord Nicholas Kaldor of Cambridge University, stipulate three laws of strong positive correlation: (a) between the growth of manufacturing and the growth of GDP; (b) between the growth of manufacturing and the growth of manufacturing productivity; and finally, (c) between growth of manufacturing output and the growth of productivity outside of manufacturing. Taken together, Kaldor's

Growth Laws should put a country in what is called a virtuous cycle of growth (see Kaldor 1966, 1967). Apparently even Kaldor himself advised protection in the early stages of economic development. According to Thirlwall (2003, 124), Kaldor told one of his Indian students at Cambridge University that developing countries could industrialize only by protection, maintaining that anyone who says otherwise is "dishonest."

5. One can, however, trace the origins of protectionist theories in the writings of the great free- market economist Adam Smith too, who wrote: " Humanity may in this case require that freedom of trade should be restored only by slow gradations, and with a great deal of reserve and circumspection. The reason for this is that if those high duties and prohibitions were taken away, all at once, cheaper foreign goods of the same kind might be poured so fast into the home market, as to deprive all at once many thousands of our people of their employment and means of subsistence " (Panic 1988, 123–24).

6. As List (1856, 188) asserts: "Having reached the highest degree of skill, wealth and power by a gradual return to the principles of free trade and free competition in their own and foreign markets, they keep their agriculture from inaction, their manufactures and their merchants from indolence, and stimulate them to wholesale activity, that they maintain the supremacy which they have acquired."

7. As mentioned in the last chapter, at a later point, in the 1980s, Spraos (1980) confirmed the historical trend, but at a lower rate of 0.5 percent per annum.

8. Prebisch's argument that prices of primary products tend to fall over the course of time has been substantiated by two major works. First, the support come from the so-called Engel's law, founded by nineteenth-century German Economist Ernst Engle. The law stipulates that as per capita income rises in the course of time, demand for primary necessities, such as food, declines, while demand for luxuries tends to rise. Therefore, rise in income globally would keep shifting demand away from food to luxuries. Second, a major study by Grilli and Yang (1988) showed that the relative price of primary products might have declined by as much as 0.8 percent during the period of 1900 and 1986. There are, however, counter-arguments that prices of primary products fall due to low income elasticity and emergence of substitutes. As Pugel and Lindert (2000, 276–277) elaborate, two other tendencies also affect the demand and output of primary products. First, nature's limit—with the increase in population and incomes, natural inputs, such as land, water, minerals, and so on, become increasingly scarce and therefore, their relative price might increase more than manufacturing products. Second, relatively slow productivity growth in the primary sector—as productivity advances more slowly in primary products, such as agriculture and mining, than in manufacturing, that translates into slower growth in supply of primary products than manufacturing. That may, in turn, increase prices of primary products, relative to manufacturing prices. Therefore, the ultimate effect would depend on the outcome of the tug of war between the two depressing factors—Engel's law and the synthetic substitutes—and the other two factors that raise demand and prices of primary products—nature's limits and slow productivity in primary sector.

9. For example, in his report to UNCTAD in 1964, Prebisch criticized the ISS, as practiced in developing countries, for frequent and considerable waste of capital, adverse effects on exports of manufactured goods owing to high costs of production and slow rise in productivity, and insulation of domestic markets through excessive protection. He also advocated for export subsidy and GSP provisions for imports of developing countries , as selective measures, as against devaluation as a means of providing uniform incentives to various products. See Shafaeddin (2000) for details.

10. For example, in 1995, only 22 nations had gross national products (GNPs) greater than the annual sales of Mitsubishi, and the total amount of money spent in Wal-Mart across the world was greater than the combined GNPs of 161 countries (UNCTAD 1996, 96). In 1997, total assets of the top 100 TNCs stood at $4.2 trillion, with the 5 largest TNCs owning 25 percent of the assets. The top 100 TNCs accounted for over 80 percent of the world's industrial output (UNCTAD 1999a). They do exercise considerable market power, thanks to their scale of economies and command over markets. In 1997, for example, sales of General Motors exceeded the GDP of Norway and Thailand, sales of Ford Motors and Mitsui exceeded the GDP of Saudi Arabia (UNDP 1999).

11. Based on mainstream economic theory, many pundits argue that after the phasing out of the quota-restricted regime in textiles and clothing, massive reallocation of resources will take place in this sector in China and India, two countries with strong comparative advantage in this sector. But given huge surplus labor in these countries, such reallocation may not hurt allocation in other sectors. As Myint (1958) pointed out long ago, in the nineteenth century much surplus labor was transferred from subsistence agriculture to plantations and mining for exports, increasing overall productivity of the economy, without decreasing allocation of the domestic consumption sector.

12. See Shafaeddin (2000) for a useful discussion on fallacious assumptions of the classical and neoclassical economics.

13. As mentioned in the last chapter, several developing countries that signed the original GATT Agreement—such as China, Lebanon, and Syria—left the organization by 1950.

14. The revised GATT Article XVIII(B) entitled developing-country contracting parties to impose QRS whenever monetary reserves were deemed to be inadequate in terms of the country's long-term development strategy, while Article XVIII(C) provided that these countries could impose both tariff and nontariff restrictions, in order to support their infant industries and raise domestic living standards.

15. The newly incorporated GATT articles—(Articles XXXVI–XXXVIII)—called for eliminating restrictions that "differentiate unreasonably" between primary and processed products, to improve market access of products of export interest to developing countries. The articles, however, fell short of calling for any specific action or making binding commitments in favor of developing countries.

16. As pointed out before, the Kennedy Round (1963–1967) brought down manufacturing tariffs by 26 percent for goods of export interest to developing countries, compared to 36 percent for goods of export interest of developed countries. The Tokyo Round (1973–1979) brought down tariffs by 26 percent for goods of export interest to developing countries and 33 percent for goods of export interests to developed countries. Moreover, many argue that such tariff cuts came more as a consequence rather than as a cause of trade expansion, and largely in the interest of developed countries, especially transnational corporations. Factors like rapidly increasing international mobility of industrial capital, fast increase in intra-industry trade, oligopolistic character of industrial production, and intracorporation trade led to internalization of tariffs, which in turn led to "painless tariff cutting" (Tussie 1987). Also see Shukla (2000).

17. The First UN Conference on the LDCs was held in Paris in 1981, which adopted what is called a Substantial New Program of Action (SNPA) for the 1980s. The Second UN Conference on the LDCs was held in 1990, in Paris, which adopted the Paris Declaration and the Program of Action for the LDCs for the 1990s.

18. For details on the Doha Ministerial Conference and the Doha Declaration see World Trade Center (WT/MIN(01)/DEC/1, 20 November 2001; and Annual Report of WTO, 2003.

19. One can guess the handwriting on the wall by looking at the press statements of delegates at the Cancun Conference. For example, Malaysian minister for international trade and industry Rafidah Aziz said "Our boys have come around. We proved that the developing countries were not to be taken for granted." An African delegate said, "When our priorities are ignored and the conference refuses to discuss them, they call it a collapse. I won't call this a collapse. It is better to have no deal than to have a bad deal" (cited in Dowlah 2003a).

20. The origin of GSP can be traced to the 1961 GATT declaration—"Promotion of Trade of Less Developed Countries"—which envisaged preferential market access for developing countries, and the 1964 GATT Framework, which allowed contracting parties to provide "more favorable and acceptable market access" to products of export interest to developing countries. The GATT Framework also granted the so-called "less-than-full reciprocity" to developing countries, and incorporated two new provisions—Articles XXXVI–XXXVIII—calling for eliminating restrictions, that "differentiate unreasonably" between primary and processed products. Then, after an UNCTAD proposal in 1968, GSP was introduced "temporarily" in 1971. It was given a permanent shape by the Enabling Clause of the Tokyo Round (1973–1979).

21. The "competitive needs limit" refers to $100 million per tariff line or $13 million if the exporting country has more than 50 percent share of US imports, while the rules-of-origin requirement for the GSP scheme beneficiaries is 30–40 percent (World Bank 2003a, 213-214).

22. The European Council, however, considers certain agricultural and food products as nonsensitive, they include: castor oil, frog's legs, grapefruit, green tea, malt beer, papayas, pepper, and sweet potatoes.

23. In contrast, in the early 1980s, four beneficiaries—Brazil, Hong Kong, Korea, and Taiwan—derived more than 50 percent of GSP benefits (Karsteny and Laird, 1987).

24. See Figure 6.3 in World Bank (2003a, 215).

25. Of course, this may change by 2009, if the EU follows through its commitments under the EBA. But there are always uncertainties and possibilities of other kinds of barriers, such as environmental, labor, and political issues. More on this later.

26. This, however, indicates a significant improvement over 1992, when 78.5 percent of all dutiable imports from beneficiary countries were covered under the EU GSP, but the utilization rate (effective GSP benefiting imports) had been 35.5 percent. See Cuyvers (1998).

27. There is, however, another side of the coin. Based on the same study of Ozden and Reinhardt, World Bank (2003a, 211–212) concluded that countries removed from the GSP outperform those remaining eligible for GSP treatment, indicating that the so-called graduated countries have indeed higher ratios of exports in their GDP than the countries that are eligible for GSP treatment.

28. In the early 1950s, the famous Prebisch-Singer thesis showed how a secular decline of terms of trade of primary commodity exporters resulted in a long-term transfer of income from poor to rich countries. The deteriorating trend in commodity terms of trade—decline in the prices of primary commodities relative to manufactured goods—still continues, of course, with some exceptions. As mentioned above, the grievances of the primary producers were acknowledged, and in 1958, the Haberler report recommended addressing com-

modity price fluctuations through maintenance of buffer stocks and reduction of internal taxes on primary products in developed countries.

29. As UNCTAD (2000a, 5) remarks, "Although there are various factors influencing growth in the LDCs, the close association between the trends in per capita GDP in the group as a whole (particularly when Bangladesh is excluded) and the movements in the terms-of-trade demonstrates the significance of the terms-of-trade."

30. Of course, the implications of declining terms-of-trade varied among the LDCs depending on the nature of their trade specializations and the composition of exports and imports. While the sub-Saharan African countries and some island economies, which are primary commodity exporters, were worst hit, the impact had been mixed for LDCs that had increased specializations in services (like Maldives) or in manufactures (like Bangladesh). But in overall analysis, the TWN (2001) is right in pointing out, "a major reason why the world trading system has not been working beneficially for many developing countries is because their main way of participating in the system has been to export commodities, whose prices have been declining, and thus their terms of trade have been deteriorating."

31. See, for example, Dollar (1992); Sachs and Werner (1995); Edwards (1993); and Dollar and Kraay (2001).

32. It is, however, notable that Rodriguez and Rodrik (2000) have criticized such studies for their failure to adequately control other economic policies, such as macrostability, rule of law, or governmental consumption.

33. Important studies that looked into the IIP issues included Little, Scitovsky, and Scott (1970); Bhagwati (1988), and Krueger (1978).

34. See, for example, Articles 3 and 8 of the ASCM. Article 3 denies any leeway to extend support to any infant industry, whether it is for exports or not, as long as the subsidy is tied to export performance. In the agricultural sector, however, subsidies are allowed in research and development, crop insurance, and so on, which are used by developed countries, while subsidies are subject to countervailing measures in input and land improvement and so on, which developing countries use (Das 1999, 157).

35. As mentioned before, while granting less-than-full reciprocity to developing countries, the newly incorporated GATT provisions of 1964—Articles XXXVI–XXXVIII—also called upon developed countries to eliminate unreasonable restrictions between primary and processed products in order to improve market access of products of export interest to developing countries.

36. The framework also calls for greater coordination of technical assistance from bilateral, regional, and other multilateral sources as well.

37. For example, agreements on SPS Measures, TBT, Customs Valuation, TRIPs, TRIMs, ATC, Settlement of Disputes, and the Balance-of-Payments contain provisions for technical assistance for the LDCs and countries in transition.

38. For example, a coordinating workshop of senior advisers to ministers of trade in LDCs, held in Sun City, South Africa in June 1999, was critical of the way the IF worked and demanded "evaluation and more practical assistance."

39. A recent report of the WTO, however, claims that there has been an increase in the level of its technical assistance activities and in the financial resources that are available for these activities, and its technical assistance programs now cover a wider range of WTO agreements and activities. The document, however, does not mention any specific amount of budgetary allocations.

40. But almost 90 percent of the World Bank's technical assistance funds comes from trust funds provided by two or three bilateral donors, which makes the commitments to technical assistance less specific.

41. For example, the Marshall Plan succeeded mainly because European countries—which had all neoclassical parameters of economic growth in place—had been experiencing the Harrod-Domar-type "savings gaps" only. As a result, massive transfer of funds under the Plan resulted in successful reconstruction of war-torn Europe. In East Asia also, foreign aid did help, but in most other developing countries foreign aid negatively affected both domestic and foreign resource allocation, undermining economic growth.

4

The GATT/WTO Trade Regimes: How Has Lackluster Liberalization of the Textiles and Clothing Sector Restrained Economic Growth of the LDCs?

INTRODUCTION

Over the last few decades, trade liberalization brought unprecedented prosperity to the world, but much of the benefits accrued to developed countries. While the share in the prosperity had been less significant for many of the developing countries, it was unmistakably abysmal for the LDCs—they literally missed the boat. One main reason for the debacle has been that while successive rounds of the GATT reduced tariff and nontariff barriers for products of export interest to industrialized countries, those were raised further for the products of export interest to developing countries. While the textile and clothing sector, in which developing countries enjoy nearly absolute advantage, was kept largely outside the parameters of GATT negotiations, the agricultural sector, in which developing countries enjoy natural comparative advantage, was effectively kept outside the GATT discipline. Such a systemic and deliberate trade protection in industrialized countries perhaps constituted one of the most protracted and prolonged processes that powerfully impeded growth potentials of many developing countries, especially the LDCs, since World War II. This chapter examines multilateral trade regimes in textiles and clothing—a crucially important sector of export interest to developing countries—in order to ascertain how protectionist trade regimes under the GATT as well as WTO have contributed to the marginalization of the LDCs. Agriculture is discussed in the next chapter.

LIBERALIZATION PROCESSES OF THE TEXTILE AND CLOTHING SECTOR

The textiles and clothing industry was at the forefront of the industrial revolution in eighteenth-century Europe. It, however, took two centuries, up to the mid-twentieth century to be precise, for this sector to lead the way to a significant scale of manufacturing production in the less developed parts of the world, when some developing countries began to demonstrate comparative advantage in this highly labor-intensive manufacturing activity. Ironically, the industrialized world, otherwise firmly committed to nonprotectionist trade regimes, found this development somewhat incompatible with its employment and growth objectives. Instead of welcoming this development as a technology-driven shift in employment structure and international division of labor, the industrial world responded to it by erecting a formidable wall of protection around this sector. As a result, as Cline (1987, 10) points out, while tariff and nontariff barriers to other manufacturing sectors fell sharply in the aftermath of World War II, this sector faced an inexorable rise in protection in developed countries.

The urgency for protection of the textiles and clothing sector in the economic agenda of developed countries can be gauged from the fact that the original GATT Agreement, signed in 1947, deliberately left this sector out of its jurisdiction. The GATT discipline, as mentioned earlier, envisaged the principles of reciprocal and mutually advantageous trade arrangements, reduction of tariffs and other trade barriers, and nondiscriminatory treatment, the so-called most-favored-nation (MFN) principle, in international commerce. But the agreement formally exempted the textiles and clothing sector from these principles, treating it as a "special case," subject to a special set of rules. It was argued that the challenge presented by "low-cost" imports was "unique" to the sector, and that employment and production in the sector was important for importing countries (Dickerson 1991, 303).[1]

Consequently, none of the GATT principles worked in international trade in the textile and clothing sector. For example, the GATT principle of reciprocity prompts trade liberalization or tariff reduction by a country when it receives similar concession from another. This principle thus gave little scope for liberalization to developing countries; being principally primary goods producers, they had little to benefit from lower tariffs or liberalized trade for manufactured goods in developed countries. The principle of nondiscriminatory trade or the MFN principle had also hardly benefited developing countries, as industrialized countries often chose not to comply with GATT rules and principles whenever such compliance was deemed to be injurious to their domestic industries, or economic and political interests.[2] Even in the 1980s, the textiles and clothing sector faced an elaborate network of internationally agreed upon trade restrictions, as discussed later.

It was the successful conclusion of the Uruguay Round in the early 1990s that for the first time brought the sector into the GATT discipline by providing a framework for gradual integration of the sector into the global trading system. What follows is a review of the pre-UR period to examine how discriminatory and restrictive trade regimes in the textile and clothing sector retarded liberation of trade in less developed countries, and thereby retarded their days of industrialization or economic growth.

Short-Term Arrangement (STA)

The first serious assault by the industrialized countries on international trade in the textile and clothing sector, however, came in the early 1960s, when coinciding with the increased demonstration of comparative advantage in the sector by some developing countries, the Dillion Round succeeded in reaching a temporary one-year GATT agreement, called the Short-Term Arrangement (STA), which enabled contracting parties to treat textiles and clothing trade as exceptions from the GATT rules. The STA came in 1961, apparently with strong support of the Kennedy Administration, which led the move for restricting imports of textiles and clothing.[3] The STA, however, covered only the cotton textile products and authorized one-year restrictions on 64 categories of cotton textiles—until a more permanent mechanism could be devised.

Officially the STA was aimed at: (a) significant increase in access to markets that were then restricted; (b) maintaining orderly access to markets that were relatively open; and (c) securing a measure of restraint on the part of the exporting countries in order to avoid market disruptions. It allowed developed countries to negotiate quantitative restraints as well as other import restrictions on "low-cost" imports from developing countries on a selective basis in case of "market disruptions."[4] Viewed from this perspective, STA could be considered as the first multilateral trade agreement that introduced a new set of trade rules—the so-called special rules—for the textiles and clothing sector alongside the existing rules of the GATT. But what followed was a plethora of discriminatory and bilateral agreements for governing trade in textiles and clothing around the world, under so-called special rules.

Long-Term Arrangement (LTA)

In February 1962, the GATT approved what is called Long-Term Arrangement regarding Cotton Textiles (LTA). Initially signed by 19 major textile trading nations, it came into force for a period of five years. Subsequently, it was extended twice, in 1967 and 1970, in each case for a three-year period. By 1973, 82 countries were signatories to LTA. The LTA retained the restrictive character of STA in the textiles and clothing trade, and allowed importing countries, facing market disruption or perceived threat of market disruption, to negotiate bilateral agreements with exporting countries, or impose unilateral restraints in case no agreements could be reached.

LTA, however, barred importing countries from lowering quota from the amount of the actual imports during the previous period, and called for five percent increase a year. This provision, however, slowed down quota growth rates once a supplier was brought under restrictions, as the maximum permissible growth rate next year would be limited to five percent. LTA was also limited to cotton textiles, defined as textiles having cotton as over 50 percent of the fiber content.[5] Also, Article 4 of LTA permitted bilateral trade arrangements on the basis of "terms not-inconsistent" with LTA objectives, allowing developed countries to impose restrictive measures even when they were not actually threatened by market disruptions. As a result, terms-of-trade in textiles and clothing essentially came under the control of developed countries, which could legally discriminate against developing-country manufacturers of textiles and clothing.

THE WORLD OF MULTI-FIBER ARRANGEMENTS

In the late 1960s, LTA began to confront some economic as well as technological developments. The technological change came from the increased use of synthetic fibers, especially polyester and acrylic, and innovations in knitting technology. The economic challenge came from a growing number of newly industrializing developing countries that began to make a dent in the global textile market. Also, facing restrictions on shipments of cotton textile products, some developing countries shifted to the uncontrolled fiber product areas. These developments called for multilateral multifiber trading arrangement. Initially, the EU countries opposed a US demand for a multilateral agreement on the ground that they had no problem in controlling the influx of wool and manufactured fiber imports into their markets through bilateral measures.[6] Facing such opposition, the United States and Canada also signed several bilateral agreements in the early 1970s –in 1971 and 1972—with developing-country exporters imposing quota restraints to limit shipments of textile goods of manufactured fibers and wool in their markets. As a result of restraints in the United States and Canada, growing quantities of Asian textile goods diverted to European markets, forcing the EC members to participate in a multifiber agreement.

Eventually, by end-1973, a GATT Negotiating Group agreed on the text of the Multi-Fiber Arrangement Regarding International Trade in Textiles, commonly known as the Multi-Fiber Arrangement (MFA). The MFA was officially aimed at achieving expansion of textiles and clothing trade and progressive liberalization of the sector. It was also expected to ensure orderly and equitable development of this trade, so that disruptive effects of the trade could be avoided in both importing and exporting countries. MFA also had the objective of furthering economic and social development of developing countries by substantially increasing their export earnings from this sector. Besides committing itself to such impressive goals, the MFA also broadened its scope beyond LTA and STA by incorporating products made of manufactured fibers and wool as well. Originally signed by more than 50 countries, the MFA came into force in January 1974, initially for a four-year period.

Although eventually it ended up as one of the most discriminatory trade regimes in the entire history of multilateral trade, the MFA did provide some mechanisms for orderly development of the textile and clothing trade. It provided an umbrella arrangement under which bilateral trade arrangements could be concluded. Such bilateral agreements established the quota restraints on the exporting country's products—on the quantities of goods to be exported, by weight, or by the number of items, according to the product description. The MFA enlarged product coverage by including textiles and clothing made of wool and man-made fibers, as well as cotton and blends, but it excluded hand-loomed fabrics and cottage products as well as traditional ethnic handicraft products from its coverage.

Second, as mentioned earlier, the MFA emphasized progressive liberalization of world trade in textiles and clothing, and set terms and conditions for governing quantitative restrictions on textile and clothing exports through negotiations or bilateral agreements or on a unilateral basis. The MFA regime granted certain flexibilities in quota restrictions for the exporters apparently to help them adjust to changing market conditions, export demands, and their own capabilities. New quotas could be large enough to accommodate the actual trade level reached during the previous 12-month period. Also, when a restraint was renewed, the new quota could not be lower than the previous level, and in the case of continuing quotas, the annual growth could not be less than 6 percent.

The MFA, however, allowed the quota level to exceed six percent provided there was a corresponding reduction in another quota, that is, in case of swing provision—transfer of a quota from one category to another.[7] The MFA also allowed carryover of up to 10 percent of the unused portion of the previous year's quota to the subsequent year, and up to five percent carry-forward—borrowing from the next year's quota or advance utilization from the following year's quota. The MFA also allowed combined use of carryover and carry-forward for up to 10 percent of the original quota. In exceptional circumstances, when a recurrence or worsening of disruptions was anticipated, quota growth, however, could be reduced below 6 percent.

Third, the MFA regime contained safeguards for avoiding disruptive effects on individual markets and individual lines of production in both importing and exporting countries. It also imposed stricter rules for determining market disruption to discourage unwarranted claims of disruption. In cases of actual market disruptions, import restrictions could, however, be imposed unilaterally if a mutually agreed solution could not be reached. In situations of real risk of market disruptions, only bilateral restraint agreements were allowed.[8]

Finally, the MFA regime provided for a multilateral surveillance institution, called the Textiles Surveillance Body (TSB). The TSB came as a major institutional invention of the MFA—it had the responsibility to make sure that the obligations of bilateral agreements or unilateral arrangements reached under the MFA were respected by all parties. Also, it required all contracting parties of the GATT to notify the TSB of all restrictive measures on textiles and clothing—no matter whether reached through bilateral agreements or on a unilateral basis. Also, a Textiles Committee was established as a management body consisting of all GATT members, which served as the final arbiter—as a court of appeal for the disputes that could not be resolved at the TSB.

How Discriminatory Were the MFA Regimes?

The MFA protocols of 1973 were extended five times, up to 1994 when the MFA regimes were replaced by the Uruguay Round Agreement on Textiles and

Clothing (ATC). The MFA II came into force for a period of four years from January 1, 1978 under a Protocol of Extension. The MFA III took effect in January 1982 and continued until 1986. It was further extended in August 1986 for a period of three years, up to July 1991. The MFA V took effect in 1991 and expired by 1993. In December 1993, The MFA VI came into force for a year, to expire by December 1994. In 1993, the MFA had 44 members and, as Table 4.1 shows, six major textiles and clothing exporters—Austria, Canada, EEC, Finland, Norway, and the United States—maintained 98 restraining agreements.[9]

With every extension of the MFA, with the exception of the last three extensions, which coincided with the negotiations of the Uruguay Round, restraints were intensified, and the country and product coverage was further enlarged. Bilateral agreements became increasingly restrictive and importing countries often resorted to additional restrictive measures despite the quota restrictions in operation under the existing arrangement. By the mid-1980s, more than 70 percent of the textiles and clothing products imported to developed countries were subject to nontariff barriers (NTBs), both within and outside the MFA (UNCTAD 1986).

The progression of the restrictive and discriminatory regimes under the MFAs has been quite intriguing. The MFA II (1977–1982) provided for "jointly agreed reasonable departures" from the terms of MFA, permitting participating countries to negotiate bilateral agreements without complying with the requirements of the original MFA. Such "departures" from the original MFA worked against the interest of developing country exporters as importing countries could reduce quotas, deny flexibility provisions, and allow less than six percent growth rates in quota as envisaged in the original MFA. The EC countries, for example, divided textile products into 114 categories and five groups, and imposed most severe limits on Group 1, which included the eight most sensitive product categories. In 1976, the year when such groups were devised, over 60 percent of the LDC imports were placed in Group 1. Also, under the provision, called "basket extractor," any unrestricted exporting country whose exports in any product exceeded certain proportion of EC imports automatically came under trade restrictions.

Negotiations for the MFA III (1982–1986) were held under intense political pressure from textiles and clothing lobbies in developed countries. Textile and clothing lobbies in both the United States and the EU believed that restrictions of MFA II were not good enough to slow down the tide of cheap imports from developing countries. Also, there had been intense political pressures during the Kennedy Round (1964–1967) and the Tokyo Round (1973–1979), both in the United States and in the EU, against further liberalization of trade barriers in the textiles sector. As a result, as Dickerson (1991, 314) points out, the United States Congress granted negotiating authority to its trade delegations to MFA III with the condition that the LTA and the MFA would be extended without further liberalization.

At the same time, however, the so-called "low-cost" exporters—developing countries—also became more organized under the auspices of the UNCTAD. While industrialized countries favored stronger restrictions, developing-country exporters, under the auspices of the UNCTAD, demanded abolition of all tariffs and quotas (quantitative restrictions) on textile imports from developing countries

Table 4.1
Bilateral MFA Restraint Agreements of Six Major Importing Countries (as of 31 December 1993)

Suppliers	Restraining importers						Number of agreements
	Austria	Canada	ECs	Finland	Norway	US	
Argentina			x				1
Bangladesh		x				X	2
Brazil		x	x			X	3
China	X	x	x	x	x	X	6
Colombia		x				X	2
Costa Rica						X	1
Czech Republic		x	x		x	X	4
Dominican Republic		x				X	2
Egypt						X	1
El Salvador						X	1
Guatemala						X	1
Hong Kong	X	x	x	x	x	X	6
Hungary		x	x		x	X	4
India	X	x	x	x	x	X	6
Indonesia		x	x		x	X	4
Jamaica						X	1
Macau	X	x	x	x	x	X	6
Malaysia		x	x		x	X	4
Mexico						X	1
Pakistan		x	x		x	X	4
Panama						X	1
Peru			x				1
Philippines		x	x		x	X	4
Poland		x	x		x	X	4
Republic of Korea	X	x	x	x	x	X	6
Romania		x	x		x	X	4
Singapore		x	x	x	x	X	5
Sri Lanka		x	x	x	x	X	5
Thailand	X	x	x		x	X	5
Turkey		x				X	2
Uruguay		x					1
Total	6	22	19	7	16	28	98

Source: International Trade Center/UNCTAD/WTO (1996).

by a fixed target date. Eventually, developing countries succeeded in eliminating the so-called "reasonable departures" clause from the MFA III. Instead, a less restrictive "anti-surge" provision granted special restraints in the event of "sharp and substantial increases" in imports of sensitive products with previously underutilized quotas. The MFA III also tightened "market disruptions" by requiring proof of a decline in the growth rate of per capita consumption. Although the MFA III protocols granted favorable treatment for small-country suppliers and new entrants. But, in aggregate, restraints under MFA III were more extensive and more restrictive than ever before. No wonder that the EC as well as the United States condemned the MFA III as a failure.

While the previous MFAs restrained cotton textiles, and eventually extended coverage to synthetic fibers and wool, the MFA IV (1986–1991) extended restraints to vegetable fibers. Apparently, developed countries were concerned that developing country exporters shifted production to goods made of still-uncontrolled fibers, such as ramie, silk, and flax, to counter increasingly restricted markets for cotton, wool, and manufactured fiber products. The extended fiber coverage applied to products in which the previously uncontrolled fibers exceeded 50 percent of the weight or value of the imported goods. The coverage, however, did not apply to "historically traded textiles in commercially significant quantities prior to 1982" (Dickerson 1991, 316). This provision was applicable to product areas such as sacks, carpet backing, cordage, and similar products made from jute, coir, sisal, abaca, maguey, and henequen. The last two extensions of the MFA protocols—the MFA V (1991–1993) and the MFA VI (1993–1994)—took place while this sector came under intense scrutiny and multilateral negotiations under the Uruguay Round. The UR eventually displaced the MFA regime altogether with the Agreement on Textiles and Clothing (ATC).

How the MFA Regimes Impeded Growth of Developing Countries

During the two-decade-long discriminatory reign of the MFA—from 1973 to 1994—there had been a significant increase, if not a surge, in developing countries' exports of textiles and clothing products to developed countries. But, as several studies suggest, developing-country exports of textiles and clothing could increase manifold more in the absence of the MFA restrictions. For example, Kirmani, Molanji, and Mayer (1984) suggested that developing country exports to major OECD countries could increase by 82 percent for textiles and 93 percent for clothing if tariffs and the MFA quota restrictions were removed. A UN study (1986) found that complete nondiscriminatory liberalization—involving both tariffs and the MFA quotas—could increase developing-country exports of clothing by 135 percent and textiles by 78 percent. Then, the United States International Trade Commission (1989) showed that the value of exports of constrained supplies to the United States market could rise by 20.5 percent for textiles and 36.5 percent for clothing, or an average of 35 percent in both product groups in the year. Then, Trela and Whalley (1990b) estimated that individual developing countries could increase their exports by several hundred percent if both quota and tariff restrictions were removed, and in 1993, Yang showed that in the absence of the MFA regimes, developing-country exports to MFA importers could increase by 26 percent for clothing and 10 percent for textiles. Thus, although estimates of potential losses differed, all these studies clearly indicate that the MFA constraints caused substantial export loss for developing countries.

Second, the MFA regimes are criticized for generating rent transfers from importing to exporting countries through export quotas. Some studies suggest that these rents could more than compensate developing countries for restricted market access. A USITC (1989) study estimated the quota premium on clothing products at 16.8 percent. Trela and Whalley (1990a) estimated quota premiums for MFA exporting countries between 78 percent and 300 percent. An Indian study (1990) suggests that quota premiums in India, averaged over product categories, ranged from 14 percent in Canada to 42 percent in Ireland. A Pakistani study (1988) suggests that quota premiums in Pakistan ranged from about 50 percent of the free-on-board value of the item for clothing and cloth to about 80 percent for cotton knitwear. Hamilton (1988) estimated that import tariff equivalents of voluntary export restraints on clothing from Hong Kong in the European Communities over the period 1980–1984 were about 14 percent, while they were about 28 percent for the United States.

Third, the quota allocation procedures of the MFA regimes had built-in weaknesses, which resulted in significant economic inefficiencies. Above all, the quota regimes sheltered inefficient producers in developing countries by guaranteeing them a share of the markets that they could lose in a competitive trade regime. Then, the MFA regimes required exporting countries to administer their own licensing system, which involved varieties of quota allocation procedures. Many developing countries did not permit trading of licenses, and, thereby, protected existing firms against more efficient ones or new ones, thwarting competition. As most of the developing countries followed what is called past performance criteria for allocating quota volumes, this policy might have forced some efficient firms to work at suboptimal levels. Also, the quota eligibility criteria, that allowed, for example, shipment to third-country markets (non-quota-restricted), might have dissipated some of the rents derivable from quota ownership. The MFA regimes also resulted in what is known as "quota hopping"—investors moving abroad in search of lower-wage and less-quota-restricted countries. For example, in the mid-1970s, Hong Kong clothing industries moved to Macau, and then to Sri Lanka and Indonesia in the late 1970s. In the 1980s, Chinese and Korean companies invested in countries like Bangladesh and Vietnam in order to evade quota restrictions (Dowlah 1999).

Fourth, the MFA concept of market disruption paved the way for an institutionalized derogation from the fundamental GATT principles and rules. Many provisions of the MFA, such as bilateral agreements, quota restrictions, noncompensation for imposing import restrictions, and so on, were contradictory to the GATT principles. The MFA regimes did not require importing countries to compensate the countries whose products were placed under restrictions, which could have been the case under the GATT rules. Moreover, the MFA established a precedent of imposing quotas on products from developing countries—but not from developed countries.[10] The MFA was originally signed as a temporary arrangement to provide a "'breathing space" for industries in the developed world to adjust to increased competition in the global markets. Subsequently, it took a permanent shape, crippling rule-based trade in textiles and clothing, and slowing down industrial structural adjustment in the developed world.[11]

Fifth, the MFA regimes, indeed, created a separate world of international trade of its own. By providing special trade rules for textile and clothing products, especially after most fibers were included in it, the MFA effectively removed a large portion of world trade from the jurisdiction of normal GATT rules. Moreover, MFA rules violated many codes and rules of the GATT. For example, GATT's principles of MFN and nondiscrimination were turned upside down by the MFA by permitting countries to regulate textile trade on a country-by-country basis, or through bilateral agreements.

Sixth, developed countries also reaped mixed benefits from the restrictive trade regimes under the MFA. In spite of decades of protection, employment, which textiles lobbies and politicians emphasized mainly to justify protection, in fact, declined significantly in developed countries. Also, textiles and clothing employment declined mainly owing to productive increases from the substitution of machines for labor through automation, computerization, and other labor-saving devices. As a result, although the MFA succeeded in stabilizing production levels in many developed countries, the loss of employment continued, and eventually, the MFA ended up protecting machines, instead of jobs.[12] In the United States, for example, more than 2.4 million people were employed in textiles and apparel in 1973; by 1996, the number dropped to 1.5 million—thus this sector experienced a 39 percent decline in employment, while employment with overall manufacturing sector dropped by 8 percent only (Mittelhauser 1997).

Finally, the MFA regimes also cost badly developed country consumers. According to the Economic Report of the United States President (1988), the protection of textiles and clothing costs between $200 and $400 a year per household. A Canadian study showed that protecting the Canadian clothing industry cost lower-income households four times as much as higher-income households. Several OECD studies in the mid-1980s found that the burden of protection in textiles and clothing fell most heavily on the lower-income households of the OECD region, in which clothing accounted for a larger share of their consumption expenditure. Then, Hufbauer and Elliott (1994, 11–13) found that annual cost to American consumers for import protection in textiles and clothing was $4.3 billion in 1994.

INTEGRATION OF THE TEXTILES AND CLOTHING SECTOR INTO GATT DISCIPLINE

In 1986, about one-fourth of world textile and clothing trade was subject to the MFA regime—40 percent of clothing and 14 percent of textiles, and including other kinds of restraints, such as bilateral agreements outside the MFA, about 60 percent of global trade in the sector was subject to some type of restraints ((Dickerson 1991, 319). In December 1994, when the MFA was replaced by the ATC under the Uruguay Round, the MFA had 44 signatories,[13] and there were 102 bilateral restraint agreements under the MFA.[14] As mentioned earlier, although all eight GATT rounds aimed at reducing tariffs, in some cases, nontariff barriers, the textiles and clothing sector had been subject to special treatment up until the Uruguay Round. The GATT MTNs, however, began to focus significant attention on the textiles and clothing sector since the Dillon Round (1961).

At the Kennedy Round (1964–1967) average level of tariffs on manufacturing fell by about one-third, but fibers and other textiles and clothing received the lowest tariff cuts of any product areas. Then the Tokyo Round (1973-1979) negotiated additional tariff cuts and reached a series of agreements governing nontariff measures, such as quotas, import licensing programs, technical standards, and other measures to keep out foreign goods, and agreed to reduce manufacturing tariffs below the levels agreed upon at the Kennedy Round. But cuts in textiles and clothing were less than on other manufactured products. Moreover, these cuts lost any significance as at the same time the MFA regime came into force, allowing developed countries to opt for discriminatory trade practices in textiles and clothing.

Finally, the Uruguay Round (1986–1993) paved the way for integration of the textiles and clothing sector into the GATT discipline. Several developments, such as restrictive trading arrangements envisaged by several extension of the MFA, retention clauses of the 1981 Protocol of MFA, and clauses such as "good will," "exceptional cases," and "antisurge," which facilitated loosening of the MFA discipline, led developing countries to work together to place the "textile issue" on the agenda of the 1982 GATT Ministerial Meeting.

The GATT Ministerial Declaration of 1982 acknowledged that exports of textiles and clothing were being chafed under the growing restrictions imposed by developed countries, and pushed for gradual dismantling of the MFA regime. The Declaration led to the establishment of a Working Party on Textiles and Clothing (WPTC) with three broad options: (a) full application of the GATT provisions with a movement toward liberalization; (2) full application of GATT provisions combined with liberalization of trade measures irrespective of their GATT conformity; and (3) liberalization under existing frameworks (GATT 1984). The WPTC, however, failed to make any headway as developed countries contended that progress toward liberalization of the sector was a responsibility of all participants, while developing countries maintained that the responsibility lay with countries that maintained restrictions inconsistent with the GATT discipline. Failure of the WPTC in 1982 resulted in rapid proliferation of restrictions and additional measures that further thwarted efforts aimed at constructive modalities for liberalization of trade in the sector.

The liberalization bid for trade in the textiles and clothing sector was taken more seriously at the GATT Ministerial Declaration in Punta del Este, Uruguay, in September 1986. The Declaration included a special mandate for the textiles and clothing sector "to formulate modalities that would permit the eventual integration of this sector into GATT on the basis of strengthened GATT rules and disciplines."[15] This mandate, for the first time, brought the textile and clothing sector specifically into the multilateral trade negotiations. Neither the United States nor the EC, however, indicated their intention of refraining from further attempts to re-negotiate the MFA, before its expiration in 1991. As a result, the negotiating process was difficult. In 1987, however, the Negotiating Group on Textiles and Clothing (NGTC) was established to examine techniques and modalities for integration of this sector into the GATT discipline, but it failed to complete its work before the Montreal Ministerial Meeting in 1988, in which developed countries sought to renew MFA beyond 1991 with renewed restrictions, while developing countries wanted a clear timetable for phasing out of the MFA and integration of this sector into the GATT discipline.

Subsequently, negotiations for integration of the sector into the GATT discipline received a definitive boost when the Trade Negotiation Committee (TNC) agreed that the modalities for the integration of this sector into GATT should involve phasing out of the MFA and other GATT-inconsistent restrictions. It also agreed that the modalities of the integration process should include a specific timespan, a progressive character, and special treatment for the LDCs. TNC also decided that the gradual process of integration should commence after the conclusion of the UR negotiations. Major issues of contention in the negotiations centered around: (a) product coverage during the transition period; (b) the phaseout of the MFA restrictions; (c) the procedures for transitional safeguards; and (d) the application of strengthened GATT rules and discipline.

Developing countries, represented by the International Textile and Clothing Bureau (ITCB),[16] proposed three elements for the phaseout: (a) liberal actions, such as immediate integration of certain products like children's clothing, products of vegetable fibers and silk blends, hand-woven fabrics and products made thereof, and immediate removal of restrictions on small suppliers and least-developed countries (LDCs); (b) a programmed elimination of the remaining restrictions, after the stages of processing. The restrictions on tops and yarns to be removed initially, followed by those on fabrics, and then on made-up articles, and, in the last stage, restrictions on clothing to be eliminated; (c) an accelerated expansion of the quotas while they were awaiting phaseout. Developing countries emphasized that the dismantling of the restrictions should commence from the very beginning and continue progressively throughout the transition period until completed.

But the ASEAN and Nordic countries emphasized progressive enlargement of quotas, so that quotas could become redundant at the end of the transition period. The EC shared this approach of progressive integration, but insisted that the existing MFA restrictions had to be the starting-point for the phaseout. Eventually, the EC and the developing countries adopted phase-wise integration to be completed at the end of the transition period. But the EC differed as regards the phaseout modality, proposing a liberalization target for each stage consisting of an agreed proposition for the volume of restraint levels. Within this target, each restraining country would be free to pick and choose quotas for removal, according to its convenience. At the same time, facing projectionist pressures domestically, the United States Congress withdrew its mandate in 1988 for its delegation to negotiate on textiles and clothing for several years by passing the Omnibus Trade and Competitiveness Act.

The negotiations for liberalization gathered pace at the end of 1990 after the United States indicated its willingness to negotiate. Progress, however, remained dismal because of wide differences on the so-called "economic package," consisting of the product coverage of the proposed agreement, the percentage for the integration of product coverage, the percentage of integration of products in each stage, increases in the growth rates for products, and the duration of the agreement. The stalemate broke on 20 December, 1991 when Arthur Dunkel, the director general of the GATT, introduced a text of the agreement on textiles and clothing as part of a package of the so-called "Dunkel Draft," which sought to resolve these issues. The textiles and clothing sector, however, remained a contentious issue up until the final document was finally adopted at the Marrakech Ministerial Meeting in April 1994.[17]

THE URUGUAY ROUND AGREEMENT ON TEXTILES AND CLOTHING

The Agreement on Textiles and Clothing, as incorporated in the Final Act of the Uruguay Round, consists of a preamble, nine articles, and an Annex. Article 1 of the ATC stipulates that the agreement will serve as the legal framework during the transition period for the integration of this into GATT 1994. The ATC called for progressive phasing out of all MFA restrictions and other discriminatory measures in a period of ten years, so that at the end of the transitional period, by January 1, 2005, the era of discriminatory, bilateral quota measures of the MFA can be eliminated completely, and the sector in its entirety can be brought under the GATT rules and discipline, as strengthened in the Uruguay Round. In contrast to the MFA regimes that were applicable to the MFA signatories only, not to all contracting parties of the GATT, the ATC is applicable to all members of the WTO Agreement. Thanks to the "single-undertaking approach" that underpinned the UR agreements, the ATC has to be accepted in toto and all trade in textiles and clothing is subject to its provisions.

Major Features of the ATC

Product Coverage. The ATC, among others, covered all MFA restrictions maintained between GATT 1947 contracting parties and in place on the day before the entry into force of the WTO Agreement,[18] required all members to provide information to the Textiles Monitoring Body (TMB) on justifications for the restrictions,[19] report all actions taken by the members under the provisions of the transitional safeguard mechanism,[20] and report all products already integrated into GATT 1994 in accordance with the integration scheme under transitional safeguard mechanisms.[21] Article 1 of the ATC distinguishes three categories of members whom it entitled for special treatments: (a) small suppliers and new entrants in the textiles and clothing sector, in order to help them develop commercially significant trading opportunities;[22] (b) those members who did not accept the MFA Protocols since 1986; and (c) the cotton-producing exporting countries.

Phases of Integration. The ATC requires full integration of the textiles and clothing sector into GATT discipline by the end of the transition period, by January 1, 2005, and Article 9 of the agreement rules out any possibility of extension of the deadline. The Annex of the ATC provides a list of products to be integrated in four stages. For integrational purposes, 1990 has been considered as the reference year—each stage's integration is based on a percentage of the total volume of imports in 1990 of the products covered by the Annex. At each of these stages, products had to be chosen from each of the following categories: tops and yarns, fabrics, made-up textile products, and clothing, but the members would have the freedom to select the products to be integrated. The integration ratios of four stages—16 percent, 17 percent, 18 percent, and 49 percent—are to be completed in four phases of three years, four years, three years, and one-day. The phases and integration ratios are as follows:

Stage One—on the date of entry into force of the WTO Agreement (that is, by 1 January 1995)—members were required to integrate into the GATT 1994 products that accounted for not less than 16 percent of their total volume of 1990 imports of the products in the Annex, in terms of HS lines or categories; Stage Two—on the first day of the 37th month—(that is by 1 January 1998)—members were required to integrate into GATT 1994 products that accounted for no less than a further 17 percent of the total volume of their 1990 imports of the products in the Annex; Stage Three—on the first day of the 85th month—(that is, by 1 January 2002)—members were required to integrate into GATT 1994 products that account for not less than a further 18 percent of the total volume of their 1990 imports of the products in the Annex; and Stage Four—on the last day of the ten-year transition period—(that is by 1 January 2005)—the entire textile and clothing sector shall stand integrated into GATT 1994, with the remaining 49 percent of the total volume of 1990 imports integrated, and thus, all restrictions eliminated.

The agreement, however, makes clear that integration ratios outlined above are neither the maximum limits nor mandatory for members. The members are free to integrate their imports into GATT 1994 to the extent they like—provided that the minimum percentages are integrated. There is no maximum limit for integration—a member can fully integrate its textiles and clothing sector into GATT 1994 at any time it prefers.[23] At the same time, Article 2.9 maintains that those members that have notified their intention not to retain the right to use the provisions of Article 6—that is, transitional safeguard measures—could be deemed to have already integrated their textiles and clothing products into GATT 1994.[24]

Also, the ATC provides for quota growth rates that would make the quota system redundant by the end of the transition period. It calls for increases in the annual growth rates for restrictions under bilateral agreements in three stages. Stage One—1 January 1995 to 31 December 1997, inclusive—the level of each restriction under the MFA bilateral agreement in force for the 12-month period prior to the date of entry into force of the WTO Agreement to be increased annually by not less than the growth rate established for the respective restrictions, increased by 16 percent. Stage Two—1 January 1998 to 31 December 2001, inclusive—the growth rate for the respective restrictions during Stage One increased by 25 percent. And Stage Three—1 January 2002 to 31 December 2004, inclusive—the growth rates for respective restrictions during Stage Two, increased by 27 percent.[25] As regards the flexibility measures, such as swing, carry-over and carry-forward, the ATC retains the provisions of the MFA bilateral agreements for the 12-month period prior to the entry into force of the WTO Agreement. The ATC, however, prohibits any quantitative limits on the combined use of swing, carry-over and carry-forward.

Non-MFA Restrictions. The ATC also deals with other non-MFA quantitative restrictions on textiles and clothing products, including all unilateral restrictions, bilateral arrangements, and other measures having a similar effect. In general, non-MFA restrictions could be grouped into three categories: (a) non-MFA restrictions imposed by some developed countries, such as Japan and Switzerland, which are also signatories of the MFA;[26] (b) restrictions imposed by the MFA signatories against non-MFA signatories;[27] and (c) restrictive measures maintained by other countries, including developing countries, both the MFA and non-MFA signatories, except those justified under the provisions of GATT 1994. The ATC provides that all GATT-inconsistent, non-MFA restrictions had to be either: (a) brought into conformity with GATT 1994 within one year, by 31 December 1995; or (b) phased out progressively according to a program not exceeding the 10-year transition period.

Transitional Safeguards. The ATC calls for progressive phasing out of all restrictions that are nonconsistent with the GATT 1994—no matter whether they are imposed under the MFA or not. But Article 6 of the agreement allows the application of the MFA-type selective safeguard actions during the transition period to protect the domestic market against damaging surges in imports. Such transitional safeguard measures can be applied to products covered by the Annex, except those integrated into GATT 1994 under the integration program and those already under restraint. The agreement, however, called upon the MFA signatories—who did not maintain the MFA restrictions—to notify TMB of their intention to retain the right to use the transitional safeguards.

Article 6 of the ATC, however, cautions that the transitional safeguards should be applied: (a) as sparingly as possible; (b) as consistently as possible with the provisions of the Article; and (c) for facilitating effective implementation of the integration process under the agreement. With respect to duration of the transitional safeguard actions, Article 6:12 of the ATC provides that a member may maintain such measures up to three years without extension or until the product is integrated into GATT 1994, whichever comes first. Article 6:13 maintains that whenever a transitional safeguard action remains in force for a period exceeding one year, growth rates and other flexibilities (swing, carryover, carryforward) be established along the same lines contained in Annex B of the MFA. No quantitative limits, however, can be placed on the combined use of carryover, carryforward, and the provisions of Article 6:14.

Circumvention. Article 5 of the ATC identifies circumvention by transship-ment, rerouting, false declaration concerning country of origin, and falsification of official documents as a major concern for integration of the sector into GATT 1994. It requires member countries to establish necessary legal provisions and ad-ministrative procedures to address and take action against the acts of circumven-tion. Member countries are required to cooperate fully in the investigation of the alleged circumvention in order to establish the facts, by exchange of documents and information, by plant visits and contacts, by investigating involved exporters and importers. Once the fact of circumvention is established, the importing coun-try can deny entry of the circumvented goods. In case goods have already entered the country, they may be debited to the quota of the country of origin. If the cir-cumvention has occurred through a country of transit, action may also be taken against such a country. False declaration concerning fiber content, quantities, de-scription or classification of merchandise, and so on are also considered as "of-fenses having effects as acts of circumvention." In such cases, members can take appropriate actions consistent with domestic laws and procedures. Article 5 of the ATC requires that the members concerned should promptly consult with one an-other with a view to seeking a mutually satisfactory solution. If such a solution is not reached, the matter may be referred by any member involved to the TMB for its recommendation.

Quota Administration. As in the MFA, all restrictions maintained under the ATC, including those applied under the transitional safeguard provisions, are re-quired by Article 4 to be administered by exporting members. Importing members shall not be obliged to accept shipments in excess of the restrictions notified under Article 2, or of restrictions applied pursuant to Article 6. Any changes in practices, rules, procedures, and categorization of textiles and clothing products, including those changes in HS codes, in the implementation or administration of the restric-tions under the agreement should not adversely affect the access available to a member, impede the full utilization of such access, or disrupt trade under this agreement. However, the member initiating the changes in the restrictions must in-form such changes and initiate consultations with the affected member(s) prior to the implementation of such changes in order to reach a mutually acceptable solu-tion. If such prior-to-implementation consultation is not feasible, or a mutually sat-isfactory solution is not reached, any member involved may refer the matter to the TMB for its recommendations.

Commitments for Integration. The ATC calls upon the members to fulfill certain commitments to facilitate the integration process. It asks the members, among oth-ers, to: (a) achieve improved access to markets for textiles and clothing products through tariff reductions and bindings, reduction or elimination of nontariff barri-ers, and facilitation of customs, administrative, and licensing formalities; (b) en-sure the application of policies relating to fair and equitable trading conditions as regards textiles and clothing in such areas as dumping and antidumping rules and procedures, subsidies and countervailing measures, and protection of intellectual property rights; and (c) avoid discrimination against imports in the textiles and clothing sector when taking measures for general trade policy reasons. The agreement also provides that tariff concessions on textile and clothing products may be withdrawn on items of specific interest to a given country, or quota growth rate increases can be denied to countries that violate market access commitments.

The ATC, however, acknowledged special circumstances of the LDCs, requiring them to undertake commitments and concessions to the extent consistent with their individual development, financial and trade needs, or their administrative and institutional capabilities. The ATC has also provided for establishment of the TMB to supervise and monitor the implementation of its provisions. Consisting of 10 members chosen from among the WTO members, the TMB is responsible for: (a) ensuring that members afford each other adequate opportunity for consultation with respect to any matters affecting the implementation of the ATC, and to make recommendations to the members concerned; (b) promptly reviewing any particular matter that a member considers to be detrimental to its interests under the ATC; and (c) exercising surveillance of the implementation of its recommendations.

WHAT DIFFERENCE DID THE ATC MAKE, ESPECIALLY FOR THE LDCS?

The ATC came as a milestone in the history of global trade. It accomplished two far-reaching goals simultaneously. First, it succeeded in bringing together all member countries—developing (exporting) as well as industrialized (importing) countries—to sign an agreement ending the discriminatory and restrictive MFA regime that pursued anti-developing-country interests in the textile and clothing trade for more than two decades. Second, the ATC succeeded in integrating the textile and clothing sector in the mainstream GATT, into the rule-based global trading system, by paving the way for phasing out of the arbitrary and discriminatory trade practices. As a delicate compromise between the interests of developing and developed countries, the ATC provides for a 10-year four-stage integration process, to be completed by January 1, 2005. Moreover, ATC grants special treatment for small suppliers with respect to base levels, growth, and flexibility provisions, and includes special provisions for the LDCs.

There is no question that ATC provides for elimination of some of the most upsetting features of the MFA, such as: (a) the provision of "exceptional circumstances," which enabled developed countries to escape from the obligations of Annex B of the MFA; (b) the concept of "minimum viable production," through which small importing countries could evade obligations and transfer the burden of import adjustment from dominant to less significant suppliers; (c) the so-called "mutually acceptable terms," which served as a vehicle for importing countries to deviate from obligations in negotiating bilateral agreements with developing countries. The agreement also succeeded in abolishing the system of bilateral agreements based on the concept of so-called "real risk" in market disruptions. As Table 4.2 shows, the ATC also brought reduction in textiles tariffs.

It is, however, notable that the restrictive and discriminatory character of the MFA continued to influence trade in the textiles and clothing sector over the entire transition period. Bilateral agreements concluded under the MFA are effective until the day of full integration of the ATC. The integration process allows the restraining countries to select their own products for integration, and it kept 49 percent of the trade in textile and clothing sector to be integrated on the last day of the transition period—on December 31, 2004. By allowing each member to select products of its own choice for integration, the ATC enables importing countries to decide which MFA restrictions to be phased out in the early stages and which to be phased out at a later stage. That explains why the most sensitive products, in which growth rates are lowest and quota levels consistently filled, are left out for the final stage of integration. Thanks to such an end-loaded integration ratio, restraining countries so far evaded the phasing out of the most sensitive MFA restrictions.

Third, as the Annex to the ATC incorporates a number of tariff lines not specifically restricted under the MFA, importing countries can use this inflated volume to avoid integrating currently restricted product areas at the earlier stages. Also, the ATC covers the whole universe of textile and clothing products (Section XI of the HS code), including many products in which there had not been significant imports from the restricted sources. Such a broader coverage brings in products like soft luggage, umbrellas, seat belts, and so on, under the ATC, although they are not strictly textile products. These loopholes have allowed developed countries to avoid liberalization of MFA restrictions at early stages, and thereby, effectively impeded meaningful trade liberalization in this sector so far.

Fourth, as explained earlier, scores of studies have shown enormous benefits to stem from the elimination of the MFA and the complete integration of the textiles and clothing sector into the GATT 1994. One estimate showed that annual world income will rise by $510 billion by the year 2005 from full integration of the sector into the rule-based global trade system. Another estimate suggested that with the elimination of the MFA regime, combined imports of textiles and clothing would increase by 244 percent in the United States, 214 percent in Canada, and 264 percent in the EU—the three principal importers of textile and clothing products from developing countries. Trela and Whalley (1990b) estimated that in aggregate, the global gains from the elimination of quotas and tariffs from this sector would be $23.4 billion, of which $8 billion, one-third, will be accrued to developing countries. Table 4.3 shows different estimates of benefits from the overall liberalization of trade under the Uruguay Round.

Much of these anticipated benefits are expected to come from increased market access to developed country markets. Although the ATC came as a death knell to the discriminatory MFA regimes, the implementation of the ATC so far has not led to significant market access for developing countries, and therefore, they are yet to see those benefits. The MFA-maintaining countries, especially the United States and the EU, have taken full advantage of the end-loaded transition schedule. As a result, even in 2004, the textiles and clothing sector remains as quota-ridden, as discriminatory and arbitrary as ever. In the first phase of integration, the values of the United States and the EU products integrated into the ATC were 6.6 percent and 8.7 percent, respectively, to the benchmark values of the 1990 level.[28] By the second phase of integration, by January 2002, the shares of integration of the top

Table 4.2
Estimates of the Annual Benefits of Uruguay Round Trade Liberalization (US$ Millions, at 1992 Prices, Percentages of GDP in Parentheses)

Model/variant	Year	World	Industrial countries	Developing countries
WTO (Francois, McDonald, Nordstrom)				
A. Static, perfect competition	1992	40	27	13
		(0.17)	(0.16)	(0.30)
B. Static, imperfect competition	1992	99	40	59
		(0.44)	(0.23)	(1.23)
C. Induced investment, imperfect competition	1992	214	90	125
		(0.94)	(0.5)	(2.6)
World Bank (Harrison, Rutherford, Tarr)				
A. Static, perfect competition	1992	93	73	18
		(0.40)	(0.41)	(0.38)
B. Static, imperfect competition	1992	96	77	19
		(0.42)	(0.42)	(0.42)
C. Induced investment, imperfect competition	1992	171	115	55
		(0.74)	(0.61)	(1.20)
GTAP (Hertel, Martin, Yanaishima, and Dinaranan)	2005	258	172	86
		(0.89)	(0.72)	(1.56)

Source: Martin and Winters (1996, 10).

three textiles and clothing markets in the world were 51.35 percent of 1990 export volumes in the United States, 51.39 percent in the EU, and 53.2 percent in Canada.

But as Knappe (2003) points out, the actual share of integrated clothing in these markets ere 7 percent in Canada, 6 percent in the EU and 6.5 percent in the USA, and only 20 percent of quota restricted imports were liberalized. An IMF (2002) study also points out that by January 2002, the actual shares of integrated clothing and textiles in these markets were only 15 percent of their quota-restricted imports of 1990. Similarly, WTO (2003b, 133) points out that although the process of quota elimination has been accelerated in stage 3, still about 80 percent of the quotas, consisting of a total of 239 quotas maintained by Canada, 167 by the European Union, and 701 by the United States, are left to be integrated by the end of 2004.

Thanks to the strategy to uphold the technical requirements of the ATC, rather than the spirit of the agreement, progress in the integration of the textiles and clothing products in the United States and the EU remains less reassuring in the third phase as well.[29] Also, integration of the textiles and clothing products has so far been largely concentrated in less-value-added products, and therefore, commercially meaningful integration of the sector, or "full and faithful implementation" of

Table 4.3
**Pre- and Post-Uruguay Round Tariffs for Textiles and Clothing
in Selected Countries**

	Pre-UR tariff	Post-UR tariff	Reduction	Pre-UR bound	Post-UR bound
US	19.6	17.5	10.9	98.9	98.9
EU	9.9	8.3	16.5	100.0	100.0
Japan	10.4	6.8	34.3	100.0	100.0
Republic of Korea	28.1	19.9	29.0	1.4	87.1
Brazil	78.5	36.7	53.2	0.3	100.0

Source: International Trade Center (1996).

the ATC, remains a far cry from achievement.[30] Unfortunately, the main reasons for still-constrained market access in this sector lies with the ATC itself—it does not specify the proportion of each of product groups that has to be integrated at each stage of integration.

A look into the global textiles and clothing market in the contemporary world will indicate how lack of liberalization or integration keeps international trade in this sector still skewed to a few importers and exporters, mainly in developed and developing countries. In 1997, for example, global clothing exports reached $177 billion and the same year textile exports were valued at $155 billion, as the value of garments exports surpassed that of textiles for the first time. According to ITC (2000), between 1985 and 1997, global textile trade increased by 182 percent and the corresponding figure for the garment trade was 259 percent. Over the past two decades, the report maintains, the textile production grew steadily at 3.6 percent per annum in developing countries, while the corresponding figure for developed countries was 0.2 percent only. Also, in the 1970s the share of Asian textile exports in the global exports was about 28 percent, in the 1980s it rose to 34 percent, and in 1997 the share was well above 40 percent. But most of this share is hold by just one country—China. In 1997, its share in global exports of textiles and clothing reached a staggering $46.6 billion, which is over a quarter of total exports in the sector in the year. China's share in textiles and clothing exports grew phenomenally, since it became a member of the MFA in the early 1980s—from about $2.5 billion in the early 1980s, its exports increased to $8.5 billion in 1986 and, as mentioned above, to $46.6 billion in 1997.

With a share of $30 billion, China was the largest exporter of clothing in the world in 1998, when the value of the global trade in this product stood at $180 billion. As Table 4.4 shows, the same year, the United States, with a share of $55.7 billion, was the largest importer of clothing in the world. But thanks to NAFTA, there had been a very fast growth of garment imports from Mexico to the US and Canadian markets in the 1990s. In 1999, Mexico emerged as the largest supplier of

Table 4.4
Major Exporters and Importers of Clothing, 1998 (US$ Billions)

Exports		Imports	
China	30.05	US	55.72
Italy	14.74	Germany	22.35
Hong Kong, China	9.67	Japan	14.72
US	8.79	UK	11.98
Germany	7.68	France	11.64
Turkey	7.06	Italy	5.86
Mexico (1996)	6.60	Belgium	5.30
France	5.75	Netherlands	5.27
UK	4.92	Mexico	3.75
India (1996)	4.32	Switzerland	3.41
Belgium	4.04	Canada	3.26
Thailand	3.56	Spain	3.15

Source: ITC (2000).

garments into the US market—it fetched $7.7 billion, or 14.8 percent of the US market. The other major suppliers to the US market in 1999 were China (8.4 percent share in US market), Hong Kong (8.4 percent), Dominican Republic (4.5 percent), Honduras (4.3 percent), Republic of Korea (4.1 percent), Taiwan (3. 9 percent), and Bangladesh (3.4 percent). In 1999, the EU was the world's second largest exporter of textiles and clothing. Between 1990 and 1998, imports of clothing into the EU increased by 72 percent to $48.8 billion and 31 percent in textiles to $18.7 billion.

In global textiles trade, Germany topped the list of exporters in 1998, with a $13.3 billion share, with China as the third biggest exporter of textiles with a share of $12.8 billion, while the United States was the largest importer of textiles, followed by China. As Table 4.5 indicates, in textiles products intra-industry trade (IIT) ratio is very high, signifying two-way international trade in this sector, that is, exports and imports of the same or similar goods. A high ratio of IIT also indicates that, like many other manufacturing products, trade barriers and transportation costs in this product are low.

As this discussion indicates, the textiles and clothing trade is still dominated by developed countries. In the early 1990s, eight developed countries were among the top 15 textile exporters in the world, with Germany and Italy amongst the top five. Similarly, out of the 15 top garment-exporting countries in the early 1990s, seven were developed nations, with Germany and Italy among the top five suppliers (Hyvarinen 2000). In fact, only one of the 50 LDCs have so far emerged as a leading exporter to

Table 4.5
Major Exporters and Importers of Textiles, 1998 (US$ Billions)

Exports		Imports	
Germany	13.26	US	13.46
Italy	13.03	China	11.08
China	12.82	Germany	10.99
Republic of Korea	11.28	UK	8.31
Taiwan P. of China	11.02	France	7.50
US	9.22	Italy	6.61
France	7.57	Belgium	4.42
Belgium	7.47	Japan	4.36
Japan	5.97	Canada	4.03
UK	5.43	Republic of Korea	3.56

Source: ITC (2000).

the United States and EU markets. The emergence of Bangladesh, from almost next to nothing of garments production in 1980, into a major exporter in the 1990s, with exports fetching more than $4 billion a year, has largely to do with the search for new potential suppliers of garments with cheap labor. But much of the success of the Bangladesh garment exports has to do with the MFA quota regime—which allowed its garments exporters to guaranteed market in the United States, the EU, and Canada. Similarly, much of the recent surge in clothing exports from CBI (Caribbean Basin Initiative) and sub-Saharan countries to the US markets has to do with the easier access granted by the US Trade and Development Act, 2000. These countries will face formidable problems in the post-UR quota-free world—as most of them lack backward linkages, as well as competitiveness in skills and efficiency, as they were largely shielded from global competition.

And then, whatever little market access has resulted from the implementation of the ATC, that has been overridden in recent years by measures such as transitional safeguards, antidumping actions, and discriminatory application of rules-of-origin principles by some importing countries.[31] Trade liberalization in textiles is also constrained by the existing quota system which has created vested interests in both developing and developed countries—some developing-country exporters, especially LDCs, benefit more from continuation of the quota system, rather than elimination of it. Removing protection is expected to improve market shares of all developing countries. But, when it comes to gains for an individual developing country, perhaps the benefits depend on what wave a country in question belongs to.

Also, as Table 4.6 shows, the share of textiles, clothing, and leather goods in their total exports declined in the high-income Asian countries—Hong Kong, Republic of Korea, Singapore, and Taiwan—from 30 percent to 13.5 percent between

Table 4.6
Historical Trade Dynamics of Developing Countries in Textiles, Clothing, and Leather Goods, 1977–1997

Regions	Share in the region's total exports (%)			Average growth (% per annum)		Contribution to the GDP growth of the region (%)	
	1977	1987	1997	1977–1987	1987–1997	1977–1987	1987–1997
High-income Asia, excluding Japan	30.0	25.1	13.5	13.8	4.9	23.7	7.7
East Asia and Pacific	5.1	14.0	22.4	23.0	23.0	18.8	24.5
South Asia	14.0	27.9	46.5	15.4	18.8	40.2	54.4
Latin America and the Caribbean	2.7	3.8	8.5	12.2	18.1	4.7	12.0
Europe and Central Asia	9.9	18.0	12.6	16.8	18.4	23.2	11.8
Middle East and North Africa	1.0	2.1	5.8	7.1	15.6	-31.6	12.2
Sub-Saharan Africa	0.3	1.2	4.7	16.5	20.8	4.0	9.7
Low- and middle-income countries*	2.6	7.1	15.5	16.1	20.3	14.8	19.8

Source: Compiled from Table 1.A1 from World Bank (2003a, 55–56), based on GTAP release 5.0.
Note: *High-income Asia—Hong Kong, Republic of Korea, Singapore, and Taiwan—is excluded from the low- and middle-income region in the totals.

1977 and 1997. During the same period, the share of these exports almost tripled in the countries of East Asia and the Pacific to 14 percent, while the share nearly doubled in the developing countries of Europe and Central Asia to 18 percent, and in South Asia to 28 percent. But for the countries of the sub-Saharan region, the share increased from 0.3 percent in 1977 to 1.2 percent in 1997. In terms of contribution of these products to the growth of these countries, during the 1987–1997 period, these products accounted for greater shares in East Asia and the Pacific, South Asia, Latin America and the Caribbean, sub-Saharan Africa, and the Middle East and North Africa, while their contribution declined, compared with the previous decade, in high-income Asia, Europe, and Central Asia. These developments explain how the dynamics of trade in textiles, clothing, and leather goods have been changing in recent years, and how significantly economic growth of low-income developing countries, such as in South Asia, sub-Saharan Africa, and in East Asia and the Pacific, depends on these products.

Also, liberalization of the textiles and clothing sector does not affect all developing countries or the LDCs in the same manner. The following list shows how three waves of global trade in textiles and clothing progressed in the developing part of the world since the early 1970s (Dowlah, 1999).

First wave (late 1970s)
South Korea

Hong Kong

Taiwan

Singapore

Second wave (late 1980s)
Thailand

Philippines

Indonesia

Malaysia

Third wave (late 1990s)
Bangladesh

Pakistan

India

Nepal

Sri Lanka

Laos

Vietnam

The higher-cost developing countries, such as newly industrialized countries like South Korea, Hong Kong, and Taiwan, which have a substantial share in textiles and clothing exports to developed-country markets under the MFA regimes, have a lot to lose with the elimination of MFA-regimes as it gave them protected market niche against the lower-cost suppliers. On the other hand, lower-cost developing countries, such as India and China, would find elimination of the MFA regime advantageous, as they would be capable of supplying more in a restriction-free market. On the other hand, the lower-cost small suppliers, most of which are LDCs, like Bangladesh and some African countries, stand to lose from quota-free trade. These countries benefited from the MFA regimes; having fixed quotas for their products, they have done little to compete in a restriction-free trade, and therefore, might well be squeezed out of international markets because of sheer size and greater productivity of exporters like China and India (Dowlah 1999; Amjadi, Reinke, and Yeats, 2000).

Also, emphasis on quota elimination in WTO negotiations has so far neglected the issue of tariff reduction in the textiles and clothing sector, leaving scope for continuation of "tariff peaks" in industrialized countries on the textiles and clothing trade even after the phasing out of the quota system. With the implementation of the ATC, as Schott (1994, 58–59) points out, the US tariff cuts will average about 24 percent, but more than 50 items will be left with tariffs above 15 percent, particularly wood and wool-blended fabrics. In comparison, textile tariffs will be cut by an average of 31 percent by the EU and 39 percent by Japan. For the apparel products, the US tariffs will be cut by only 9.2 percent and will average about 18 percent after the ATC is fully implemented, while apparel tariffs will be cut by 12 percent in the EU and 34 percent in Japan. Another study, by Supper (2000), also shows that Quad countries–the United States, the EU, Japan, and Canada—will retain significant tariff peaks in sectors in which developing countries have a realistic chance of exports, such as textiles, clothing, shoes, and wood products. That means, even after the complete phasing out of the MFA regimes, that liberalization of this sector might not be achieved, and significantly higher tariffs might remain in this sector compared with other manufacturing activities.

But a major challenge to developing country exporters of textiles and clothing in recent years has been stemming from increased deployment of antidumping actions by developed countries. According to UNCTAD (2000c), of the 1,229 anti-dumping cases registered between 1995 and 1999, 67 percent targeted developing countries, resulting in reduction in their trade volumes and market shares in their exports. The report points out that nearly 20 percent of the EU's antidumping measures during 1995-99 were related to developing-country exports of textiles. The EU's repeated investigation into gray cotton fabrics originating from six developing countries—China, Egypt, India, Indonesia, Turkey, and Pakistan—resulted in decline of import volumes from these countries by about 28 percent, while their market share fell from 59 percent to 41 percent, according to ITCB (TWN 2001). Eventually, however, no antidumping duties were imposed. But proliferations of antidumping and countervailing duty actions in recent years send a worrying signal for developing countries that protection of the textiles and clothing sector could shift from quotas to antidumping measures after the phasing out of the transition period.[32]

CONCLUDING REMARKS

In sum, international trade in the textiles and clothing sector has long been characterized by a very high level of protection, almost systematically orchestrated by the developed world against the interests of developing exporting countries. The cost of protectionism had been exorbitant for the consumers in the developed world and bitter for the developing exporting countries as restricted access and discriminatory trade practices under the MFA regimes gravely hindered their growth potentials. The biggest achievement of the UR agreement on textiles and clothing would be complete elimination of the MFA regime and full integration of the textiles and clothing sector into GATT 1994. While estimates differ about the gains and losses of the liberalization of trade in this sector and the potential beneficiaries and losers of such liberalization, it can be safely argued that in general the effect of liberalization as well as trade expansion under a freer regime would be far greater than the continuation of a restrictive and discriminatory regime that is being dismantled now under the ATC.[33]

Although during the transition period, the benefits to developed countries would outweigh the gains in the developing countries, in the end, the complete removal of the MFA quotas should be favorable to growth of developing countries. Much of the benefits of developing exporting countries would, however, depend on their technical ability to expand markets in the developed world under a freer regime, in their skill and strength for complex negotiations, and finally, in putting their own houses in order by carrying out necessary structural reforms. Also, trade in this sector might remain heavily protected even after the successful phasing out of the MFA-regimes by January 1, 2005. Many high tariffs or tariff peaks will remain in developed countries in the aftermath of the transition period. Therefore, truly commercially meaningful integration of the sector into the WTO discipline may not be accomplished even with full integration of sector by the last day of the transition period.

NOTES

1. Especially two articles of the GATT—Article XII, "Restrictions to Safeguard the Balance of Payments," and Article XIX, "Emergency Action on Imports of Particular Products"—provided legal protection to such a special status to trade in the textile and clothing sector.

2. Apparently several factors facilitated such moves by developed countries. First, the GATT was a voluntary organization, which lacked coercive power. Here contracting parties signed multilateral treaties, submitting themselves to certain code of rules. It could hardly resist a powerful contracting party when it violated rules by raising its domestic concerns. Second, as mentioned earlier, certain GATT Articles, indeed, allowed them to do so. And third, up until the launching of the UR negotiations in 1986, the GATT was essentially a club of rich countries, where developing countries were mere onlookers.

3. President John F. Kennedy, during his election campaign, committed himself to protect the domestic textile industry, which felt threatened with imports from the "low-cost" developing countries. His administration made good with his election pledge by providing leadership at the GATT for restricting imports of textile and clothing.

4. Another reason for the United States to play a dominant role in framing STA was that it wanted to be even with the European countries, which had already imposed quantitative restrictions on textile imports from the "low-cost"' exporters, and the United States believed the Europeans were not taking their share of textile exports from developing countries.

5. Although the 50 percent formula was based on the fiber content, the United States followed the principle of value, called "chief value method," under which the value of the textile product had to contain more than 50 percent for cotton.

6. The EU also opposed the US proposal for multilateral agreement because of the fact that the EU countries themselves exported a substantial volume of textile products to the US markets.

7. That is, if the quota of a product were not filled, another product could be shifted to take advantage of the unused quota.

8. Diagnosing "market disruption" under MFA, however, had always been difficult and controversial. Market disruption was linked to the existence, or threat, of serious damage to the domestic industry, which could be assessed by examining factors like sales, market share, profits, employment, and production. The damage was linked to a sharp and substantial increase in imports from a particular source, and/or at the prices lower than those prevailing in the market for similar products from domestic as well as other import sources.

9. Two MFA members—Switzerland and Japan—however, never applied restraints. Also, Sweden left the MFA in 1991, but with the joining of the EC in 1995, the EC quotas were imposed on the Swedish market. Also, China was not a contracting party of the GATT, but it was a member of the MFA (Hyvarinen 2000).

10. Developed countries, under the MFA, chose not to impose restrictions on imports from other developed countries. There are, however, some instances when developed countries did take actions against each other outside the MFA. For example, during 1980–1983, the EC members initiated three antidumping actions against exports from the United States—two resulted in the imposition of a definitive duty, and the other one found no evidence of dumping.

11. Perpetuation and proliferation of the MFA regime disrupted the autonomous processes of structural adjustment and equilibrium of world economy. Gradually, voluntary export restraints (VERs), such as those inherent in the MFA, were extended to other areas, such as steel, automobiles, consumer electronics, footwear, metal products, wood products, machine tools, and semiconductors.

12. This is quoted from UNCTAD (1994, 109), according to which, "the MFA is increasingly becoming a regime for protecting machines rather than jobs." Job loss in this sector in developed countries is, however, a reality. According to the International Labor Organization (ILO), during 1980–1993, job loss continued in textile, clothing, leather and footwear industries, as the following table (cited in ITC 2000) shows:

Employment fell by (in percentages)

Finland	61.7
Sweden	65.4
Poland	51.0
Syria	50.0
France	45.4

Employment increased by (in percentages)

Mauritius	344.6
Indonesia	177.4
Morocco	166.5
Jordan	160.8
Jamaica	101.7

13. It is notable that two important industrialized countries—Australia and New Zealand—were not signatories to the MFA, and Japan and Switzerland were members of the MFA, but they did not maintain quotas under bilateral agreements under the MFA regimes.

14. Of the 102 bilateral restraint agreements, 32 were in the United States, 25 in Canada, 15 in the EU, 17 in Norway, 7 in Finland, and 6 in Australia (GATT 1994, 16).

15. Among others, the Punta del Este Declaration included a special mandate for the textiles and clothing sector as follows: "Negotiations in the area of textiles and clothing shall aim to formulate modalities that would permit the eventual integration of this sector into GATT on the basis of strengthened GATT rules and disciplines, thereby also contributing to the objectives of further liberalization of trade."

16. The International Textile and Clothing Body (ITCB) is an independent intergovernmental organization aimed at strengthening the process of cooperation and coordination among developing countries in the field of textile and clothing products.

17. It was the Montreal Midterm meeting that asked Arthur Dunkel, the chairman of the Textile Negotiations Committee (TNC), to reach a compromise on the issue through negotiations. While presenting the so-called Dunkel Text to a TNC meeting, Mr. Dunkel maintained that reopening or changing of any parts of the texts would require consensus. But whenever developing countries raised questions, Mr. Dunkel insisted on "consensus for reopening," while whenever such requests came from the United States or the EU, negotiations were reopened. Mr. Dunkel's successor, Mr. Peter Sutherland, followed the same practice (see Raghavan 1993).

18. Article 2:1 of the ATC provides that all quantitative restrictions within bilateral agreements maintained under Article 4 or notified under Article 7 or 8 of the MFA in force on the day before the entry into force of the WTO Agreement shall be notified in detail, including the restraint levels, growth rates, and flexibility provisions, by the members maintaining such restrictions, to the Textiles Monitoring Body (TMB), within 60 days of the entry of a member into the WTO. It also states that all such restrictions maintained between GATT 1947 contracting parties shall be governed by the ATC.

19. Article 3 of the ATC requires the members to bring such restrictions into conformity with GATT 1994 within one year after the entry into force of the WTO Agreement.

20. These products include those in Section XI of the HS Code (textiles and textile articles except the lines of raw silk, raw wool and raw cotton) and other products from certain other chapters of the HS Code that are included in this category by the MFA-restraining countries.

21. Article 6 of the ATC calls upon the members—who do not maintain restrictions falling under Article 2—to notify TMB—within 60 days after the coming into force of the WTO Agreement—whether or not they wish to retain the right to use the transitional safeguard provisions.

22. Article 1:2, Article 2:18, and Article 6:6(b) and footnote 1 of the ATC. Article 2:18 provides that small exporters who are subject to the MFA quotas and whose restrictions in volume terms are 1.2 percent, or less, of total restrictions in an importing country as of 31 December 1991 move ahead one stage in the growth process. Article 6:6b provides for favorable treatment to the small suppliers in the application of quota base levels, growth rates, and flexibility.

23. Article 2:10 maintains that nothing in the ATC shall prevent a member—which has submitted an integration program to TMB pursuant to Article 2:6 or 2:8—from integrating products into GATT 1994 earlier than provided for in the agreement.

24. In cases of such members of WTO—which did not retain the transitional safeguards—Articles 2:6, 2:7, 2:8, and 2:11 do not apply. There are, however, not many members who have not opted for such transitional safeguards. Article 6 of the agreement provides that members opting for transitional safeguards must notify TMB to this effect within 60 days of the coming into force of the WTO Agreement. The time limit was, how-

ever, up to six months from the date of coming into force of WTO, for those members who did not accept the MFA Protocols since 1986.

25. For specific limits and annual growth rates contained in the MFA bilateral agreements of major importing countries see calculations by the UNCTAD secretariat based on data in GATT document COM.TEX/SB/1799 & 1873 and ITCB database. Also see tables 1.2 and 1.4 in Dowlah (1998), which show illustrative increases in growth rates provided for in the ATC under the Uruguay Round.

26. For example, Japan imposed import restrictions on silk yarn against China and the Republic of Korea, and on cotton yarn against Pakistan. Switzerland instituted a price surveillance system on imports of textiles and clothing products.

27. For example, the EC has applied restrictive measures against Morocco, Tunisia, Turkey, Malta, Japan, some Latin American countries, and some Eastern European countries in transition. The United States has applied restrictive measures against Bahrain, Mauritius, Haiti, Lesotho, etc.

28. Also, it is interesting to note that both the United States and the EU notified integration of 16 percent of its 1990 volume of textiles and clothing imports into GATT discipline, including many nontextile and clothing products.

29. According to some observers, only 2.6 percent of the clothing products on which US restrictions are currently at their highest is likely to be integrated in the third phase of the integration.

30. A major review of WTO (1998a), for example, found the opening of this sector by the developed countries "not commercially meaningful" for developing countries as "products selected for integration were concentrated in less-value added products" and pointed out that over 96 percent of restricted trade might remain to be integrated even after seven years of implementation.

31. For example, facing protectionist pressures from domestic industry, the United States initiated as many as 24 safeguard actions on textiles and clothing items at the very outset of the transition period. Developing countries, of course, can take advantage of the Textiles Monitoring Body (TMB) and the WTO Dispute Settlement mechanism, but they have to bear in mind that until the dispute is resolved, exports of the affected products to industrialized countries remain restricted. Two developing countries, Costa Rica and India, used the dispute settlement mechanism of the WTO by challenging the safeguard measures initiated by the United States. In both cases, the United States was forced to withdraw its safeguard measures (Mukerji 2000).

32. The complete abolition of the MFA regime itself may, indeed, create more pressures on developed countries to resort to antidumping as a safety valve. Also, as Hoekman and Kostecki (2001, 318) point out, dumping is not prohibited by the WTO. "All the WTO does is to establish certain rules that apply to governments that seek to offset dumping. Why dumping occurs is not considered relevant under GATT rules."

33. As Martin and Winters (1996, 9) explain, the exporting developing countries as a whole gain from the abolition of the MFA, as they increase their exports into the developed world, benefit from increased prices in other markets, and eliminate the distortions associated with quota allocation and administration.

5

The GATT/WTO Trade Regimes: How Lack of Liberalizatiori of the Agricultural Sector Impedes Growth of the LDCs

INTRODUCTION

This chapter explains how lack of liberalization in agricultural trade under the GATT/WTO trade regimes impeded growth of least developed countries (LDCs) before the successful conclusion of the Uruguay Round (UR), and how the implementation or lack of it of the UR Agreement on Agriculture (URAA), which brought the agricultural sector for the first time under the strengthened GATT discipline in 1994, continues to hinder the actual or potential economic growth of the LDCs in the post-UR period. As pointed out earlier, two major sectors of international trade—agriculture and textiles and clothing—in which developing countries have great export interests and on which their economic prosperity hinged on profoundly—had experienced the most protracted, prolonged, systematic, and deliberate trade protections in industrialized countries during the entire GATT period. While successive rounds of GATT brought down tariffs and nontariff barriers for goods of export interests to developed countries, textiles and clothing and agriculture, faced ever-increasing protections in the developed world. While the textiles and clothing sector faced steep protections in developed-country markets, the agricultural sector was kept almost absolutely outside the GATT discipline.[1] In fact, at every stage, the GATT and the major industrial countries, suiting the parameters of what we called the second wave of globalization, moved only reluctantly to enable developing countries to draw benefits from the global trading system.[2]

Thanks to the "unique" and "sensitive" character of agriculture, the bearing of this sector on national food security, the fear of food deficiency, and parochial nationalistic expediencies, many countries, especially developed ones, erected elaborate mechanisms of trade protection around this sector. Up until the UR negotiations, agriculture was effectively excluded from multilateral trade negotiations (MTNs). This exclusion from the GATT discipline eventually led to proliferation of various types of protectionist measures throughout the world. To justify such a massive scale of protection in agricultural trade, governments, in both developed and developing countries, used wide-ranging pretexts, such as concerns for stabilization and growth of firm income, guaranteeing of food security and improving balance of payments, need for promoting development of other sectors of the economy, and increasing domestic agricultural output (Fitchett 1987).

Even as almost every government intervened in agricultural trade, developed countries most certainly excelled in the race. Through regulations, domestic subsidies, and export supports, industrialized countries erected high walls of protection around agriculture, insulating this sector from international competition, which meant, in most cases, competition stemming from developing countries. Some developed countries, indeed, acquired comparative advantage in agriculture through massive domestic supports and export subsidies, and then traded subsidized agricultural products internationally. Such explicit and large-scale distortions in developed countries depressed the world price of agricultural commodities to uncompetitively low levels and generated global market instability in the mid-1980s. Agricultural protection in developing countries, on the other hand, led to higher food prices, negative taxation of agriculture, prolonged dependence on food aid, lowering of domestic output, and subsidization of foodstuff for the politically vocal urban population.[3]

Eventually, however, the agricultural sector came under the GATT negotiation following the Punta del Este Declaration in 1986, which sought "to achieve greater liberalization of trade in agriculture and bring all measures affecting import access and export competition under strengthened and more operationally effective GATT rules and disciplines" (FAO 1998, 8). At the time of the rounding up of the UR, which resulted in the replacement of the GATT by the World Trade Organization (WTO) with effect from January 1, 2005, international trade in this sector was subject to a complex mosaic of nontariff barriers, such as quotas, quantitative restrictions (QRS), variable import levies, minimum import prices, discretionary import licensing, voluntary export restraints (VERs), and so on. Only 55 percent of agricultural tariffs in developed countries and only 18 percent of such tariffs in developing countries were bound at that time (Dowlah 1998). The URAA, reached at the fag end of the arduous UR negotiations, sought to break such entrenched and vested interests in agriculture by bringing this sector, for the first time, under the rule-based GATT trading system.

The chapter is organized as follows. The next section explains the processes that led to eventual integration of agriculture into the GATT discipline, and the following section explains the main features of the UR Agreement on Agriculture (URAA). Next I explore the benefits of the URAA from theoretical perspectives, and then I examine the actual implementation of the URAA. Next I look into the stakes of developing countries and the LDCs in the implementation or lack of implementation of the URAA, followed by a concluding section.

INTEGRATION OF AGRICULTURE INTO THE
GATT DISCIPLINE

Interestingly, the major impetus for bringing agriculture before the GATT nego- tiating table did not originate in developing countries; it rather came from sharp differences in the positions of the major industrialized countries, especially of the United States and the EU (Bergsten 1998). The EU countries—which by the 1970s through the 1980s acquired comparative advantage in agriculture through the con- troversial Common Agricultural Policy (CAP)[4]—insisted on managed interna- tional trade in agriculture to keep the CAP beyond the scope of GATT negotiations. The United States, which enjoyed comparative advantage in many agricultural products but at the same time protected special interests, on the other hand, stood for greater liberalization of agricultural trade while seeking to protect special interests. While such a deadlock hindered progress toward agricultural trade liberalization for decades, in the early 1980s a GATT Committee on Agricul- ture was established to look into so-called codes of domestic and export subsidies and government procurement procedures. Its role, however, was very limited–it mainly focused on the settlement of disputes.

In the mid-1980s, however, "ideological balance swung towards greater reli- ance on markets, competition and deregulation" (Hoekman and Kostecki 2001, 215), which eventually pushed the agricultural trade liberalization agenda in the GATT ministerial meeting in Punta del Este in 1986. Several factors contributed to the eventual push at Punta del Este. First, by the mid-1980s major agricultural ex- porting countries began to face increasing surplus stocks, as supplies increased faster than domestic and international demand. This was a period when major in- dustrialized countries, such as the United States and the EU, reinforced subsidized exports of agriculture, and major food-importing countries sought to attain food self-sufficiency, leading to a sharp decline in international agricultural prices.[5] While world grain imports increased at an annual rate of six percent in the 1960s through the 1970s, in the 1980s world grain imports stagnated, with the decline of demand from the EU countries and slower growth of import demands in develop- ing countries (Tangermann 1994). Several studies showed how government inter- vention distorted agricultural production and led to economically costly and inefficient policies in many countries, and how high levels of export subsidies greatly depressed the world price of agricultural commodities.[6]

Second, there had been growing awareness that nontariff barriers, such as vari- able import levies, which fluctuated with the movements in the world price in or- der to maintain a fixed internal price, insulated domestic producers from exposure to international prices, and thereby artificially debased global demand and supply conditions in agricultural commodities (FAO 1998). And finally, tensions were mounting in developing countries as agricultural protectionism imposed high im- plicit taxes on farmers in countries where public-sector support to farmers had been absent or negative. As Hathaway and Ingco (1996, 31) point out, while in de- veloping countries artificially orchestrated low prices of agricultural commodities created downward pressure on domestic prices, threatening livelihood of the peo- ple whose incomes depended on agriculture, in the developed world, on the other hand, a small number of powerful farm producers forced their governments to provide increasing export subsidies and domestic supports.

Given the sensitive and unique character of agriculture and the diverse interests and objectives of negotiating parties, it is imaginable that multilateral negotiations in agriculture were quite strenuous. The conflict between major industrialized exporting countries, primarily between the United States and the EU, as mentioned above, proved the hardest to begin with.[7] From the beginning the industrialized countries were divided into two opposing groups—one led by the United States and the other by the EU—the two biggest agricultural exporters, who jointly controlled 40 percent of international trade in agriculture.[8] The United States advocated for reform and liberalization and wanted to reduce the protection and support enjoyed by producers in the EU under the CAP. The US position was also shared by the Cairns Group—14 traditional agricultural exporters, from both developed and developing countries, Argentina, Australia, Brazil, Canada, Chile, Columbia, Fiji, Hungary, Indonesia, Malaysia, New Zealand, the Philippines, Thailand, and Uruguay. The Cairns Group sought binding commitments for eliminating domestic supports and export subsidies.

The EU, on the other hand, opposed far-reaching liberalization of agricultural trade. It rather sought a more moderate agenda to limit protections without major shake-up in the rules of domestic supports or export subsidies. To correct structural imbalance between supply and demand in world agriculture, it proposed to reduce domestic support slowly, until "balanced markets" were achieved, without disturbing "the basic policy structure and mechanisms" of domestic support. In respect to external protections, it proposed some "readjustments" to reduce distortions in the market. The EU position would uphold the right of all member countries of GATT to keep their agricultural policies.

Both the United States and the Cairns Group found the EU position aimed more at protecting its sacred cow—the CAP—or a clear attempt to block liberalization of agricultural market. At the same time, net food importing developing countries took strong interest in the liberalization of the sector, apparently being buoyed by the stipulation that liberalization would further lower their food import bills. Japan and Korea, which had highly protected rice markets and strong domestic opposition to reforms and no appreciable export activity in agriculture, supported the prohibition of export subsidies, but vigorously opposed proposals for abolition of quantitative import controls and reduction of tariffs. They sought continuation of domestic subsidies, up to certain levels, for the sake of national security.

With the world community remaining sharply divided on the liberalization of one of the most sensitive areas of international trade, the UR negotiations, scheduled to end by December 1990, took three more years for completion, mainly because of the thorny issue of farm subsidies. The pace and progress toward the completion of the URAA were determined by the progress made by the United States and the EU in resolving these differences. While the United States demanded what is called zero-zero option—for phasing out of all agricultural subsidies and quantitative restrictions over a period of ten years and harmonizing world health and safety measures—the EU dogmatically resisted such liberalization and rather sought short-term measures, without disturbing the existing levels of protection.

As a result, at the midterm review in Montreal in 1988 the agricultural group failed to produce a text for discussion, while the Cairns Group refused to approve the draft of other negotiating groups unless there was a text on agriculture. In April 1989, however, a midterm review was resumed, which paved the way for the so-called Blair House Accord in November 1992, when the United States and the EU reached an agreement under which the United States dropped its demand for zero-zero option and agreed to adopt a series of short-term measures that involved a freeze in the current levels of domestic support, export subsidies, and border protection, at the same time requiring commitment of the negotiating parties to long-term objectives of reducing government intervention in these areas of agricultural policy.

MAIN FEATURES OF THE UR AGREEMENT ON AGRICULTURE (URAA)

To bring the agricultural sector into the strengthened GATT discipline, the URAA required all member countries to submit a Country Schedule,[9] providing quantitative commitments on a commodity-by-commodity basis covering: (a) market access (tariffs and nontariff barriers); (b) domestic support; and (c) export subsidies. The commitments were to be implemented in six years, by 2000, by developed countries and within 10 years, by end-2004, by developing countries.

Market Access

The market access measures of the URAA encompass four major areas: tariffication, tariff reduction, maintenance of current access level, and special treatment and special safeguard. Under the tariffication scheme, members are required to convert average rate of protection provided by nontariff barriers (NTBs) during the base period (1986–1988) into a tariff equivalent and establish a base rate of duty for each product covered by the URAA. No tariff could be increased without negotiations with other countries.[10] In order to bring down tariff rates, the URAA requires, as Table 5.1 shows, developed countries to reduce unweighted average tariff by 36 percent, with a minimum of 15 percent reduction in each tariff line, over a six-year period, while developing countries are to reduce the unweighted average tariff by 24 percent, with a minimum of 10 percent in each tariff line, by the end of the transition period. At the end of the implementation period, all tariffs will be bound at the final level, and in the future the tariff rate may not be raised above these levels, except under specific circumstances. There were no reduction commitments for the LDCs.

The URAA requires member countries to maintain current access level for each individual product, as determined by the volume of imports in the base period (1986–1988). In case the current level is negligible, a minimum access has to be established at not less than 3 percent to 5 percent of domestic consumption during

Table 5.1

Main Measures of the UR Agreement on Agriculture (1995–2000)

Measures	Developed countries	Developing countries (LDCs exempted)
Market access reduction in tariffs	36%	24%
Minimum reduction per tariff line	(15%)	(10%)
Transition period (base 1986–1988)	6 years	10 years
Market access opportunity	5%	4%
Deadline	2000	2005
Domestic support reduction commitments (in AMS)	20%	13.3%
Transition period (base 1986–1988)	6 years	10 years
de minimis rule (% of value of production)	5%	10%
Exceptions	Blue and green boxes	Blue and green boxes and S+D
Exports reduction in value of export subsidies (per product)	36%	24%
Reduction in volume of subsidized exports	21%	14%
Transition period (base 1986–1990 or 1991–1992)	6 years	10 years
Exceptions	—	Support for marketing and domestic and international transport

Source: Compiled from Mathews (2001).

the base period.[11] This implies that a proportion of the imports of a commodity that had previously been subject to NTBs would be allowed into the importing country at a reduced tariff rate.

The special-treatment provisions of the URAA allow countries to claim exemptions from tariffication commitments for certain sensitive products, and the special-safeguard provisions enable a country to apply additional tariffs to certain specified commodities, where import prices are particularly low or where there is a sudden surge in imports. In both cases, normal tariffs may be supplemented by additional duties when actual import volumes rise above a specified trigger level or when import prices, denominated in domestic currency, fall below a certain trigger level.[12] The minimum-access opportunities of the URAA are to be implemented on the basis of tariff quota at a low or nominal rate according to the MFN principle. The URAA also allowed what is called tariff rate quotas (TRQs)—a minimal tariff rate for a limited volume of imports—to address situations where tariffs replaced NTBs.[13]

Domestic Support

To reduce trade-distorting domestic supports to agriculture, the URAA adopted what is called Aggregate Measure of Support (AMS), which quantifies all domestic supports deemed to have a distorting effect on trade. The domestic support reduction commitments of the URAA, as Table 5.1 shows, require cuts in the base-total AMS (value of total AMS during 1986–1988) by 20 percent for developed countries and by 13.3 percent for developing countries, to be implemented in equal installments over the specified period. For developing countries, where agricultural support services are considered to be essential for the country's overall development, the obligations are generally less demanding. For measuring domestic support to agriculture, the URAA introduced four different measures: (a) product-specific AMS—meaning support provided to an agricultural product; (b) non-product-specific AMS—meaning supports directed at the agricultural sector as a whole; (c) equivalent measure of AMS—meaning calculation of support through alternative means for the supports that cannot be measured by AMS methodology; and (d) total AMS—the total value of all nonexempt domestic support provided to agricultural producers.

For the purposes of AMS calculation, agricultural policies are placed in three boxes—the Amber Box, the Green Box, and the Blue Box. The Amber Box includes those policies that have a substantial impact on the patterns and flow of trade. The Green Box includes policies that are deemed not to have major effect on agricultural production and trade. These policies include a variety of direct-payment schemes that subsidize farmers' incomes, such as programs for product or resource retirement, environmental protection, certain types of investment aid, research, training and extension, and marketing information. Certain types of direct payment to producers that may be included in the Green Box include decoupled income support—supporting the incomes of the producers to be exempt from AMS calculations, provided that support does not influence production decisions. The support, however, should be decoupled from production so that it in no way affects what is produced or how much is produced.

The Blue Box includes those policies that fit neither the Amber nor the Green Boxes and fall in between. These policies mostly relate to compensatory payments and land-set-aside programs of the EU and deficiency payments programs of the United States. Such direct payments under production-limiting programs are exempted from AMS reduction if such payments are based on fixed area and yields, or such payments are made on 85 percent or less of the base level of production, or livestock payments are made on a fixed number of head. The AMS calculation, however, is conditioned by what is called *de minimis* exemption, which allows any support to a commodity to be excluded from the total AMS, provided the total support for the particular commodity is not greater than 5 percent of the total value of production of that product. The support ceiling is, however, 10 percent for the developing countries. This exemption also applies to non-product-specific supports; in that case its value cannot exceed 5 percent for developed and 10 percent for developing countries of the value of total agricultural production.

Export Subsidies

The URAA firmly addresses the issue of trade-distorting export subsidies to agriculture, which were mainly provided by industrialized countries, especially by the EU and the United States. In order to eliminate such distortive practices, the URAA requires developed countries to reduce the volume of subsidized exports by 21 percent and the expenditures on subsidies by 36 percent over a six-year period (see Table 5. 1). Developing countries are required to reduce the volume of subsidized exports by 14 percent and the expenditure on subsidies by 24 percent over a 10-year period. The starting level of export subsidy reduction commitments was, however, modified by what is called "front loading," which enabled the countries to locate the level of subsidies prevailing in 1991–1992, provided the level of subsidies at this period exceeded that in the base period. This was done apparently to make the transition less demanding at the initial period of implementation. No new export subsidies, however, can be introduced and the subsidies that are allowed should be applied in a way that would not undermine the cuts in export subsidies. The subsidies covered by the agreement include: payments in kind, subsidized stock exports, producer-financed export subsidies, export marketing, cost subsidies, export-specific transportation subsidies, and subsidies on goods incorporated into exports. The LDCs are exempted from such reduction commitments.

WHAT DIFFERENCE DOES THE URAA
MAKE—THEORETICALLY ?

After decades of discriminatory and protectionist trade practices, the integration of agriculture in the GATT discipline, indeed, came with sweeping promises and great expectations, as well as some reservations. The URAA aims at gradual phasing out of restrictive trade regime in agriculture, but even its full implementation will not fully integrate this sector into a rule-based, market-controlled global trading system as expected under the WTO. At least two reasons can be cited for this. First, the URAA leaves out much of the reforms necessary for liberalizing the agricultural trade regime to diverse interpretations, country discretions, and future negotiations (Dowlah 2001). Article 20 of the URAA called for another round of MTNs on agriculture one year after the expiration of the agreement to evaluate implementation of its reduction commitments, their effects on agricultural trade, and other agriculture-related issues. Second, global trade in agriculture continues to be treated differently from trade in manufactured goods, and unlike manufacturing NTBs, which are guided by the Technical Barriers to Trade (TBT) Agreement, agricultural NTBs are brought under the Agreement on Sanitary and Phytosanitary Standards (SPS).[14]

However, the significance of the URAA can hardly be overemphasized—it is, indeed, a giant first step toward liberalization of global trade in agriculture. The benefits of such liberalization have variously been estimated. Table 5.2 shows findings of Anderson (1999), based on Version 4 of the Global Trade Analysis Project (GTAP) database, that global economic welfare from removing trade distortions in goods will be $254 billion annually in 2005, of which 165 billion will

Table 5.2
Impact on Economic Welfare of Removing Post-UR Trade
Distortions in Goods in 2005 Using Version 4 of the GTAP
Database, 1995 (US$ Billions)

Liberalizing region	Benefiting region	Agriculture and food processing	Other primary	Textiles and clothing	Other manufac-tures	Total
High-income						
	High-income	110.5	-0.0	-5.7	-8.1	96.6
	Low-income	11.6	0.1	9.0	22.3	43.1
	Total	122.1	0.0	3.3	14.2	139.7
Low-income						
	High-income	11.2	0.2	10.5	27.7	49.6
	Low-income	31.4	2.5	3.6	27.6	65.1
	Total	42.6	2.7	14.1	55.3	114.7
All countries						
	High-income	121.7	0.1	4.8	19.6	146.2
	Low-income	43.0	2.7	12.6	49.9	108.1
	Total	164.7	2.8	17.4	69.5	254.3

Source: Anderson (1999).

accrue from liberalization of agriculture and food processing, and of this amount $43 billion will accrue to low-income (developing) countries and $121 billion will accrue to high-income (developed) countries. Earlier, simulations of GTAP Version 3 of 1992 showed that global economic welfare from removing trade distortions would be $260 billion annually in 2005, of which 32 percent, or one-third, would stem from liberalization of agriculture and food processing in OECD countries alone (Anderson, Erwidodo, and Ingco 1999). These estimates, however, do not capture factors like gains from liberalization of services trade, government procurement policies, benefits of increasing the degree of competition, the scope for scale economies, or the dynamic effects of reforms (Mathews 2000). Also, there are other estimations of the benefits of liberalization of agricultural trade.[15]

Several studies undertaken in the 1990s indicate that complete liberalization of agriculture—elimination of tariff and nontariff barriers, export subsidies, and domestic supports—would lead to significant cutbacks in agricultural production in the OECD countries, significant rise in agricultural production in developing countries, and significant rises in world prices of agricultural goods. Liberalization of agricultural trade, as Robinson (1994) points out, will result in major cutbacks in EU's agricultural production, significant increase in the United States share in wheat and food grains trade, some gains for Australia, while Canada would retain its share and the former Soviet Union would benefit from significant reduction in its import requirements. Obviously, higher grain prices will help exporters and hurt importers, but as Robinson points out, higher prices will also help offset the policy bias against agriculture that is characteristic of many developing countries. Therefore, benefits of developing countries from a liberalized agricultural trade would depend on potential efficiency gains from domestic policy reforms and improved market access.

Moreover, the phasing out of trade-distorting supports is expected to lead to structural change in world agricultural production, whereby production would shift from highly subsidized regions to low-subsidized or nonsubsidized regions, as in the absence of subsidies agricultural production would decline in the developed world, while greater opportunities and market access would lead to higher production in countries with real comparative advantage—the developing part of the world (Mathews 2001, 23). At the same time, consumption in the developed world is expected to rise as prices will be cheaper for them, while consumption in developing countries will fall because prices will be higher for them. These shifts in production and consumption would eventually lead to greater advantages for developing countries, scholars predicted (Valdes and McCalla 1996, 420).

But this prediction comes with a caveat—all developing countries do not stand to gain from agricultural liberalization, especially when it comes to higher prices for imports. Under the URAA, import prices of wheat, maize, beef, and dairy products, which many developing countries import, are likely to increase, while prices of coffee, cocoa, and cotton, which many developing countries export, are likely to fall.[16] That means that many developing countries, especially the LDCs, most of whom are net food-importing countries, stand to lose, as world prices of many basic foodstuffs that they import may increase while the price of many temperate agricultural commodities that they export may fall (more later).

WHAT DIFFERENCE HAS THE URAA MADE SO FAR—EMPIRICALLY?

As mentioned earlier, prior to the UR, agriculture was not only a highly protected sector in international trade, it was almost completely out of the jurisdiction of the GATT discipline. Therefore, the most significant practical contribution of the UR is that this sector is now subject to the GATT discipline, although full integration of this sector into the rule-based global system presumably will take a long time—thanks to the sensitive character of the sector as well as the acrimonious nature of multilateral negotiations in this sector. The progress in respect to the implementation of the URAA has been evaluated on the basis of three major pillars of the URAA: (a) market access; (b) domestic supports, and (c) export subsidy.

Market Access

Under the URAA's "strengthened and more operationally effective" GATT rules in agricultural market access, all member countries were required to submit a Country Schedule, providing quantitative commitments on a commodity-by-commodity basis on market access covering four major areas: (a) tariffication; (b) tariff reduction; (c) current access level; and (d) special treatment and special safeguard. Such market access provisions were aimed at reducing barriers to trade and, at the same time, increasing transparency. Also, promise of greater market access in agricultural goods underpinned developing country's supports to the UR negotiations. But available literature indicates that the URAA's mandate for tariffication of all tariff and nontariff barriers at the existing level of protection has led to something called dirty tariffication, as many countries fixed high levels of bound tariff although their applied tariffs were much lower.

Such dirty tarriffication, pursued in both developing and developed countries, affected similar products everywhere—cereals, oilseeds, meat, and dairy products, with tariff quota commitments the highest for cereals, followed by vegetable oils and oilseeds. In many cases, tariff quotas have simply been used as a means of converting voluntary export restrains (VERs), with the quotas allocated to the same countries. As a result of such dirty tariffication, as Norgues (2002) points out, agricultural protection in many countries, especially in industrialized ones, might have increased in the post-UR world, compared to the pre-UR period. Developing-country importers are less willing to make larger cuts in agricultural-bound tariffs, because the URAA requires them to commit to a smaller percentage tariff reduction over a longer time period, and also for some countries, high bound tariffs allow them not to alter tariff rates in order to stabilize domestic farm prices in the face of low world prices (Tangermann and Josling 1999).[17] On the other hand, the URAA requires developed countries to cut tariffs by 36 percent, but they can do so on the basis of unweighted average of all tariffs. Thus, the goal of tariff cuts could be accomplished by cutting tariffs sharply on least sensitive items while applying maximum tariff to important and sensitive products. Developed countries are required to cut individual tariff lines by only 15 percent, which leaves agricultural tariffs at a much higher level than manufactured goods, even after the full implementation of the URAA.

As Table 5.3 shows, agricultural tariffs are still shockingly high throughout the world compared with manufacturing tariffs. In Quad countries, average agricultural tariff in 2001 was 10.7 percent, compared with only 4.0 percent in manufacturing. In developing countries, tariff rates are still very high for both agricultural and manufacturing products, but agriculture is still more protected than manufacturing. This hurts developing countries badly, as in the 1990s, about 56 percent of the growth of developing country agricultural trade was accounted for by sales to other developing countries, while the rest—44 percent—went to developed-country markets (World Bank 2003a, 104). In the post-UR period, some developing countries, especially the middle-income ones, succeeded in increasing their share in global agricultural markets. But the increased share came principally from exports shares with other developing countries, rather than with developed countries. Developing countries' agricultural exports increased to 7.2 percent annually during the 1994–1997 period, from 6.1 percent during 1990–1994, although only 40 percent of this trade was with developed countries (Mathews 2001).

Table 5.3
Agricultural and Manufacturing Tariffs in Post-UR World,
1999–2001 (Most-Favored-Nation, Applied, Ad Valorem,
Out-of-Quota Duties) (in Percentages)

	Agriculture	Manufacturing	Percentage of lines covered
Quad countries	10.7	4.0	86.7
Canada (2001)	3.8	3.6	76.0
EU (1999)	19.0	4.2	85.9
Japan (2001)	10.3	3.7	85.5
US (2001)	9.5	4.6	99.3
Large-middle-income countries*	26.6	13.1	91.3
Other-middle-income countries**	35.4	12.7	97.7
Lower-middle-income countries***	16.6	13.2	99.8

Source: Compiled from World Bank (2003a, 118), attributed to WTO Integrated Database.
Notes: *Based on 2001 data of Brazil, China, India, Korea, Mexico, Russian Federation, South Africa, and Turkey. **Based on 2001 data of Bulgaria, Costa Rica, Hungary, Jordan, Malaysia, Philippines, Morocco (1997), and Romania (1999). ***Based on 1999 data of Bangladesh, Guatemala, and Indonesia, 2001 data of Kenya, Malawi, Togo, Uganda, and Zimbabwe.

One reason for still subdued market access to developed country markets has to do with high tariff peaks in industrialized countries in agriculture and food products. Although average agricultural tariffs declined from about 30 percent in 1990 to around 18 percent in 2000, tariff peaks remain substantial, especially in Quad countries. In the post-UR era, protection in agriculture ranges from tariff protection, subsidies, tariff peaks, tariff rate quotas (TRQs), tariff escalations, to opaque tariffs, and "the entire interlinked system of protection" is heavily biased against developing countries (World Bank 2003a, 118). Table 5.4 shows how average agricultural tariff ranged from 3.8 percent (Canada) to 19.0 percent (EU) in the Quad countries in 2001, while their tariff peaks ranged from 50 percent in Japan to 506 percent in the EU.

But as Table 5.5 shows, effective ad valorem tariffs in Quad countries on agricultural products from the LDCs range from 3.4 percent in Canada to 29.1 percent in the EU, and even taking overall OECD countries, the tariff comes to about 20

Table 5.4
Agricultural Tariff Peaks in Quad Countries, 2001
(Most-Favored-Nation, Applied, Ad Valorem, Out-of-Quota,
Percentages, and Standard Deviation)

	Average tariff	Maximum tariff	Standard deviation	Percentage of lines covered
Canada	3.8	238.0	12.9	76.0
EU	19.0	506.3	27.3	85.9
Japan	10.3	50.0	10.0	85.5
US	9.5	350.0	26.2	99.3

Source: Compiled from World Bank (2003a, 119), attributed to WTO Integrated Database.

Table 5.5
Effective Ad Valorem Tariff Equivalents on Bilateral Agriculture
Trade Flows

Importers	Exporters				
	Least-developed countries	Other low-income countries	Middle-income countries	All developing countries	OECD
Canada	3.4	18.7	16.3	17.5	33.7
EU	7.6	13.4	24.8	20.0	41.6
Japan	29.1	16.3	21.2	21.9	28.3
US	28.1	9.5	13.0	12.7	14.5
Other OECD	19.6	28.0	35.4	32.5	42.1
Developing countries	—	—	—	17.0	14.5
Middle-income countries	18.2	18.4	23.1	—	—

Source: IMF and World Bank (2002).

percent. What is more significant is that in both the US and the EU, agricultural products face higher ad valorem tariffs than products from other OECD countries. Similarly, TRQs—a minimal tariff rate for a limited volume of imports—although applied limitedly, have also been powerfully affecting market access for developing-country products, as TRQs cover some of the main commodities produced in the OECD countries. About 28 percent of domestic agricultural production in the OECD countries is protected by TRQs, while the rates are 38 percent and 26 percent, respectively, for the EU and the United States (World Bank 2003a, 125).

And, there are tariff escalations—rise of tariffs with levels of processing of products. Tariff escalations in developed countries have long been viewed as one of the major impediments to the developing-country efforts to move to value-added and processed products. The manufacturing component of agriculture and food processing has been a prime target for high tariff escalations for a long time. The trend continues. In 2002, for example, average tariff escalations were: (a) final product of coffee—12.1 percent in the EU, 10.1 percent in the United States, and 19.8 percent in Japan; (b) final product of cocoa—30.6 percent in the EU, 15.3 percent in the United States and 21.7 percent in Japan; and (c) final product of fruits—22. 5 percent in the EU, 10.2 percent in the United States, and 16.7 percent in Japan. But these averages mask very high peaks on individual products. For example, in 2002, in the United States, the tariff on final fruit products and cocoa was 136 percent and 186 percent, respectively, while in the EU, the respective rates were 98 percent and 63 percent.[18] Also, many agricultural products, such as live, fresh, chilled, or frozen crustaceans, face tariff escalations of more than 100 percent in Japan and the United States (Bacchetta and Bora 2003). Obviously, the forgone income from such tariff escalations is huge for developing countries.[19]

Developing countries' prospect of market access is also impeded by the nature of international food production, trade, and distribution system. The world's largest wheat producers are China, the EU, India, and the United States, whose production in the last half of the 1990s averaged at 109 million metric tons (mmt), 99 mmt, 70 mmt, and 63 mmt, respectively. But the United States was the largest wheat exporter in the world, with 23 percent share in global wheat trade, compared with 40 percent share in the early 1980s. In corn production, the United States was the largest producer and exporter—in 1999/2000, its share in global corn exports was 67 percent, China came second in corn exports with a 14 percent share, followed by Argentina with a 12 percent share. In global rice trade, key exporters are Thailand, Vietnam, China, the United States, India, and Pakistan. That means that in major agricultural products only a handful of countries are exporters—indicating the oligopolistic character of the market.

Moreover, only a small proportion of global food production is traded internationally, and some food products do not have global markets at all. In 2000, for example, only 17 percent of world wheat production, 11 percent of coarse grains (maize, barley, oats, and others), and 6 percent of rice were traded internationally. Global agricultural trade is further compounded by dominance of a few transnational corporations—in 2000, almost 85–90 percent of agricultural trade was controlled by the top five transnational grain businesses—Cargill, Continental, Louis Dreyfus, Andre, and Bunge. They also substantially controlled marketing of agricultural inputs—such as fuel, fertilizer, seeds, pesticides, and irrigation equipment. By controlling trade of both agricultural inputs and outputs, as well as banking, processing, and shipping operations, these transnational corporations powerfully distort agricultural trade around the world, while their operations and influence remain outside the purview of the WTO (Murphy 2002).[20]

Also, lack of progress in agricultural trade negotiations thwarts prospects of greater market access for developing countries. Agricultural negotiations remained acrimonious in all the post-UR trade negotiations held so far. The Doha Ministerial, which promised "substantial improvement in market access," failed to make any headway in "substantial reductions in trade-distorting subsidies," facing vehement opposition from the EU, especially from France. The post-Doha agricultural negotiation, which revolved between a radical US proposal that called for reduction of trade-distorting domestic subsidies by $100 billion to 5 percent of agricultural production, cutting average tariffs from 62 percent to 15 percent, and abolishing export subsidies by 2010 and the EU proposal, which sought to cut tariffs by 36 percent, domestic-production-linked subsidies by 55 percent, and export subsidies by 45 percent, also failed to make any headway (Sally 2003).[21]

Then, throughout the year 2003 WTO members discussed the so-called Harbinson Draft, proposed by Stuart Harbinson, chair of the special negotiating session of the WTO Committee on Agriculture. The draft called for tariff cuts on farm products by at least 25 percent and eliminating export subsidies within nine years.[22] The draft, however, failed to satisfy any of the major players in agricultural negotiations. While the United States and the Cairn Group expressed disappointment with the draft for lacking ambition in cutting tariffs and trade-distorting supports, the EU complained that the draft modalities were biased toward agricultural exporting countries such as the United States and those of the Cairns Group. The EU also criticized the Harbinson Draft for not sufficiently taking into account of agricultural nontrade concerns (NTCs), such as environment and food safety. Some developing countries, including India, Kenya, and Nigeria, however, welcomed the draft, noting that it would provide poorer countries with the flexibilities they needed to address their developmental needs.[23]

Among the NGOs, the reaction was mixed as well. While several NGOs, such as the Bangkok-based "Focus on the Global South" and the Institute for Agriculture Trade Policy (IATP), criticized the Harbinson Draft for failing to even out the systemic pro-developed-country bias in international agriculture rules, some other NGOs, such as the Like-Minded Group (LMG) in India, Kenya, and Nigeria, welcomed the draft as a "small victory" for the developing countries. Finally, the last WTO Ministerial, held in Cancun in September 2003, collapsed mainly on the issue of farm subsidies, as discussed earlier.[24]

Domestic Supports

Trade-distorting domestic support reduction has been a hallmark of the URAA, but commitments made by the member countries in this regard so far show no remarkable signs of promise. At the time of the launching of the UR negotiation in 1986, agricultural subsidies in OECD economies totaled $326 billion, but as UNCTAD (1999a) points out, these countries spent on average $350 billion a year in agricultural support between 1996 and 1998, which was more than double the agricultural export earnings of developing countries, which totaled $170 billion during the period. In 2002, subsidies and other supports to agriculture in high-income countries were running at $1 billion a day, more than six times all development assistance in the world (Ingco 2003), and government production supports accounted for up to 39 percent of farm income in the EU countries, while the percentage was 15 percent for US farmers (World Bank 2003a, 107). Thanks to such a massive scale of government supports to farmers, the average income of farmers in most of the industrialized countries is much higher than their national average.[25]

During 1999–2001, as Table 5.6 shows, direct production subsidies accorded to the OECD-country farmers—through higher domestic prices—totaled $248 billion, out of a total of $329.6 billion of total farm supports given during the period. As expected, the EU topped the list with $112.7 billion—accounting for more than one-third of total OECD supports. The United States ranked second with $95.5 billion, while Japan's support stood at $65 billion. Benefits to consumers were estimated at $26.2 billion only, or about 7 percent of the total agricultural support of $329.6 billion. Also, of the total support to producers of the $248.3 billion—about two thirds—$160 billion—came from border measures, such as tariffs and quantitative restriction designed to support domestic markets, which accounted for 70 percent of all protection in the OECD countries. The bulk of these supports went to producers of corn ($12.9 billion), meat ($47.3 billion), milk ($42.1 billion), rice ($26.4 billion), and wheat ($17.3 billion). But as World Bank (2003a, 121) points out, the protection rate for producers—measured as a percentage of gross agricultural output at world prices—has decreased in the OECD countries from 62.5 percent in 1986–1988 (the URAA base period) to 49 percent in 1999–2001.[26] Also, overall levels of agricultural support in the United States and the EU have declined between 1986 and 2001. For example, in the EU, farmers' prices were 65 percent higher than international prices in 1986–1988, which has come down to 34 percent in 1999–2001.[27] Similarly, in the United States domestic prices came down to 10.8 percent in 1999–2001, from 16 percent in 1986–1988.

One main reason for continuation of the agricultural production support in the New Millennium has to do with the URAA itself, which provides for exclusion of certain expenditures, such as expenditures for public stockholding for food security purposes and expenditures for domestic food aid to vulnerable sections of the community, from AMS calculations under certain conditions.[28] This exemption allows continuation of some of the most retrenched support structures for subsidizing agriculture, especially in industrialized countries. Even at the current levels of subsidized exports, a third or more of the trade in beef, wheat, and vegetable oils and a fifth of poultry and coarse grains can still be subsidized. As the earlier discussion indicates, industrialized countries continue to provide domestic supports to individual commodities, such as sugar, rice, vegetables, wheat, beef, coarse grains, and dairy products, while meeting their commitments with the URAA by reducing overall supports.

Table 5.6
Agricultural Supports to the OECD Countries, 1999–2001
(US$ Billions)

	US	EU	Japan	Other OECD countries	Total OECD
Where total support goes:					
Consumers	21.4	3.8	0.1	0.2	26.2
General services	22.8	9.6	12.7	2.3	55.1
Producers	51.3	99.3	52.0	12.3	248.3
Total	95.5	112.7	64.8	14.9	329.6
Where producer support goes:					
Corn	8.3	2.7	—	0.2	12.9
Meat (beef and pork)	2.6	34.0	4.1	2.8	47.3
Milk	12.4	16.7	4.9	4.7	42.1
Rice	0.7	0.2	18.0	-0.2	26.4
Wheat	4.9	9.5	0.8	0.9	17.3
Other	22.3	36.2	24.1	3.6	102.2
Where producer support comes from:					
Domestic measures (direct payment to producers)	32.6	38.5	5.0	6.3	88.2
Border measures (tariff and tariff equivalent)	18.7	60.9	47.0	5.7	160.1

Source: World Bank (2003a, 120), attributed to OECD 2002.

Export Subsidies

Reduction of export subsidies—that is, subsidized agricultural exports—has been another pillar of the URAA. The URAA limits ability of member countries to subsidize agricultural exports, but does so with some flexibility. Between 1995 and 1998, as the World Bank (2003a, 125) points out, "WTO members used 42 percent of budgetary expenditures and 64 percent of the volume allowed for export subsidies, with the European Union accounting for 90 percent of all OECD export subsidies." Even in 2001, in the United States production subsidies reduced cost of production of farmers by 51 percent; the percentages was 58 percent for wheat, 67 percent for corn, and 77 percent for rice (Watkins 2003). Thanks to such export subsidies, global markets of important consumption goods like sugar, cotton, rice, peanuts, and wheat are still heavily distorted. These supports end up supporting subsidized exports, depressing global prices, and badly affecting developing countries and the LDCs, in terms of lost income and welfare.[29]

Sugar is one of the most glaring examples of international trade protection, regressive subsidies, and low prices. High domestic prices of sugar in industrialized countries, especially in the Triad countries –the United States, the EU, and Japan—have long been promoting inefficient and high-cost production of sugar and sugar substitutes. Trade liberalization of sugar would result in $4.7 billion annual gains in global welfare and raise sugar prices by about 40 percent, increasing sugar exports in the triad countries by about 15 percent per year. In cotton production, a small number of cotton growers in the United States receive about $3 billion of government support annually,[30] while the EU provides cotton growers about $0.6 billion annually. But producer prices of cotton in the United States were 91 percent higher than world market prices in 2001–2002.[31] Removal of protection and support to cotton would increase world cotton price by 13 percent annually over a 10-year period, while global trade would increase by 6 percent. But cotton exports from the United States will drop by 6.7 percent and from the EU by 70.5 percent, while increasing the share of cotton exports from Africa by 13 percent, from Uzbekistan by 6 percent, and from Australia by 3 percent (World Bank 2003a, 129).

Government supports to rice farmers averaged 40 percent globally and up to 200 percent in some countries. In 1999–2001, the OECD countries provided more than $26 billion support to rice production, and in Japan, government supports to rice farmers were 700 percent of production cost at world prices. Liberalization of international trade in rice would lead to average price increases by 33 percent, 90 percent for medium- and short-grain rice, benefiting rice-growing countries like Cambodia, China, and Vietnam. Currently, the OECD countries provide more than $17 billion support to their wheat producers, $10 billion just by the EU alone. With discontinuation of such a massive support, the EU will retreat back to net importer of wheat. Similarly, major growers and exporters of peanuts—China, India, and the United States—still protect this sector through high subsidies and price supports. Liberalization of this trade would help countries like Gambia, Malawi, Nigeria, Senegal, South Africa, and Sudan to regain their global share in the market.

STAKES FOR THE DEVELOPING COUNTRIES AND THE LDCS

Agriculture is the predominant economic activity in developing countries—more than 70 percent of their populations live in rural areas, and 97 percent of them are engaged in agriculture (Ingco 2003). The URAA boosted aspirations in developing countries that eventually elimination of trade distortions in the sector in industrialized countries would lead to what the pundits called structural shifts in global agricultural production and consumption, benefiting developing countries more than the developed ones. As mentioned earlier, GTAP version 2 estimated global economic welfare from liberalization of agriculture at $165 billion annually, with $43 billion, about 26 percent, accruing to low-income countries.[32] Some indications, in the immediate aftermath of GATT 1994, indeed, showed some progress in this direction. As mentioned earlier, developing countries' agricultural exports grew by 7.2 percent annually between 1994 and 1997, compared to 6.1 percent during 1990–1994, but around 40 percent of those exports went to other developing countries, while developed-country imports from developing countries did not show much improvement.

The picture grows bleaker as one moves to the LDCs—where an overwhelming proportion of the population live in rural areas and depend preponderantly on agricultural activities for their income and food entitlements. But thanks to lack of productivity growth, continued underutilization of agricultural potentials, decline in international commodity prices, subsidized agricultural exports by some developed countries, and decline in food aid, the LDCs have been losing ground, even in agriculture, in which they could enjoy natural comparative advantage. According to FAO (2000), many of the LDCs that were net food exporters in the 1960s transformed into net food importers in the 1980s and 1990s, and given the rates of growth in their agricultural production and population growth, dependence on food imports is likely to increase in most of the LDCs, at least up to 2015. In the 1960s, net exports of rice from the LDCs totaled 2.4 million tons, but by the mid-1990s, they, instead, imported 3.5 million tons, and this import figure, worse still, is projected to rise to over 7.5 million tons per year by 2015. At the same time, net imports of wheat by the LDCs increased from 1.1 million tons in 1961–1963 to 6.1 million tons in 1995–1997, and are projected to reach 15 million tons by 2015.

One main reason for this debacle has, however, to do with the increasing gaps between annual growth rates of food and population in the LDCs. The gap is widening, although not in Malthusian proportions. During 1990–1997, as Table 5.7 indicates, consumption of basic foodstuffs in LDCs grew by an annual rate of 2.3 percent, well below the population growth rate of 2.6 percent. As a result, while in the 1970s domestic production of cereals met up to 96 percent of their demands, the ratio fell to 85 percent in 1990–1998. As FAO (2001a) suggests, population growth in the LDCs as a whole rose from 2.5 percent in the 1980s to 2.6 percent in the 1990s, and is projected to grow at 2.3 percent annually up to 2015.

Table 5.8 shows agricultural output of the LDCs and developing countries in the 1980s and the 1990s. Although the figures show an increase in agricultural production in the 1990s—an annual average growth rate of 2.5 percent, compared

Table 5.7
Agricultural Production, Consumption, and Trade of the LDCs, 1970–1997 (Average Annual Growth Value, in Percentages)

Commodity group/ Commodity	Production			Consumption			Imports			Exports		
	1970– 1979	1980– 1989	1990– 1997	1970– 1979	1980– 1989	1990– 1997	1970– 1979	1980– 1989	1990– 1997	1970– 1979	1980– 1989	1990– 1997
Basic foodstuffs	1.78	1.91	2.40	2.40	2.33	2.26	4.43	3.12	2.51	-5.95	-7.92	9.23
Cereals	0.65	2.05	2.32	1.96	2.79	2.21	4.07	0.79	2.66	-5.70	-10.66	-1.99
Wheat	2.53	0.67	5.53	3.59	2.73	4.49	3.25	3.40	4.21	-15.57	20.51	35.72
Rice, milled	0.51	2.24	1.75	1.93	3.09	1.69	4.22	-0.61	1.20	-6.31	-13.98	-10.24
Coarse grains	0.80	1.54	3.98	1.60	1.71	3.45	6.13	-2.45	3.26	0.39	0.83	-1.26

Source: Compiled from FAO (2001b), attributed to FAOSTAT (2000), and World Bank (1999).

Table 5.8
Agricultural and Food Production in the 1980s and 1990s in LDCs and Other Developing Countries (Annual Average Percentage Increase)

	Agricultural production			
	Total		Per Capita	
	1980–1990	1990–1999	1980–1990	1990–1999
LDCs	1.6	2.5	-0.8	-0.1
All developing countries	3.6	3.7	1.5	2.0
	Food production			
	Total		Per capita	
	1980–1990	1990–1999	1980–1990	1990–1999
LDCs	1.7	2.5	-0.8	-0.1
All developing countries	3.7	3.9	1.5	2.2

Source: FAO (2001b).

with 1.6 percent in the previous decade—in terms of per capita terms, however, the output actually declined. Also, as FAO (2001a) points out, more than 25 LDCs experienced negative per capita agricultural growth during 1990–1999, only five had positive growth rates ranging between 2 to 5 percent, and in only 15 LDCs was per capita agricultural production in the 1990s higher than in the 1980s. The whole sub Saharan Africa—the third world of Third World—experienced massive decline in agricultural output. Also, slow food production growth and sharp annual fluctuations in output had contributed to rising poverty and food insecurity in the LDCs. Between 1969–1971 and 1996–1998, the proportion of undernourished in total population in the LDCs increased from 38 percent to 40 per cent, while the absolute number of undernourished increased from 116 million to 235 million.[33]

The LDCs' capacity to import foodgrains is also constrained by the fact that their export earnings have been declining due to fall in export prices of commodities and increasing burden of foreign debt. At the same time, food aid flow has been declining, especially since the 1990s, adversely affecting food availability in many LDCs, although the WTO members pledged at the Marrakech Declaration in 1994 to provide food aid sufficient to the needs of developing countries, especially LDCs and net food-importing countries. Available data suggest that the commitments of major donors at the Food Aid Convention (FAC) dropped from 7.5 million tons in 1986 to 5.4 million tons in 1995, and to 4.9 million tons in 1999. Actual food aid shipments also fell from 10.4 million tons in 1992/1993 to 5.8 million tons in 1996/1997, but then increased to 8.1 million in 1998/1999 and 8.3 million tons in 1999/2000. At the same time, overall food aid deliveries, from FAC members as well as other countries and NGOs, has declined by almost 60 percent, falling from 17.3 million tons in 1993 to 7.2 million tons in 1996.[34] Also, as discussed in Chapter 1, food aid, as a component of total aid from the OECD countries has been declining in recent years, especially since the mid-1980s.

At the same time, consumption of cereals by domestic production in the LDCs declined from 96 percent in the 1970–1980 period to 85 percent in 1990–1998 period. As mentioned earlier, while during the 1960s LDCs were net exporters of rice, by the mid-1990s they were importing 3.5 million tons a year, which is projected to more than double by 2015. As Table 5.9 indicates, during 1996–1998, the LDCs spent $5.2 billion for food imports, 15 percent of their total merchandise imports. Of the food imports, $2.7 billion went for cereals alone. The table also shows how the aggregate figures conceal the magnitude of actual share of food imports in merchandise imports of some heavily import-dependent LDCs. For example, for the Democratic Republic of Congo the food bills were 45 percent of its total merchandise imports, and the share was 46 percent for Guinea-Bissau, 70 percent for Mauritania, 76 percent for Sierra Leone, 50 percent for Somalia, and 51 percent for Yemen.

Continued export subsidies in the developed world hurt production and potential export incomes of developing countries and LDCs. As mentioned earlier, subsidies to cotton growers in the United States and EU result in billions of dollars in lost income for cotton-producing sub-Saharan African countries, subsidies to peanuts in the world's largest exporters—China, the United States, and Argentina—have crippled global market share of countries like Gambia, Malawi, Nigeria, Senegal, South Africa, and Sudan—whose share dropped from 17 percent in 1976 to only 5 percent in 2001. Similarly, subsidies to rice production in many industrialized and advanced developed countries retarded the share of Cambodia, China, and Vietnam in global markets. Massive subsidies in sugar, wheat, and peanuts in industrialized countries distort global markets for these products by depressing world prices and depriving welfare to countries enjoying real comparative advantage in these products.

Also, developing countries are yet to see benefits from reduction of agricultural tariffs. If agricultural tariffs are slashed just by a half, according to one estimate, it will enhance global welfare by $89bn. One of the main concerns of developing countries with domestic support is that commitments would make it more difficult for them to pursue desired food security and rural development policies. Only 20 developing countries reported positive Total Base AMS and, of these, only 12 reported Total Base AMS above the 10 percent *de minimis* allowed (FAO 1998). Thus, for many developing countries, their ability to provide direct subsidies to agriculture in the future will depend either on these being exempt under the special and differential treatment (SDT) or *de minimis* provisions. Another issue is whether negative AMS (where domestic prices are below external reference prices) could be explicitly set off against positive AMS. The URAA does not discipline taxation of production and negative AMS is ignored in calculating the AMS level.

Then, there are so-called "second-generation" or the "new trade agenda" issues in agriculture—involving intellectual property rights, trade-related environment and labor issues, food safety, investment, and competition policy. These issues, discussed in the next chapter in greater detail, have already generated considerable heat throughout the developing world. Some developed countries are interested in ensuring that the URAA disciplines on domestic support do not inhibit pursuit of their "nontrade concerns" (NTCs). The URAA does call for consideration of such NTCs in areas such as food security, protection of the environment, and viability of rural areas. This provision of the URAA, in turn, bolstered demand in some advanced countries, especially in the EU, to push for what is called "multifunctionality" of agriculture, which would allow governmental intervention for continuation of production-linked support, in the pretext of protection of the environment or maintenance of the countryside.

But use of trade policies for achieving nontrade concerns remains a controversial issue. Also, developing countries, which lack budgetary resources to embark on such programs and also view the NTCs as a new form of NTBs (nontrade barriers), would find it hard to swallow. Already, the share of developing countries, especially of the LDCs, has been declining in global agricultural exports. As Table 5.10 shows, the share of agriculture in sub-Saharan Africa's exports fell from 24 percent in 1977 to 13 percent in 1997, and, during the same period, contribution of agriculture to the region's GDP growth fell from 8.8 percent to 2.8 percent. With respect to low- and middle-income economies, the share of agriculture in their global exports fell from 13.4 percent in 1977 to 5.2 percent in 1997, while during the same period, the sector's contribution to their GDP growth fell from 11.2 percent to 1.4 percent. Inclusion of the NTCs will further marginalize these countries, as their exports will face greater NTBs.

CONCLUDING REMARKS

The inclusion of the agricultural sector into the GATT 1994 at the end of the strenuous negotiations of the Uruguay Round multilateral trade negotiations does not signify the integration of the sector into the rule-based global trading system—it is, at its best, a grand milestone toward that goal. The URAA leaves much of the reforms necessary for liberalizing agricultural trade regimes across the world to diverse interpretations, country discretions, and future negotiations, which, in turn, not only complicate interpretations of the agreement, but also make its implementation complex and problematic, especially because of deeply entrenched and powerful vested interests, primarily in industrialized countries. Therefore, liberalization of the sector—removal of export subsidies and domestic supports and opening up of the markets in industrialized countries for developing-country agricultural products—has not happened so far at a scale that was professed or postulated. Resistance to agricultural trade liberalization has not diminished in developed countries, reduction of governmental support to domestic production as well as exports has not materialized at

Table 5.9
Food Imports of Least Developed Countries, 1996–1998
(Annual Average)

Country	Total food imports (million US$)	Cereal imports (million US$)	Share of food imports in total merchandise imports (percent)	Share of cereals in food imports (percent)
All LDCs	**5 179**	**2 710**	**15**	**52**
Afghanistan	124	35	28	28
Angola	275	104	13	38
Bangladesh	598	363	9	61
Benin	98	43	15	43
Bhutan	14	9	10	62
Burkina Faso	97	63	13	66
Burundi	22	13	17	58
Cambodia	59	13	10	22
Cape Verde	49	11	21	23
Central African Republic	24	9	10	38
Chad	37	22	16	59
Comoros	22	11	38	48
Dem. Rep. of the Congo	196	103	45	52
Djibouti	54	24	17	43
Equatorial Guinea	8	2	8	24
Eritrea	69	57	14	82
Ethiopia	113	93	10	82
Gambia	63	31	26	49
Guinea	155	77	16	50
Guinea-Bissau	29	22	46	77
Haiti	224	134	32	60
Kiribati	11	4	27	38
Lao People's Dem. Rep.	37	24	6	66
Lesotho	143	70	13	49

Table 5.9 (continued)

Country	Total food imports (million US$)	Cereal imports (million US$)	Share of food imports in total merchandise imports (percent)	Share of cereals in food imports (percent)
Liberia	67	46	17	69
Madagascar	52	35	11	67
Malawi	43	30	7	69
Maldives	45	13	13	28
Mali	91	29	12	32
Mauritania	171	108	70	63
Mozambique	120	68	15	57
Myanmar	34	12	1	37
Nepal	84	20	6	23
Niger	76	28	18	37
Rwanda	66	48	25	72
Samoa	27	7	27	25
Sao Tome and Principe	5	2	22	50
Sierra Leone	130	94	76	73
Solomon Islands	17	11	10	64
Somalia	88	36	50	41
Sudan	239	146	14	61
Togo	48	26	11	54
Tuvalu	1	0	11	34
Uganda	48	34	6	70
United Rep. of Tanzania	137	71	10	52
Vanuatu	15	7	15	48
Yemen	969	442	51	46
Zambia	85	61	10	72

Source: FAO (2001b).

Table 5.10
Historical Trade Dynamics of Developing Countries
in Agriculture, 1977–1997

Regions	Share in the region's total exports (%)			Average growth (% per annum)		Contribution to the GDP growth of the region (%)	
	1977	1987	1997	1977–1987	1987–1997	1977–1987	1987–1997
High-income Asia, excluding Japan	5.1	1.8	0.3	4.6	-5.9	0.9	-0.4
East Asia and Pacific	19.1	13.1	2.2	7.0	-1.8	9.9	-0.6
South Asia	27.8	22.1	5.9	5.3	-1.1	16.9	-1.0
Latin America and the Caribbean	26.0	17.8	10.0	4.3	2.8	11.1	4.1
Europe and Central Asia	22.8	14.7	5.2	5.2	10.6	9.6	3.8
Middle East and North Africa	1.8	2.4	1.9	2.5	2.1	-15.9	1.0
Sub-Saharan Africa	23.9	20.4	13.2	1.1	0.9	8.8	2.8
Low- and middle-income countries*	13.4	12.6	5.2	4.1	1.9	11.2	1.4

Source: Compiled from Table 1.A1 from World Bank (2003a, 55–56), based on GTAP release 5.0.
Note: *High-income Asia—Hong Kong, Republic of Korea, Singapore and Taiwan— is excluded from the low- and middle-income region in the totals.

the scale as was expected, and developing countries are yet to receive the promised benefits from agricultural trade liberalization—the so-called structural transformation in global agricultural production and consumption still remains a pipe dream. In the meantime, marginalization of the LDCs continues, as their food import bills have been soaring in recent decades, and their growth potential from liberalized agricultural trade is being eaten up by border protection, repressive export subsidies, and lower world prices for goods of export interest to them. Agriculture is the key sector for income or growth potentials of the LDCs, or reduction of poverty in these countries, as shown by the green revolution in the 1970s. With their agriculture effectively in jeopardy, thanks to continued tariff and nontariff barriers, subsidies, and supports, even the so-called nontrade concerns, in industrialized countries, and their stubborn stances in all the post-UR agricultural trade negotiations, it is not surprising that the LDCs are being effectively turned into backwaters of global prosperity.

NOTES

1. Certain agricultural products, however, were included in GATT negotiations in pre-UR Rounds, especially as individual commodities. For example, the Dillon Round (1960–1961) cut tariffs on soya beans, cotton, vegetables, and canned fruit, and the Kennedy Round (1962–1967) sponsored negotiations on wheat, dairy, and meat products. Agriculture, as a whole sector, however, remained outside the GATT discipline.

2. Whatever market access the GATT and the major industrial countries conceded to provide, they did so, as Raghavan (2001a) points out, "always without contractual rights and obligations" (cited in TWN, 2001). Some observers even termed such developments as outright fraud. Lal (2000), for example, remarks, "In agriculture, as in textiles and clothing, a fraud has been perpetrated on developing countries in terms of liberalization of trade and improving market access to their exports" (cited in TWN 2001).

3. See Hoekman and Kostecki (2001, 212); (Dowlah 2001); and Hathaway and Ingco (1996, 30).

4. The origins of the CAP program can be traced to the Treaty of Rome (1957), which initially sought to achieve food self-sufficiency in the then net food-importing EU countries. Under the program, which came into force in the early 1960s, the EU countries provided massive domestic supports, price intervention and external protection to stimulate domestic agricultural production, especially focusing on some key products, such as grains, sugar, beef, and milk. It, however, took up to the mid-1980s for the EU to transform itself into a net-exporter of agricultural products, when its subsidized exports began to depress global agricultural prices.

5. In 1990, as Tangermann (1994) points out, export restitutions represented 39 percent of the total EU budget, when the EU shielded its CAP program by creating separate exchange rates for agriculture, setting variable levies, paying export restitutions, and developing a set of administratively complicated policies.

6. Evidently, the agenda was pushed by some pioneering works on huge income transfers and market distortions stemmed from agricultural support and protection policies in the OECD countries (OECD 1997).

7. The magnitude of the conflict can be gauged from the fact that about 60 percent of all trade disputes submitted to the GATT for settlement between 1980 and 1990 were concerned with agriculture, and most of those were between two major trading partners—the United States and the EU.

8. In the 1980s, the EU accounted for 24 percent of world imports of foodgrains and 11 percent of world exports, while the United States had a 22 percent share in global export volume in foodgrains. See Tangermann (1994).

9. All signatories to the WTO, except the LDCs, were to submit the Schedules by April 1994, prior to signing of the UR Agreements, while the LDCs were given an extra year, up to April 1995.

10. Article 5 of the URAA, however, allows members to raise tariffs above the level stipulated in their respective Country Schedules under particular circumstances, while Annex 5 permits a member to retain NTBs for certain sensitive products. The NTBs prohibited by the URAA include: quantitative import restrictions (QRS), variable import levies, minimum import prices, discretionary import licensing, nontariff measures maintained through state trading enterprises, voluntary export restraints, and similar border measures other than ordinary customs duties.

11. This minimum level is to rise to 5 percent by the year 2000 in case of developed countries and by 2004 in case of the developing countries. The market access provisions, however, do not apply when the commodity in question is a traditional staple of a developing country.

12. The agreement also protects preferential tariff rates for the developing-country exporters as specified under bilateral trade agreements.

13. The initial TRQ is the quota of imports that is permitted to enter the country at below the normal tariff rate, and the final TRQ reflects any changes in the initial quota due to increased quota size or reduced tariff. TRQs are applicable to developed countries, as few developing countries were engaged in such practices of tariffs.

14. The UR agreement on SPS remains highly controversial, as it is believed to have been designed to impose Western standards on health of plants, animals, and humans, which might pose serious nontariff barriers to exports originating from developing countries. More on this later.

15. See, for example, Martin and Winters (1995); Harrison, Rutherford, and Taylor (1995); FAO (1998) ; and Dowlah (1998).

16. See, for example, forecasts based on modeling researches conducted by Anderson and Tyres (1995), Valdes and Zietz (1995), and World Bank (2003a, 103–139).

17. Also, the actual, but usually unbound, tariff rates in some developing countries are in many cases currently lower than in the base period mainly because of the so-called Structural Adjustment Programs (SAP), rather aggressively pursued by the Bretton Woods institutions. See Table 5.3.

18. See World Bank (2003a, 123).

19. Hoekman, Ng, and Olarreaga (2000), for example, maintain that full duty- and quota-free access for LDCs in the Quad for tariff peak products would result in an 11 percent increase in the LDC exports—around $2.5 billion per year.

20. Also see Einarsson (2000) and McGuire (2001), who provide excellent accounts of global food trade in recent years.

21. Among the other key players in agricultural negotiations, while the Cairns Group share the radical position of the United States, the EU position, which also emphasizes nontrade concerns, such as environmental protection and animal welfare, is supported by countries like Japan, Korea, Norway, and Switzerland (Sally 2003).

22. The discussion on the Harbinson Draft is based on several issues of *Bridges Weekly*, from February to July 2002.

23. In fact, the Harbinson Draft faced uphill opposition from the very beginning. It was first suggested at a ministerial meeting of the WTO, joined by trade and agriculture ministers from 22 countries, in Tokyo in mid-February 2003. Japan, the host country, was outright in rejecting the suggested tariff cuts proposed by the Draft, presumably on the ground that such cuts would threaten its uncompetitive rice farmers and favor exporting countries (as the EU complained). The United States also found the initial plan for slashing export subsidies in developed countries as "problematic."

24. That explains why developing country agricultural exports to developed countries did not increase appreciably in the post-UR period, although developing countries' agricultural exports increased to 7.2 percent annually during 1994–1997 period, compared to 6.1 percent during 1990–1994.

25. According to OECD (2002), farmers' income was 250 percent of national average in the Netherlands, 175 percent for Denmark, 160 percent for France, 110 percent for the United States and Japan.

26. But as Table 3.11 in World Bank (2003a, 121) shows, the protection rate dropped to 41.5 percent in 1995–1997, and then rose to 49 percent in 1999–2001, indicating that such supports are on the rise again in developed countries. This rise in support to agriculture apparently came in response to declines in world agricultural prices.

27. At the same time, however, direct production-related payments to farmers increased from 10.5 percent to 21.7 percent.

28. Provided that the volume and accumulation of such stocks must correspond to predetermined targets related solely to food security, and the process of accumulation and disposal is financially transparent.

29. The following discussion on export subsides, especially the figures used, are based on World Bank (2003a, 125–130).

30. The United States has about 25,000 very affluent cotton growers, with average net worth of $800,000. Thanks to billions of dollars of subsidies each year, as columnist Nicholas D. Kristof points out in the *New York Times* (July 5, 2002), the United States cotton production has almost doubled over the last 20 years—even though the United States is an inefficient, high-cost producer, creating a glut that costs African countries $250 million each year.

31. According to Daniel Summer, professor of agricultural economics at the University of California, Davis, the United States exports of cotton would have declined by 41.2 percent and the world price of upland cotton would have increased by 12.6 percent had the framers not received subsidies (*New York Times*, January 24, 2004).

32. An earlier version of GTAP, as mentioned before, put the share of benefits for low-income countries at 32 percent.

33. For the rest of the developing countries, by contrast, the proportion of undernourished in the total population in 1996–1998 was 18 percent. In addition, indicators of poverty show that the proportion of people living below the poverty line (defined as $1 per day) has risen in many LDCs. In sub-Saharan Africa—home of 34 of the world's poorest countries—the proportion of poor people increased from 38.5 percent in the late 1980s to 39.1 percent (of a larger population) in the mid-1990s (World Bank 2000).

34. These figures are taken from Mathews (2001), who attributes those to the Report of the Committee on Agriculture (G/L/417, 20 November 2000).

6

The WTO and the LDCs: How Conducive Is the WTO Platform for Safeguarding and Promoting the Interests of the LDCs?

INTRODUCTION

With globalization sweeping across the world in momentous speed and magnitude—by abolishing physical distances, integrating national economies, undermining sovereignties of nation-states, moving finance, trade, technology, and labor across the world in unprecedented scale, flourishing democracies and market economies, making information instantaneous, and raising consciousness of ordinary people around the world in unthinkable proportions—it is hardly surprising that the question of global governance has emerged as one of the most controversial and frequently discussed issues in the contemporary world. Mounting evidence suggests that the existing mosaic of global institutions, the Bretton Woods institutions of the World Bank and the International Monetary Fund (IMF), the United Nations, and the World Trade Organization (WTO), are hardly capable of dealing with the enormity of economic, social, political, and humanitarian challenges of the contemporary world. Gaps between global challenges and global capabilities are, however, nothing new. What is remarkable is that in the current phase of globalization, since the 1980s, the gap has been widening in a breathtaking speed that the world community has never experienced before—thanks to a series of modern-day revolutions in information, technology, transports, trade, and finance, that heralded a thorough paradigmatic shift in the way the global community networks, interacts, and exchanges goods and services in the contemporary world.

What is still more startling is that the need for "the new paradigm for world governance," as Nayyar and Court (2002) call it, has been intensifying with every passing day, as economic activities are becoming more global than before, spillover effects of both production and consumption processes are penetrating across national boundaries, domestic rules and regulations are increasingly coming under global scrutiny, the processes of globalization keep marginalizing the world's poorest nations, and the existing multilateral institutions are failing increasingly in providing global public goods—such as world peace and sustainable development[1]—or dealing with global public bads—such as stopping international trade in drugs, arms, peoples, organs, and terrorism. It is, therefore, no wonder that the roles and functions, operations, approaches, and attitudes of the multilateral institutions, such as the WB, the IMF, the UN, and the WTO, are increasingly coming under meticulous scrutiny of peoples, states, civil societies, and observers and scholars from around the world. Never before has the world community demonstrated such a passion, as well as obsession, for the transparency and accountability of these multilateral institutions that constitute the core of contemporary global governance.

This chapter focuses mainly on the structures and negotiation processes of the WTO, and its predecessor the GATT, to see how this multilateral platform promotes or hinders the interests and concerns of developing countries, especially of the LDCs. As all four major multilateral institutions—the World Bank, the IMF, the UN, and the WTO are rather intricately interlinked, the next section examines major factors responsible for heightened global scrutiny on these institutions to see how their structure and composition, how forces of liberalization and democratization, and the phenomenal growth of nongovernmental organizations (NGOs) and civic societies condition the capabilities of these institutions in the current wave of globalization. The following section discusses the structures and compositions as well as mandates of the WTO, to show how little the developing countries, especially the LDCs, can influence the processes and the outcomes of multilateral trade negotiations under the WTO. The following section looks into the so-called new-generation issues, such as the General Agreement in Services (GATS), the Trade-Related Intellectual Property Rights (TRIPS), labor standards, and environmental issues. The following section examines proposals put forward in recent years to improve WTO governance, transparency, and accountability, and concludes the chapter highlighting the stake of developing countries, as well as the LDCs.

FACTORS RESPONSIBLE FOR HEIGHTENED GLOBAL SCRUTINY ON MULTILATERAL INSTITUTIONS

This section highlights major factors that have contributed to a heightened level of global consciousness and concerns with the existing multilateral institutions in the contemporary world, especially since the onset of the third wave of globalization.[2]

Institutional Factors

First, the "logic of 1945"[3] that entrusted the Bretton Woods institutions with the "single overarching mission" to promote growth and stability through progressive liberalization of economic activities (Sutherland and Sewell 2000) has rapidly been losing grounds, as deepening integration and interdependence of economies and the consequent decline in the authorities or jurisdictions of nation-states make the post-World War II Keynesian consensus of full employment and welfare state increasingly redundant in the current wave of globalization. The multilateral institutions of the second wave of globalization—the World Bank and the IMF—emerged in the immediate aftermath of the World War II mainly in response to the perceived failure of the global economic management (or market failures) between the two World Wars when the industrialized countries witnessed the Great Depression and the entire world experienced an upsetting reversal of globalization.

These institutions, as conceived at the Bretton Woods Conference of 1944, were aimed at promoting growth and stability in world economy through progressive liberalization of tariff and trade, deregulation of economies, and greater integration of world economy. The World Bank was supposed to help finance reconstruction of war-damaged economies and development projects, the IMF was expected to manage the international monetary system in order to promote financial stability around the world, and the International Trade Organization (ITO) was expected to oversee expansion of global trade through reduction of tariff and nontariff barriers. Although the ITO could not be established, the General Agreement on Tariff and Trade (GATT) gradually took over the responsibility of promoting liberal global trade regimes. And then, there was the UN, which provided a diplomatic platform for promoting global peace and security.

A careful look into the founding principles of such an impressive architecture of post–World War II multilateral institutions would reveal that they were invariably guided by the overarching principle of nonintervention in "matters which are essentially within the domestic jurisdiction of any state" (Article 2 (7) of the UN Charter). By accepting the status of a specialized agency under the UN system, the World Bank, the IMF, and the GATT—all of them—subscribed to such a principle of nonintervention in domestic affairs of states, not to impinge on sovereignties of states. In the UN, all members enjoyed equal status, while the World Bank and the IMF were accountable to member states through their boards of governors that represented all member states. While the UN has the Security Council to make major decisions, the World Bank and the IMF have their respective Board of Executives to oversee their operations, but the GATT lacked any such top decision-making body—all contracting parties had equal rights in its decision-making processes, and decisions were made through what is called negative consensus—nobody present in the negotiation opposing.

The experience with the United Nations over the course of the last five decades have at best been mixed. Like the negative-consensus-based decision making principle of the GATT, perhaps the greatest contribution of the UN has been that the world has so far had no third World War. This, again, cannot be solely attributed to the UN alone—the other global institutions have contributed to this achievement as well. Over the last decades, the UN's role has expanded overwhelmingly—from peacekeeping to famine prevention, handling international political crises to holding domestic elections, from refugee care to promoting education and culture—but at the same time, the moral authority of the UN, as Nayyar and Court (2002, 11) point out, has seriously been undermined "because its laws or principles are enforced selectively when it suits the interests of the rich and the powerful." As the events in the 1990s through the beginning of the new century showed—especially with respect to Bosnia, Rwanda, and Iraq—the UN's credibility and effectiveness have substantially eroded—it has no teeth, often it cannot even bark, forget about biting. There could be at least three root causes for this debacle: (a) a kitchen cabinet of decision making—political and financial control of the UN by the five security council members, with complete disregard of global transformations that have literally reshaped the world since the establishment of the UN in 1945; (b) a bureaucratic leviathan—leaving the entire operation of the UN system to bureaucrats selected largely on the basis of a complex mosaic of quotas, concessions, and compromises, seriously undermining consideration of merit and accountability so critically needed for responding to global challenges; and (c) the democratic deficit—making mockery with the one country-one-vote by literally transforming the General Assembly into a mere talking forum.

When it comes to accountability and transparency, the World Bank and the IMF fare even worse. These institutions, indeed, began their journey with a lopsided sense of accountability. The IMF, originally created to manage the international monetary system on the basis of the gold exchange standard, that is, to manage a regime of fixed exchange rate, has over the decades moved to a regime of floating exchange rate, and in recent years attempting to "cope with the move from capital controls to capital mobility" with little success, "is no longer able to manage the international monetary system" (Nayyar and Court 2002, 13). At the root of the increasing marginalization of the IMF in managing global capital flows and exchange rates, as the East Asian Financial Crisis demonstrated in the late 1990s, and Stiglitz (2000) forcefully pointed out, the entire operation of the IMF is pegged to capital account liberalization and capital account convertibility—as if these twin principles are the greatest and the only recipes for economic growth. Second, the IMF's operations are shrouded in secrecy, the organization lacks accountability almost completely, and the conditionalities that it imposes often undermine sovereignty of recipient countries. Third, the voting rights in the IMF are based on quotas that allow countries like the United States, the UK, France, Germany, Russia, China, and Saudi Arabia to have their own executive director on the Board, while all other countries are lumped together under some groups, entitling each group to have one executive director to represent it on the Board. Another peculiarity with the IMF is that although the Executive Board does supervise its operations, the institution is, in fact, staff-driven. It is not the Executive Board, but the staff of the IMF, that negotiates with member countries and strike deals with them. Of course, the Executive Board's approval is needed for implementation of those agreements.

The World Bank's institutional structure is "asymmetrical and unequal;" like the IMF, voting rights are concentrated in a small number of countries—the principal shareholders of its paid-up capital—while countries from the rest of the world, who are the principal stakeholders, control a small proportion of voting rights (Nayyar and Court 2002, 16). Like the IMF, although the Executive Board supervises its operations, the World Bank is also a staff-driven organization. It is not the Executive Board, but the staff of the World Bank, that negotiates with member countries and strikes deals with them. The performance of the World Bank has been questionable as well—there are questions about the so-called Washington Consensus, pursued by the Bank in the 1980s and 1990s—whether they contributed to eradication or exacerbation of poverty in poor countries—the principal business of the Bank. The Bank's prescriptions for development, funding of development funds, claims of achievements, even methodologies of measuring poverty eradication have often invited serious criticisms.[4]

The WTO—the successor of the GATT—essentially a multilateral institution of the third wave of globalization—has emerged with very different parameters. The WTO is responsible for providing a common institutional framework for multilateral trade negotiations, trade dispute settlement mechanisms, surveillance of international trade policies, and achieving greater economic policy coherence in cooperation with the Bretton Woods institutions. The supreme decision-making authority of the WTO lies with the Ministerial Conference, composed of trade and commerce ministers of all member countries, not with a Board of Governors, as with the World Bank and the IMF. Also, unlike the World Bank and the IMF, the WTO is a member-driven organization, where key decisions, such as ministerial conferences or dispute settlement, are made by the members themselves, and the Director General of the WTO acts as a broker, not as a decision maker.[5] Major decisions of the WTO are made at the biannual Ministerial Conferences of the WTO, and the functions of the WTO are carried out by a General Council, composed of permanent officials, headed by the Director General. But unlike the World Bank and the IMF, the WTO is not a specialized agency of the UN—it has not entered into any agreement with the UN to be treated as such, although the Marrakech Declaration of 1994, which founded the WTO, clearly stipulates that the WTO should cooperate with the Bretton Woods institutions to achieve "greater coherence in global economic decision making" (Article III.5). The Marrakech Declaration emphasized cooperation with the Bretton Woods institutions, but it has not mandated the WTO to continue the GATT tradition of being treated as a specialized agency of the UN.

Also, the WTO, being an institution of the third wave of globalization, has began its journey with greater commitment to transparency than perhaps was demonstrated by the Bretton Woods institutions over five decades ago.[6] All member countries of the WTO are entitled to take part in all General Council meetings through their Geneva-based delegates. Member countries can also participate in the deliberations of the General Council when it turns itself into trade adjudication body—called the Dispute Settlement Body—and into Trade Policy Review Body (TPRB) to review trade policies of member countries. Similarly, member countries can participate in the deliberations of three subsidiary councils of the WTO: the Council for Trade in Goods, the Council for Trade in Services, and the Council for Trade-related Aspects of Intellectual Property Rights, and numerous committees, subcommittees, bodies, standing groups, or working parties. But certain committees and deliberations are not open to all member countries, such as the deliberations of the Appellate Body, Dispute Settlement Panels, the Textiles Monitoring Body, and committees dealing with Pluralist Agreements.[7]

Although the WTO provides wider arrays and scopes for participation in its negotiations and deliberations than perhaps the World Bank and the IMF, for example, only a few developing countries are capable of maintaining active presence in WTO headquarters in Geneva. Only a few of the LDCs have delegations in Geneva, and in many cases, such delegations show little interest in WTO deliberations and consultations, reportedly because of lack of interest in their own capitals. Also, as Sutherland and Sewell (2000) rightly point out, the agenda of the poorest nations in the WTO seem more defensive—they are more concerned with technical assistance from the WTO and multilateral agencies to enable them to participate more effectively in the WTO and to ensure duty-free access to developed-country markets, while their trade and commerce remains limited in both scope and depth—about 75 percent of their exports are unprocessed raw materials and about 70 percent of their export earnings come from three top exports.

Liberalization of Economies and Democratization of Nations

The current wave of globalization, which has witnessed the end of the Cold War and triumphant victory of capitalism over socialism, has also been witnessing momentous developments toward liberalization of economies and democratization of nations around the world. In fact, in the contemporary world democratization and liberalization have emerged as twin pillars of globalization.[8] The exorable forces of the free market, driven by efficiency of production and sovereignty of consumers across the world, have been pushing forward the ideals of a self-regulating market as the normative basis of global order. According to the 2004 Index of Economic Freedom, among 161 countries surveyed, in 75 economic freedom scores were better than before.[9] With the current pace of liberalization of global trade and commerce continuing, the proponents of globalization believe, humankind will eventually move to a borderless global market, where the virtues of free enterprise and the vices of state intervention will rule supreme. The neoliberal ideals of a self-regulating market, which underpin the contemporary momentum toward economic liberalization and political democratization, by design equate laissez faire capitalism and Western democracy as the synonyms of progress, and assure that such globalization will bring prosperity to all parts of the world, and that market forces will eventually correct irregularities associated with unequal global-distribution patterns.

By pushing such an aggressive ideological agenda, the neoliberal globalists have brought into question the credibility of the leading multilateral institutions that assumed an internationalist role in the post–World War II period. As a result, the Bretton Woods institutions, the United Nations, and the GATT and its successor WTO—all are now widely criticized for merely carrying out the inflexible imperatives of rich nations under the guise of so-called "Washington Consensus" or what is often called "Golden Straightjacket" formula for growth and prosperity. At the core of the issue is the real transfer of power to the multilateral institutions

away from the nation-states over the last few decades—in the name of liberalization—which has already made the nation-states less capable of controlling the
lives or welfare of their own peoples. As national governments lose control of their
economic policies, because of ever penetrating interventions of the World Bank,
the IMF, the UN, and the WTO, sovereignty of states, especially of the poorer
ones, is coming under increasing threats. On top of that, there are transnational
corporations (MNCs), with their vast capital, technology, and outsourcing operations, that national governments must reckon to.[10] Criticisms of these institutions
have grown to such a proportion that almost all these institutions have been facing
serious problems in the contemporary world (more on this later).

The current wave of globalization, especially since the end of the Cold War, has
also been accompanied by what Scholte (2000, 263) terms as the "third wave of
democratization," when democracy has engulfed much of Africa, Asia, Latin
America, and the former Soviet bloc. In 1974, only 39 countries—one in four in
the world—were elected democracies, but by 2001, the number increased to 121
countries —three in four in the world (Moore and Pazzle, 2001). Of course, democracies differ from country to country, and have divergent manifestations in
different countries depending on their customs and traditions, institutions, cul-
tures, and history, which, in turn, gives birth to, what Bhgawati (2004) calls
"highbred democratization." Freedom House (2002), for example, defines democracies as political systems, whose leaders are elected in competitive multiparty and
multicandidate processes in which opposition parties have a legitimate chance of
attaining power or participating in power.

Obviously, not every country that claims to be a democracy would satisfy all
these parameters. While countries do differ in forms, styles, or substance of democracy that they embrace or cherish, a democratic governance would usually
conform to certain norms, such as collective decision making, as opposed to au-
thoritarian or dictatorial rule; participatory governance, as opposed to majoritarian
tyranny; commitment to transparency, as opposed to secretive conducts of the
statecraft; and accountability to the public, through periodic elections, representative institutions, rule of law, and so on, as opposed to unresponsive, unaccountable, and tyrannical rule by unelected rulers, and inaccessible civil and military
institutions (Scholte 2000, 263–67). These parameters are obviously synonymous
with Western, especially American liberal democracy, which is marked not only
by free and fair elections, but also by constitutional liberalism—the rule of law,
separation of powers, and protection of basic liberties of speech, assembly, reli-
gion, and property. Democracies are now flourishing across the world, but as
Zakaria (1997) points out, in most cases without accompanying constitutional liberalism. In the absence of constitutional liberalism, what Zakaria calls illiberal democracies have been proliferating in many parts of the world.

As momentum toward democratization—liberal or illiberal—spreads hand in
hand with globalization—with or without marriage between democracy and capitalism, not only the traditional states that essentially command sovereignty over a
territory, but also multilateral institutions that exercise intraterritorial or
supraterritorial authority, are increasingly coming under the magnifying glass of

ordinary people across the world. One reason for this is that—thanks to the momentum toward globalization—by design, default, or simply fascination, more and more domestic issues are being brought under the formal or informal, direct or indirect jurisdiction of multilateral institutions.

Emergence of NGOs and Civic Societies

Phenomenal growth of NGOs—in both developed and developing countries—be that in economic, business, trade, social, or cultural sectors— has made them unavoidable, and often very powerful, partners in both national and international decision-making processes in the contemporary world. Generally speaking, NGOs are non-profit entities, ideally composed of voluntary membership, and they strive to promote sustainable development, mainly addressing various social and ecological objectives. According to the World Watch Institute, there are literally millions of NGOs in the world—the United States alone is the home of more than two million NGOs, and there are about one million NGOs in India and thousands of such bodies strewn across the Europe, Africa, and other continents. Among others, as *Economist* (December 11, 1999) points out, the end of communism, the spread of democracy in poor countries, technological change, economic integration, and globalization have provided a fertile soil for their phenomenal growth in recent decades. The *Economist* also claims that the NGOs now deliver more aid than the whole United Nations system. Another article in the *Economist* (January 29, 2000), claimed that NGOs provided over eight percent of all jobs in North America and six percent in the United Kingdom.

No wonder, most international organizations have to reckon with the growing presence and pressures of NGOs, some of which are multinational in their operations and outreach, and capable of exerting formidable pressure around the world. The NGOs that play an active role in the multilateral trade arena usually press for labor and human rights, environmental protection, consumer rights, sustainable economic development, and so on. For example, the International Federation of Free Trade Unions (IFFTU—based in Brussels) and AFL-CIO (federation of trade unions in the United States), are engaged in trade union activities; the World Wildlife Fund (WWF), the Sierra Club (US), the Worldwide Fund for Nature (WFN), and Greenpeace are engaged in environmental protection; Consumer International and Transatlantic Consumers Dialogue are engaged in consumer rights; and Oxfam, the South Center, and the Third World Network (TWN) are engaged in economic development.

In the context of international trade and the WTO-related issues, Scholte, O'Brien, and Williams (1999) divide such a wide variety of NGOs into three categories: (a) the conformers—who accept the WTO's mission to promote global integration of economies on the basis of rule-based trading system and reliance on market-economic principles; (b) the reformers—who do not oppose basic premises of the WTO, but believe that existing rules and regulations result in inefficient outcomes; and (c) the radicals—who challenge the WTO trade regimes and seek to destroy the institution or reduce its scope and power. Obviously, there are not many NGOs that belong to the first category, most of them belong to the other categories, and second, most of the NGOs that play an active role in international trade or WTO-related matters are based in developed countries.

Major concerns of NGOs, with respect to the WTO-related issues, can be summarized as follows: (a) that the WTO is dominated by industrial lobbyists and multinational corporations, and thus promotes policies that neglect environmental concerns, labor, and human rights, and issues related to sustainable development; (b) the WTO needs to adopt a more participatory approach through formation of consultation mechanisms and advisory bodies in order to generate greater trust and ownership in its activities; and (c) the WTO should grant the NGOs direct access to the WTO to increase government accountability in trade negotiations (Hoekman and Kostecki 2001, 470).

THE WTO STRUCTURES AND DEVELOPING COUNTRIES AND THE LDCS

This section explains how the current structure and composition of the WTO discriminates against the interest of developing countries, especially the LDCs, in terms of their influence on both the processes and the outcomes of multilateral trade negotiations under the WTO. The question is addressed from the perspectives of: (a) the structural context of negotiation processes of the WTO—the so-called Green Room processes; (b) the Dispute Settlement process; and (c) the Accession process.

The Green Room Process

The Green Room processes refer to the traditional processes of multilateral negotiations evolved under the GATT, in which four major players of the GATT—the so-called Quad members; Canada, the EU, Japan and the United States—played key role. They played a dominant role in the GATT negotiation process for so long that the Quad came down as an informal steering committee for the WTO system. Normally, the Quad members would meet together in Green Rooms, along with key parties involved in the issue being discussed, to thrash out solutions, and then the decision would be passed to the GATT decision-making body for official stamp. The so-called Green Room process did function well under the GATT, even up until the Seattle debacle of the WTO, when lack of transparency as well as the informal and nonrepresentative character of these processes had infuriated the developing country participants so much that the Ministerial had to be suspended even before any declaration could be presented for its adoption.

The failure of the Green Room process, during the third wave of globalization, has to do with a number of factors. First, during the period of the GATT, most of the developing countries remained passive observers to the GATT negotiations, as long as trade agreements reached at the GATT did not inflict any demands on them, and they presumably gained from trade accords that gradually opened MFN status to them. Also, developed countries had nothing much to negotiate with the developing countries, which had commanded a very small share of global trade and the share of trade was predominantly in agriculture, which remained effectively outside the GATT negotiation. The whole spectrum changed with the Uruguay Round, which brought two of the major sectors in which developing countries have export interest, agriculture and textiles and clothing, into the GATT discipline. Moreover, the UR also brought many other issues, such as service sector, copyrights, and sanitary and phytosanitary measures, into the GATT discipline, making it difficult for the developing countries to remain passive anymore. In fact, the UR, for all practical purposes, brought an end to the era of seclusion for the developing countries.

Second, a good number of developing countries have become successful exporters over the decades. Between 1963 and 1997, for example, the share of developing countries in world exports of manufactures increased from 4 percent to 24 percent (WTO, 1999). With a command of almost a quarter of manufacturing exports worldwide, developing countries thus developed greater stakes in the WTO negotiations and their outcomes. Third, an overwhelming majority of the WTO members are now developing countries—65 of them participated in the formation of the WTO at the Marrakech Ministerial Conference, and as of April 2003, out of 146 members of the WTO, more than 100 were developing countries. The sheer number also counts, and domination of the Quad in the Green Room negotiations, leaving most of them in the cold, does send a chilling message to them. Fourth, although their representation is still less than adequate in Geneva, only about one-third of developing countries having resident diplomatic missions in Geneva, they are becoming more and more involved, mainly because of greater consciousness in their own backyards, thanks to the information revolution, and more specifically the vocal role of civic societies (discussed below). Fifth, unlike the GATT period, the WTO members could not be "free riders" on negotiated agreements; the "Single Undertaking" clause of the UR demands that the developing countries participate in all trade negotiations, as those are mandatory for all members.

Finally, the so-called Green Room process has perhaps outlived its usefulness. The concept of the Green Room evolved in the early years of the GATT, when the global trade body had just a couple of dozen members, and consensus-based decision making was neither inconceivable nor unwieldy. But with the third wave of globalization, everything has changed. As shown at the Seattle Ministerial in 2000 and then at the Cancun Ministerial in 2003, the old paradigm of consensus-based decision making, with the Green Room playing a key role, turned out to be totally ineffective. In fact, the conception that the old paradigm is not working and a new paradigm is needed has received universal acquiescence—across the great digital divide or the economic divide of the world. After the Seattle Ministerial, the US Trade Representative Charlene Barshefsky bluntly commented, "The WTO has outgrown the processes appropriate to an earlier time," and the EU chief trade negotiator Pascal Lamy said that the WTO negotiating process "itself has to be reassessed and may be rebuilt" (Sutherland and Sewell 2000, 99). Similarly, reactions to the so-called Green Room process have been blunt from developing parts of the world as well.[11]

As the Green Room process is turning out to be counterproductive, the WTO will have to reinvent its decision-making mechanisms, unless it wants to fall into the UN syndrome of losing credibility and turning itself into a talking platform, or invite more debacles or fiascos in its ministerial conferences. Besides, leaving aside some controversial issues—such as the environment, labor standards, and intellectual property rights, which might belong to more appropriate agencies than the WTO, any thought of reinventing the decision-making process of the WTO should consider the following realities: (a) stakes of developing countries in global trade, and for that matter in the WTO decisions and deliberations, are growing, and developing countries have been asserting their positions through various coalitions; (b) the days of passing on decisions, reached through the Green Room process, are all but ended; (c) the roles, functions, and decisions of the multilateral institutions, like the World Bank, the IMF, the UN, and the WTO, are being scrutinized by the citizens around the world more intensely than ever before; (d) the NGOs and civic societies around the world are rapidly emerging as a formidable force in affecting and shaping WTO agendas; and (f) liberalization of economies and democratization of nations have been reinforcing the needs and demands for greater accountability and transparency of all major multilateral institutions, including the WTO.

Reforming the Green Room Process

Obviously, frustrations with the decision-making processes of the WTO have been mounting, especially among the NGOs and civic societies, and governments in many developing countries, who saw how they were left out in the cold in consultations and negotiations, and eventually handed down deals reached by powerful countries in secretive and nontransparent Green Room processes. Over the years several proposals sprung up to address this issue of WTO governance. One proposal seeks to move away from the existing decision-making process based on consensus, and create a decision-making structure, such as an Executive Board, as can be found in the Bretton Woods institutions. Obviously, such a modeling of the WTO governance enjoys little support in the developing part of the world—thanks to the rather unsatisfactory experience with the management of the World Bank and the IMF in the last five decades. Also, transferring decision-making power to an Executive Board—presumably to a small group of elected or selected countries—will imply giving up opportunities to maximize their interests under consensus-based decision making, and paving the way for further marginalization of their status in the WTO decision-making processes.

Some developing countries would rather prefer procedural improvements under the existing consensus-based decision-making processes so that the deliberations of the WTO, even in committees or under the so-called Green Room processes, are transparent, inclusive of all members, small or large, so that their views are heard and that the outcome of those deliberations are reported in a timely manner. Of course, there are also proposals to create an independent international public-interest body—to examine technical, such as economic and scientific, aspects, as well as nontechnical, such as social aspects of the WTO policies—which could work as a "discovery mechanism through which greater understanding could be obtained regarding the effects of national policies on various constituencies and stakeholders, both within and across economies" (Hoekman and Kostecki 2001, 473).

In the new world of more transparent and more accountable decision-making processes of the WTO, developing countries will be facing an even greater challenge. There is no reason to expect that economies with dominant roles in global trade will not find new ways and means to wield powers and maneuver to outdo rights of equal say guaranteed in the WTO decision making for all member countries. Throughout the GATT period, developed countries, especially the Quad—the United States, the EU, Japan, and Canada—maintained a form of coalition in almost all respects, except perhaps agriculture, in which the United States and the EU positions sharply differed for several years. The GATT negotiations, therefore, were essentially conditioned by what Drahos (2003) describes as "inequalities of bargaining power," whereby the Quad countries exerted strong bargaining power derived from greater control over market power, networks of commercial intelligence, enrollment power, and superior institutional arrangements.

While greater market power underpinned the capacity of developed countries to make credible threats, as Drahos (2003) explains, an effective network of commercial intelligence underpinned the capacity of developed-country negotiators to enter into informed and persuasive negotiations. The enrollment power, on the other hand, allowed developed countries to form coalitions of both government and nongovernment actors in the negotiating issues, and the institutional arrangements allowed them to use negotiating authority or bargaining power of the negotiators. On top of that, each of the GATT rounds typically saw "prenegotiation cooperation" between the United States and the EU. On the other hand, the GATT negotiations experienced no "counterweight to the Quad" up until the UR, during which the Cairns Group demonstrated that "collective action by weaker states can result in a positive payoff." Taking clue from the "positive payoff" of the Cairns Group during the UR negotiations, Drahos suggests that developing countries could come up with a formalized group, what he calls a "Counter Quad," in which major developing countries, such as Brazil, China, Egypt, India, and Nigeria, would take up the leadership role, monitor developments in various parts of the WTO regime depending on their expertise and interests, share analytical capacities with each other, and eventually adopt recommendations or positions on WTO-related issues in a manner of participatory democracy. Drahos, however, emphasizes building trust among developing countries, through effective communication among developing country negotiators, with the group structure firmly rooted in developing country capitals, not in Geneva alone.

The Counter-Quad of Drahos is, however, focused on developing countries; it does not include the LDCs or their interests. Also, unlike the developing countries, the LDCs have a forum—the LDC leaders meet annually to hammer out their positions, as exemplified by the Zanzibar Declaration of 2000, the Brussels Declaration of 2001, and the Dhaka Declaration of 2003—and they have a platform—the UNCTAD provides secretarial support to the LDC issues, although not to the LDC group directly. Second, in many cases, the interests of the LDCs are very different from those of developing countries—they are, for example, either exempted from or granted a longer period for transition under the UR, and most of them enjoy more lavish special and differential treatment (SDT) rights, for example, under the Generalized Systems of Preference (GSP), the US Trade and Development Act of 2000, and All-but-Arms (EBA) initiative of 2001 of the EU. Third, in many respects the interests of the LDCs are diametrically opposite to that of the developing countries. For example, the phasing out of the quota regimes in textiles and clothing would be less advantageous for the LDCs than for many developing countries. At the same time, agricultural trade liberalization, elimination of export subsidies in the Western world, will benefit food-exporting developing countries, but this will hurt net food-importing LDCs, whose import bills are set to go up. Finally, advanced developing countries would be interested in obtaining greater market access in developed country markets as their share in global manufacturing trade has been increasing, while most LDCs still are predominantly agricultural, with unprocessed raw materials constituting the bulk of their exports.

Such differences between the developing countries and the LDCs would call for a separate platform for the LDCs, but the ideas of leadership of some major countries, effective network of commercial intelligence, enrollment, and institutional arrangements, as emphasized by Drahos with respect to "Counter-Quad" for the developing countries, could constitute integral parts of the LDC platform that would enhance the monitoring and analytical capacity of LDC negotiators to enter into informed and effective negotiations under the WTO. Integration of the LDCs into the global economy would require serious efforts to build their developmental capabilities, raising efficiency levels, lowering wastages, and enhancing their trade participation and negotiation capacities. One way to accomplish such a feat, as Dowlah (2003a) suggests, would be establishment of an exclusive LDC think tank, maybe titled the Organization of the Least Developed Countries (OLDC), which will work as the central secretariat of the LDCs, just as the OECD works for the interests of industrially advanced countries.

The resources currently going to build trade and development capacities, for example, under the so-called Integrated Framework, can be pooled together so that all LDCs, under the guidance of the centralized institutional capabilities of OLDC, may be able to articulate their needs and concerns more rigorously, and with world-class expertise at par with their counterparts in the OECD. Currently, UNCTAD serves a great purpose in projecting the case of the LDCs, but it works under the UN, and like the UN, it is not controlled by the LDCs. Perhaps, the UNCTAD itself could be placed under the direct control of the OLDC to serve as a catalyst for identifying opportunities and challenges associated with the globalization and liberalization processes. With a command over an institution as such, the LDCs themselves would be able to control their research agenda and other activities through annual meetings to work out common LDC positions for the WTO negotiations.

The Dispute Settlement Procedures (DSP)

Although the GATT record of international trade dispute settlement can hardly be considered unsatisfactory,[12] the WTO came with a much more strengthened dispute settlement mechanism than what existed under the GATT. Unlike the GATT, however, the WTO dispute resolution procedures are formal and binding for all members. The Dispute Settlement Procedures (DSP) can be initiated by any member of the WTO against any other member when it believes that the other party has done any of the following: (a) "nullified or impaired" a concession, such as tariff binding, that was negotiated previously; (b) broke a WTO rule; or (c) impaired the attainment of an objective of the WTO. Complaints with the DSP also can take three forms: (a) a charge of violation of WTO rules—a claim that the other party violated one or more WTO disciplines or negotiated commitments; (b) a charge of non-violation-but-nullification—a claim that the other party may not have violated WTO rules or discipline, but nullifies a previously granted concession; or (c) a situational complaint—a charge that the other party nullifies or impairs a previously negotiated benefit.

Under the provisions of the Uruguay Round Dispute Settlement Understanding (DSU), the WTO follows almost the same dispute resolution procedures for most of the disputes brought for its disposal—whether concerned with goods, services, or intellectual property. The dispute settlement authority lies with the Dispute Settlement Body (DSB), which, in fact, is the General Council of the WTO. Settlement procedures of disputes, as Hoekman and Kostecki 2001, 74–78) explain, follow the following sequences: (a) consultation and mediation—initially members are required to make an attempt to resolve the dispute through bilateral negotiations, when mediation of the WTO Director General can also be sought; (b) establishment of a panel—if the parties fail to resolve the dispute through bilateral negotiations within 60 days, the DSB appoints a three- to four-member panel, composed of officials, ex-officials and academics with expertise in the relevant area of trade; (c) the panel, after examination of facts and arguments of both parties, submits its report to the DSB with recommendations; (d) the panel's report and recommendations are then adopted or rejected by the DSB within 60 days. Any party to the dispute is, however, allowed to appeal to the Appellate Body in case the panel report or its recommendations, as adopted by the DSB, are not to its satisfaction. But the decision of the Appellate Body, which normally consists of seven persons taken from WTO membership, is final, which must be adopted by the DSB; and finally (e) the recommendations adopted by the DSB must be enforced, although the offending country can negotiate a reasonable time for implementation, and in case of failure of implementation of the DSB recommendation, the complainant party is automatically entitled to retaliate against the offending party.

The strengthened WTO dispute settlement procedures have been believed to be friendlier to small countries. In fact, as Jackson (1997) points out, the DSU is widely considered to be one of the positive outcomes of the Uruguay Round, which pushed the whole dispute settlement procedure to an automatic and rule-based system, away from the power-based system that often blocked such procedures requiring "consensus" of the parties involved. The GATT system of dispute settlement, as Hudec (2002) explains, was based on consensus decision making, which required consent of the defendant in creating a panel, defining its terms of references, appointing its members, adopting its ruling, and authorizing retaliation. These procedures often led to effective blocking of the dispute settlement procedures. Under the DSU, powerful countries can no longer block establishment of panels or adoption of panel reports. At the same time, the DSU provides for clear time limits for each stage of dispute settlement, guidelines for selection of panelists, clear appellate procedures, and strengthened implementation mechanisms. The new procedures have led to higher participation in the DSU by developing countries. As Delich (2002) points out, of the 207 dispute settlement cases filed between 1995 and 2000, 53 were filed by developing countries alone, and 35 of those were complaints against developed countries.

But the WTO dispute resolution mechanism has been criticized on several grounds. First, only the governments enjoy the legal standing of filing a dispute settlement case with the WTO—concerned industries or other affected parties or advocates, such as NGOs, are not entitled to bring a case. Second, the DSB generally asks the offending party to comply with the WTO rules, without specifying how it can bring itself to compliance with the WTO rules. More specifically, although the recommendations of the DSU are legally binding, they do not provide remedy for the harm done. The recommendations are rather future-oriented; they direct the defendant to comply in the future. Developing countries have long been challenging such a forward-looking measure, demanding monetary compensation for the actual damages done to their fragile economies and their development prospects.

Third, completion of the dispute settlement course under the DSB takes a long time, usually from two to three years, including time needed for exhausting appeals and the implementation period. That's a very long time for any industry to cope with. Fourth, the ultimate penalty of noncompliance with the DSB recommendation is retaliation, which may not be an effective or practicable option for small countries. As Hudec (2002, 86) points out, a small country does not have a large enough market to mount a scale of retaliation that would cause noticeable pain in a large industrial country—the only way to achieve significant retaliation would be through collective action, under which many developing countries, not the complainant alone, would be entitled to retaliate.[13]

Finally, although the DSU provides better chance for developing countries to defend their interests, as Delich (2002) points out, it does not provide a "neutral" playing field to developing countries—they are less equipped to participate in the process. Most of the developing countries, especially the LDCs, lack necessary financial, legal, informational, and human resources necessary to reap benefits of the dispute settlement system. Also, the promised technical assistance from the WTO has so far been extremely unsatisfactory.

The Accession Rules

The WTO membership is open to any country in the world, but Article XII of the WTO requires an agreement between the applicant country and the WTO members on the accession process. Generally, a country has to submit an application for membership with a request to grant it observer status with the WTO. While granting an observer status, the General Council establishes a Working Party with interested WTO members to consider the application. The applicant country then submits a memorandum detailing its trade rules and regulations. The Working Party then examines the trade regime of the applicant country to determine its consistency with the WTO trade regulations, asks for removal of inconsistencies, and works out a special agreement, called market access negotiations, with the applicant country. The Working Party then forwards the application, along with the Protocol of Accession, to the General Council. A two-thirds majority is needed for approval of accession of a new member into the WTO.

But unlike under the GATT, when the accession process to the global trading system had been more flexible and pragmatic, the process has become much more complex and burdensome under the WTO. Only about 30 new members could be approved since the WTO came into existence—still many countries, including Russia, many Eastern European countries, as well as developing countries and the LDCs, are in the process of accession. Out of the 50 LDCs, so far only 29 are the members of the WTO. Between 1995 and 2001, the WTO established 28 Working Parties to consider accession; with a few exceptions, the accession process took a little over five years from the establishment of the Working Party to entry into force of WTO membership.[14]

Major reasons for difficulties involved in the accession process can be summarized as follows: (a) every existing WTO member has the right to present specific demands to the applicant country, with respect to both tariff and nontariff issues; (b) unlike the Cold War period, when the United States was willing to forgo its economic interests for the sake of political interests, now not only has its commitment to such obligations diminished, but also it seeks its economic interests more persuasively;[15] (c) many existing WTO members, especially industrialized ones, want to have firm commitment of new members to liberalization of trade, even privatization of their economies, before approving their membership; (d) "the country that desires to enter the WTO is *demandeur*. It must negotiate with incumbent club members, and more often than not will have little bargaining power" (Hoekman and Kostecki 2001, 67); and finally, as Michalopoulos (2002, 69) points out, the accession process seems to be riddled with contradictions—while insistence on adherence to all WTO commitments at the entry point without any transition period raises serious problems for many LDCs and transitional economies that lack necessary institutional capabilities, providing generous transition periods, instead, would create "inequities between existing and new members" as for most of the existing members transition periods are now expiring.[16]

NEW-GENERATION ISSUES AND DEVELOPING COUNTRIES

This section looks into the so-called "second-generation" issues or the "new-trade agenda"—involving the issues of intellectual property rights, trade in services, trade-related environment and labor issues, investment, and competition policies—to ascertain challenges that developing countries face with the WTO regimes currently.

The General Agreement on Trade in Services (GATS)

Integration of the service sector—trade in services—into the GATT discipline has been controversial ever since the United States pushed the agenda for its integration at the GATT ministerial meeting in 1982. One main reason is that services—from construction to transport, hotels to health care, accounting to finance, education to telecommunication—constitute a bulk of every economy, with about 30 percent of GDP in developing countries to over 70 percent in many developed countries. Moreover, trade in services is different from trade in manufacturing—services are often intangible, nonstorable, nonstandardized, and often it requires physical proximity between providers and demanders to make a service transaction feasible. Also, barriers to trade in services do not come in the form of import tariffs, as in manufacturing trade; most barriers to service trade come rather in the form of prohibitions, quantitative restrictions, price-based instruments, and government regulations, such as standards, licensing, and procurement rules (Hoekman and Kostecki 2001, 23–248).[17] Moreover, liberalization of the service sector has been found to be more difficult than of the manufacturing sector, as in many countries service sectors, such as telecommunications and transportation, are highly regulated and subsidized sectors, which enjoy deep-rooted support from vested interests as well as regulatory agencies (Bhagwati 1984).

Despite such unique dimensions of trade in services, which were fiercely defended by developing countries, especially countries like India, Brazil, and Argentina, developed countries, especially the United States and the EU succeeded in putting the service sector in the agenda of multilateral negotiations under the Uruguay Round.[18] The eventual GATS agreement, reached at the UR, included the following features: (a) it brought trade in services to the GATT 1994 discipline, by establishing rules and regulations, such as the MFN principle, as envisaged in Article I; (b) it required members to commit to certain GATT articles for trade in services—such as Article VIII, which envisages nonabuse of the dominant position of monopolies, Article XIV, which envisages market access commitments, and Article XVII, which envisages commitment to national treatment of foreign entities; (c) it provided for periodic negotiations for progressive liberalization of trade in services, as at the close of the UR negotiations, negotiations in several service sectors, such as financial services, telecommunications, and maritime transport remained incomplete and unsatisfactory; and (d) it contained sector-specific, mode-specific implementation mechanisms regarding market access and national treatment conditions. The GATS covers both trade in the balance of payments–national accounts—and local sales by foreign affiliates, but excludes services supplied in the exercise of government functions (Adlung and others 2002).[19]

The GATS identifies four standard modes of supply through which trade in services can take place: mode 1—cross-border trade—electronic or physical transactions across borders, such as air and maritime transport and financial trading, not requiring physical movement of supplier or consumer; mode 2—movement of the consumer to the country of the supplier for reasons such as tourism and education; mode 3—commercial presence—services sold in the territory of a member by foreign entities, such as local telecommunications or electricity; and mode 4—presence of natural persons, provision of services requiring the temporary movement of natural persons, such as business consulting and construction. Liberalization of services requires reduction of regulatory barriers to market access and discriminatory national treatment across all these modes of services, but all sectors are not equally dominant in trade in services. For example, modes 1 and 3—cross-border trade and commercial presence—accounted for almost 80 percent of world trade in services in 1998, when global trade in services totaled $2.2 trillion (Maurer and Chauvet 2002).

Benefits from the implementation of the GATS have been estimated to be almost the same from the full liberalization of trade in agriculture and manufactures, as services have a strong intermediate role, having both direct and indirect effect on other sectors of the economy (Dee and Hanslow 2001).[20] Empirical evidence shows that in the 1990s, world trade in commercial services increased by 6.2 percent per annum, with higher growth rates in the first half of the 1990s than the second half. One reason for this is that in the second half of the 1990s, the share of developing countries in trade of commercial services fell drastically, thanks to the East Asian financial crises.[21] Also, as Maurer and Chauvet (2002) point out, in the second half of the 1990s, the Triad countries—the United States, the EU, and Japan—accounted for about 66 percent of world trade in services, and 42 percent of the trade was among themselves.

Obviously, GATS so far has not led to greater market access for developing countries. Although some agreements were reached as a follow-up of the UR agreements, with respect to financial services, telecommunications, and maritime agreements, they have benefited primarily developed countries. As Das (1998) points out, these agreements further tilted the balance in favor of the developed countries, as they are the major providers of these services, while developing countries hardly have any export capacity in these sectors. On the other hand, while developing countries made progress with respect to their commitments to national treatment for utility services and greater market access, developed countries have yet to make a substantial concession with respect to Mode 4, which calls for liberalization of movement of natural persons; no progress can be seen in respect to cross-border movement of workers on the basis of temporary contracts or permanent basis. No wonder developing countries allege that developed countries are more interested in liberalization of GATS modes that are particularly beneficial to them, while blocking liberalization in the modes in which developing countries stand to gain.

At the same time, one should not undermine the fact that the GATS commitments for developing countries far outweigh those envisaged for the developed world. Under GATS, developing countries are to liberalize their financial services—banking, insurance and insurance-related services, utility services—such as telecom and energy services, and air, land, and maritime transports—all these would require sweeping reforms and liberalization in developing countries. Although GATS provides for "voluntary offer" or liberalization according to the pace and sectors preferred by the member country, developing countries face constant pressure from Bretton Woods institutions and the new rounds of negotiations. For example, the World Bank and the IMF have aggressively been pursing the agenda of liberalization of the financial sector and capital account in developing countries for about a decade now. At the same time, in the ministerial meetings of the WTO, at Singapore, at Seattle, at Doha, and at Cancun, developed countries doggedly pushed for agreements in the so-called Singapore Issues.

Failures or fiascos in recent WTO Ministerials should send a clear signal to developed country negotiators that no enduring results will emerge from WTO negotiations unless the interests and concerns of developing countries are addressed properly, that developing countries are not capable of further liberalization without visible rewards or reciprocal benefits stemming from the developed part of the world. It is now clear that the more the developing countries liberalize their service sectors, the more they widen market access for the developed country-based companies, and the more they make it difficult for developing country-based companies to survive. Moreover, even in the long term, the prospect of developing countries gaining substantially from GATS does not seem to be a credible proposition—they not only lack technological and professional resources needed for making a dent in developed country markets, their export potentials in services are further constrained by anticompetitive practices, subsidies, and regulatory practices in the developed world (UNCTAD 1999a, 9).

The Trade-Related Intellectual Property Rights (TRIPs)

The TRIPS is perhaps the most comprehensive multilateral agreement on intellectual property rights in the history of humankind. This comprehensive character of the agreement, as Watal (2002) points out, is demonstrated not only in the breadth of the subject matters covered, but also with respect to its near-universal applicability. The agreement provides for minimum substantive standards of protection for wide-ranging areas of intellectual properties, covering copyrights of authors, broadcasters, performers, trademarks, industrial designs, patents, inventions, and innovations, and provides member countries with procedures and remedies to enforce those rights (UNCTAD 1996).[22] By encompassing such a broad range of products—industrial as well as informational and cultural—the TRIPS blurred the traditional distinction between commercial and cultural inventions in the age of information technology and digital products (World Bank 2003a).

Obviously, the drive for such a comprehensive, as well as effective, intellectual property rights regime came mainly from the developed world, especially from the United States. The arguments put forward were straightforward—with a rising share of manufactures in global trade and the increasing role of technology in such products, the producers needed protection from piracy and counterfeit products in order to recoup their investment in research and development, as well as protect their comparative advantage. Developed country businesses, especially multinational corporations, also argued that infringements on intellectual property rights constituted a straightforward matter of piracy and theft. And, there are no dearth of studies that would show positive relations between patents and research and development (Maskus 1997).

The TRIPs agreement modified and strengthened several international treaties that were in existence at the time and were administered by the UN body—the World Intellectual Property Organization (WIPO).[23] For example, sound recordings and performers are to be granted protection for 50 years, broadcasters are to be granted protection for 20 years, patents are to be granted for 20 years for almost all inventions, including both processes and products, and layout designs of integrated circuits are to be granted a minimum of 10 years' protection. In addition, the agreement extends GATT principles of national treatment to persons and the MFN principle to intellectual property rights with some exceptions. All members are obliged to change their domestic legal and regulatory regimes to provide for effective implementation of TRIPs, including providing for nondiscrimination between domestic and foreign intellectual property rights. All members were asked to implement the TRIPs within a year—although developing countries could delay the full enforcement of the agreement for four years, with the exception of national treatment and MFN. The LDCs were granted a 10-year transition period for compliance.[24]

Although the TRIPs agreement does not call for harmonization of intellectual property rights (IPRs) across the world, the agreement does reflect what the US pharmaceutical, entertainment, and information industries had long been demanding. These companies "were largely responsible for getting TRIPs on the agenda," and they "obtained much of what they sought when the negotiations were launched" (Hoekman and Kostecki 2001, 297). As Table 6.1 indicates, with the implementation of the TRIPs, net static rent transfers to major industrialized countries, such as the United States, Germany, France, Italy, Sweden, and Switzerland, would cross $8 trillion, while almost all other countries in the world stand to lose.

Quite naturally, the TRIPs has generated considerable concern throughout the world, especially in the developing countries, mainly because of the fact that they are the net importers of technologies and other knowledge-intensive goods and services, and as a result, their cost of imports is likely to rise due to monopoly rights enjoyed by copyright or patent right holders in developed countries.[25] Many developing countries are concerned that stronger legal rules on IPR would be detrimental to their welfare and development prospects, as stronger patent protection might lead to socially wasteful patent races, duplicate researches or block patents, hinder further innovation, and retard technological progress (Watal 2002).

Developing countries are especially concerned with the impact of the IPR regimes on agricultural trade, pertaining to plants and animals, plant variety protection systems, and food security and agricultural biodiversity.[26] The IPR regimes obviously shift bargaining power toward the producers of knowledge and technology in the industrial countries, and many industrial- country firms are acquiring strong intellectual property rights, often involving fundamental research tools as well as marketable products, which put the developing countries and their firms

Table 6.1
Estimated Static Rent Transfers from TRIPs Implementation (1995, US$ Millions)

Country	Outward transfer	Inward transfer	Net transfer	Country	Outward transfer	Inward transfer	Net transfer
US	92	5852	5760	South Africa	183	15	-168
Germany	599	1827	1228	Greece	197	2	-195
France	0	831	831	Finland	281	47	-234
Italy	0	277	277	Norway	277	25	-252
Sweden	13	230	217	Denmark	330	77	-253
Switzerland	474	510	36	Austria	358	83	-275
Panama	0	0.3	0.3	Belgium	470	111	-359
Australia	177	154	-23	India	430	0	-430
Ireland	71	12	-59	South Korea	457	3	-454
New Zealand	79	8	-71	Spain	512	31	-481
Israel	125	32	-93	Mexico	527	1	-526
Colombia	132	2	-130	Japan	1202	613	-589
Portugal	138	0	-138	UK	1221	588	-633
Netherlands	453	314	-139	Canada	1125	85	-1040
				Brazil	1714	7	-1707

Source: Maskus (2000), updating McCalman (1999), copied from Hoekman and Kostecki (2001, 292–293).

and researchers in a disadvantageous position in catching up with the knowledge gap as well as adoption of technologies. With such patent rights or patent protection of plant varieties and seeds, farmers in developing countries would have to procure seeds from developed country seed producers at exorbitant cost, which would badly affect the local seed industry and increase the cost of agricultural production, and thereby increase the price of agricultural goods.[27]

Also, TRIPs' call for conforming legal standards across the world to its parameters—irrespective of level of development of member countries—in effect, it asks developing countries to raise their standards "up to developed-country norms," and by doing so, as Sally (2003) elaborates, the agreement "poisons the international trading system" in several ways. Politically, it tramples on national sovereignty; legally, it is a Procrustean approach that smacks of Cartesian, top-down legal symmetry, which could be wonderful for lawyers and Utopian constructors of global governance, but it effectively slams the door for bottom-up national policies; economically, by imposing regulations that raise costs out of line with national productivity levels, it restricts developing-country labor-intensive exports as surely as any antidumping action; and morally, it is reprehensible, as "it is tantamount to extraterritorial invasion of private property rights"—individual liberties "are the first to be sacrificed on the altar of standards harmonization."

Labor Standards

The labor issue, or the so-called labor standards, popped up in multilateral discussions in the final stage of the Uruguay Round, mainly at the instigation of the United States and France. In the name of labor standards, developed countries sought to include a "social clause," which would specify certain minimum specifications as a precondition for market access. Maskus (1997) identifies five general rights that the proponents of social clause sought recognition and enforcement of: (a) ban on exploitative use of child workers; (b) elimination of forced labor, such as prison labor; (c) prevention of discrimination in the workplace; (d) allowing free association of workers, such as trade unions; and (e) allowing collective bargaining. The advocates of labor standards argue that lower labor standards in developing countries put companies operating in industrialized countries at a cost disadvantage, and free trade will spark more human misery, as developing countries would "race to the bottom" to attract foreign investors (Rodrik 1997).[28]

One main reason for bringing the labor issue before the WTO by the developed countries is that, unlike the International Labor Organization (ILO), the WTO has an effective enforcement mechanism under which member countries can seek to impose multilateral trade sanctions against members that do not protect such labor rights. Main stakeholders in developed countries—such as trade unions and the government—view that the ILO, which has adopted numerous provisions governing working conditions and workers rights, and also provides a tripartite platform—for employers, labor unions, and governments—to address labor issues, is an "ineffective institution" that has not "done enough for their confidence" in improving labor rights protection worldwide (Sutherland and Sewell 2000). Labor advocates in the Western countries are specially critical of the ILO's enforcement mechanism—they tend to argue that the ILO was never effective in ensuring compliance of the members with its mandates.

Developing countries, on the other hand, saw strengthened labor standards and enforcement mechanism as another nontariff barrier to their exports, and argued that the ILO platform was adequate to safeguard globally acknowledged rights and standards of workers, and this area should remain under the jurisdiction of the ILO, which has decades of experience and expertise to address the issue more judiciously. Developing countries also cite GATT Article XX, which asks member countries not to apply measures arbitrarily or in an unjustifiably discriminatory manner. They also point out that the concerns for labor standards mostly relate to production and process methods (PPM), not to the products, and by directing attention to PPM, the developed countries were showing more interest in using trade as an instrument for attaining noneconomic objectives or nontrade concerns (Tay 2002). As a result, the labor issue still remains highly controversial, as developed countries' attempt to include labor standards into the WTO met fierce opposition from developing countries at the Singapore Ministerial in 1996 as well as the Seattle Ministerial in 1999.

Environmental Issues

Linkages between trade, development, and environment can hardly be overemphasized. The issue of environment, however, figured prominently under the GATT in 1971, when a Working Group was established on Environmental Measures and International Trade. The 1970s, however, were hardly a period of heightened concerns for the environment—the world was scouting through the Great Oil Shocks, among others. Even in the 1980s, the GATT environmental group remained dormant, until the dispute over tuna fish broke out between Mexico and the United States in 1991.[29] Under the WTO, the task to examine trade-related aspects of environment became the responsibility of the WTO Committee on Trade and Environment (CTE). The CTE primarily "looks at the effects of environmental measures on trade, rather than the reverse" (Jha 2002, 472). The environmental issue, however, was taken earnestly at the Seattle Ministerial in 1999, especially in the context of negotiations in agriculture, GATS, TRIPs, and the SPS. After the Seattle fiasco, the environmental issue was taken up in every ministerial held so far.

At the core of the environmental issue in the WTO lies the concern of the developed world to integrate considerations of environmental and sustainable development in all multilateral trade negotiations. Developed countries seek to link trade measures with environmental issues by emphasizing three interrelated concepts—production and process methods (PPMs), internationalization of environmental costs, and eco-dumping. The underlying logic is that environmentally harmful trade can negatively affect sustainable development and trade. Developed countries argue that countries with lower environmental standards, by failing to internalize environmental costs, unfairly subsidize their products, which can be viewed as "eco-dumping." To counter such eco-dumping, or harmful environmental effects, proponents of trade and sustainable development argue, importing countries should be allowed to impose unilateral restrictive measures, such as trade sanctions, import bans, and countervailing duties.

While developing countries do not deny links between trade and environment, or sustainable development, or do not underestimate the effect of ecological damage, they tend to argue that under the guise of environmental concerns, industrial countries might attempt to use trade-restrictive measures against developing-country exports. They oppose amendment of the GATT Article XX, which would allow "a system of blanket and automatic WTO approval" of trade measures, arguing that such ex-ante environmental measures could lead to "abuse and protectionism" (TWN 2001) . They also argue that given unequal bargaining strengths of developed and developing countries, a more appropriate forum for negotiating environmental issues could be the United Nations, especially because the UN Conference on Environment and Development (UNCED) addresses the issues of environmental concerns in the context of sustainable development (Khor 1999). Developing countries also find a universal environmental standard as out of synch with their levels of economic development, and measures like eco-labeling—labeling products environmentally friendly or not—as a form of technical barrier to trade (TBT).

CONCLUDING REMARKS

The WTO suffers from what is called the framer syndrome—the UR agreements were driven by the interests and concerns of industrialized countries, and the platform discriminates against the interests of developing countries and the LDCs. The agreements like the URAA, ATC, TRIPS, GATS, SPSS—all are direct testimony to the fact that a deliberate attempt has been made to impose what developed countries found in their own interests. Developing countries were herded into signing the WTO agreement at Marrakech—with promises of benefits that have not materialized—crucial sectors of export interests to the developing countries still suffer from trade protection and are subject to tariff escalations or tariff peaks in developed countries. The so-called Green Room Process needs to be done away with, and it should be replaced with a more transparent, democratic, and accountable mechanism for decision making that would be acceptable to all parties to the WTO. Developing countries need to come up with something like Counter-Quad, while the LDCs need to work out something like OLDC, as illustrated above, to make the WTO platform beneficial to them.

NOTES

1. Nobel laureate economist Joseph Stiglitz (2000) has identified six such global public goods, whose benefits are global in nature, not limited to a particular country: global security, global economic stability, knowledge, global environment, humanitarian assistance (such as famines), and global health (such as, contagious diseases).

2. For different waves of globalization, see Chapter 1.

3. The so-called "logic of 1945," originally developed by Kapstein (1999), emphasizes three major convictions: (a) a liberal international order would maximize international economic stability and growth, but it was also emphasized that successful international liberalization would depend on addressing social welfare needs of the people so that their supports can promote such liberalization; (b) a sound international economy required the widest possible participation of economies around the world; and (c) national governments were the only actors of any consequence for international economic diplomacy. See Sutherland and Sewell (2000).

4. While Professor Stiglitz, in his book *Globalization and Its Discontent*, criticized the World Bank staff for passing on their aid memorandums to countries often without erasing the name of the country for which it was originally prepared, Professor Bhagwati, in his forthcoming book *In Defense of Globalization*, criticized the World Bank for what he calls "data-mongering" with its abundance of economists and funds. Professor Bhagwati (2004, 67) criticizes the way the World Bank puts "all the households of the world onto one chart to measure worldwide inequality of incomes." He asks, "What sense does it make to put a household in Mongolia alongside a household in Chile, one in Bangladesh, another in the United States, and still another in Congo?"

5. The Director General cannot even determine topics for the WTO agenda. Hoekman and Kostecki (2001, 54) cite a comment made by a diplomat, who told the Director General during the Uruguay Round: "Sir, there is a difference between you and me; I am a Contracting Party and you are a Contracted Party."

6. Of course, over the course of last two decades or so, especially since the mid-1990s, there have been sea changes in the commitment of the World Bank and the IMF with respect to transparency and accountability. Although there is no dearth of critics who would still find the reforms less than adequate, it is only fair to say that these institutions do understand the ramifications of changes happening in the contemporary world, especially with the momentum of the third wave of globalization, and are slowly but surely trying to cope with the changes.

7. Pluralist Agreements do not apply to all members of the WTO; these are applicable only to those members that sign such agreements.

8. Barber (1992) explains how four major imperatives—market imperative, resource imperative, information-technology imperative and the ecological imperative—push for trananational, transideological, and transcultural globalization as a form of "universal rational society" built around commercialized, homogenized, and depoliticized market forces, as opposed to forces that a counter doctrine—which he calls Jihad—stands for. Barber, however, emphasizes that the relationship between capitalism and democracy is less than marriage—as the free market flourished "in junta-run Chile, in military-governed Taiwan and Korea, and earlier, in a variety of autocratic European empires as well as their colonial possessions."

9. The index categorizes 16 countries as "free," 55 countries as "mostly free," and 72 countries as "mostly unfree." See the Heritage Foundation and *the Wall Street Journal* (2004).

10. After all, many national economies are too small compared to some MNCs. For example, Wal-Mart's annual revenue is greater than the GDP of Greece, IBM's annual revenue exceeds the GDP of Egypt, Sony's annual revenue surpasses the GDP of the Czech Republic, and General Electric's annual revenue equals the GDP of Israel (Dowlah 2003a).

11. At the end of the Cancun Ministerial in September 2003, Malaysian minister for international trade and industry Rafidah Aziz remarked, "Our boys have come around. We

proved that the developing countries were not to be taken for granted." An African delegate said, "When our priorities are ignored and the conference refuses to discuss them, they call it a collapse. I won't call this a collapse. It is better to have no deal than to have a bad deal" (cited in Dowlah 2003a).

12. As mentioned earlier, the GATT's success rate in trade dispute settlement was around 90 percent.

13. This constrained ability of small countries to retaliate effectively against larger countries makes the WTO dispute settlement system even more one-sided than before. "By making access to retaliation more available," Hudec (2002, 84) argues, "the WTO provides larger countries still greater advantage over smaller countries that cannot effectively retaliate."

14. See Michalopoulos (2002), especially Table 8.1, which provides completion of different stages, such as establishment of working party, memorandum, tariff offers, service offers and draft working party reports for 28 countries. The author also outlines major benefits associated with WTO membership, and argues that smaller countries found the accession process easier than larger countries, as their trade regimes are more liberal than those of larger non-WTO members.

15. This, however, should be taken with a grain of salt. For China, for example, it took a long and arduous process to become a member of the WTO. It would be wrong to suggest that only economic considerations made the process so difficult—politics played a significant role all along. At the same time, unlike most countries that became members of the WTO after the Marrakech Conference, China demonstrated strong bargaining power in its accession to the WTO, with respect to several areas of GATT 1994, for example, quantitative restrictions, licensing, state trading, tariff quota in agriculture, and product-specific selective safeguards in textiles and clothing. Also, in February 2004, the WTO accepted Iraq's application for accession to the WTO (that is, established working party), while Iran's application remains in deep freeze for several years now—demonstrating that politics still plays an important role in the accession process.

16. Another potential area that could be problematic for developing countries, including the LDCs, could be the Trade Policy Review Mechanism (TPRM). Article X of the GATT, Article III of the GATS, and Article 63 of the TRIPs require all WTO members to maintain transparency with respect to their trade policies. This requirement is implemented at two levels. Domestically, every WTO member must publish its trade regulations, even trade-related administrative decisions, notify them to the WTO, and respond to queries made by other members with respect to its trade regulations. Then, at the multilateral level, the WTO secretariat is responsible for preparing country-specific Trade Policy Reviews for review of the Trade Policy Review Body (TPRB). Such trade policy reviews and surveillance, in turn, is expected to serve two purposes: (a) it helps the WTO to ensure that member countries are obliging to their commitments to the WTO; and (b) it helps the members themselves to send powerful signals to their trade partners as well as potential investors by presenting their trade regimes, rules, and regulations more transparently. The schedules for country-specific reviews are, however, not the same for all members—the four largest members of the WTO—the United States, the EU, Japan, and Canada—are subject to review every two years, the next 16 largest members are subject to review every four years, and the rest of the WTO members are subject to review every six years. These reviews, although less frequent for the developing countries and the LDCs, could be problematic for these countries, as indicated in the following section, with respect to new-generation issues.

17. See Stern (2002), who explains price-based, quantity-based, financial-based barriers of trade in services, and shows different estimates of welfare effects of liberalization of trade in services.

18. Developing countries resisted the inclusion of trade in services in the GATT discipline arguing that they might not gain from greater market access in this sector as local companies would lose out in competition with bigger foreign companies. But developed countries talked them into the agreement with the understanding that they would gain from greater market access in other areas, such as agriculture and textiles and clothing (TWN 2001). Also, in the absence of reliable data on the trade-in-service sector, developing countries took part in the GATS negotiations like a "blindfolded person in a dark room chasing a black cat" (Raghavan 2000).

19. That the ultimate GATS agreement was reached at the UR with the following elements bears distinct marks that the agreement was pushed by transnational businesses.

20. Stern (2002, 253–257) summarizes various estimates of welfare affects of trade liberalization in services, ranging between $9.6 billion and $42.4 billion annually (see Table 26.6). Some of these estimates show substantial increases in welfare "both in absolute terms and as a percentage of GNP in both industrial and developing countries," when all sectors—agriculture, manufacturers, and service—are taken into consideration.

21. Developing countries less affected by the financial crisis, such as China and India, however, had a dynamic growth rate in their trade in commercial services in the second half of the 1990s. India, for example, had an average annual growth rate of almost 20 percent, mainly accounted for by computer and information services. See Maurer and Chauvet (2002).

22. Disputes between WTO members about compliance of the TRIPS agreement are subject to the WTO dispute settlement procedures, and between 1995 and 2002, the dispute settlement procedures were invoked 24 times—the United States was the complainant 16 times and the EU was the complainant six times.

23. Of course, the jurisdiction of TRIPs is much wider than that of the Geneva-based WIPO, which is mainly concerned with the administration of the Paris Convention on patents, the Berne Convention on copyrights, the Rome Convention on sound recording and music, and the Treaty on Intellectual Property in respect of Integrated Circuits. For details on these treaties see Hoekman and Kostecki (2001, 280–283).

24. Many developing countries, on the other hand, opposed the agreement, arguing that adoption of stronger intellectual property rights would be an infringement on their domestic policy, that the alleged piracy hardly affected businesses in the Western world, and stronger legal rules on intellectual protection would be detrimental to their welfare and development prospects.

25. Some even challenge the motive of developed countries in imposing IPR regimes in the fag end of the twentieth century, while they themselves took advantage of nonprotection of intellectual rights when they grew a century ago. Some also challenge the patent rights obtained by developed countries decades or a century ago, which are "deficient" by contemporary standards (Chang, 2000). Others point out the relatively recent adherence of patent laws in advanced countries, especially with respect to pharmaceuticals and chemical products. For example, Germany and France patented pharmaceutical products in 1967, Italy did so in 1979, while Spain did it in 1992. When it comes to chemical substances, Germany established patent rights in 1967, while Nordic countries did do in 1968, Japan did it in 1976, while Spain did in 1992. "Yet the developing countries of today are asked to adhere to IPR standards that would effectively prevent them from taking the same technological path as

the developed countries" (TWN 2001). Pharmaceutical patents are particularly hurting IV/AIDS patients, as the price difference between patent-protected brands and the generic nonprotected versions is just outrageous. For example, a year's supply of three patent-protected HIV/AIDS medicines costs $10,000–$15,000 in the United States, while the similar combination offered by an Indian generic drug producer costs around $350–$600. Similarly, a 2001 Oxfam study, cited in TWN (2001), found that generic drug producers are marketing the AIDS drug fluconazole in Thailand at $0.29, in India at $0.64, whereas patent-protected brands are sold at $10.50 in Kenya, $27 in Guatemala, and $8.25 in South Africa.

26. Aside from the TRIPS, developing countries are also concerned with the implications of the Sanitary and Phytosanitary Measures (SPM) on their agricultural exports. The SPM seeks to impose Western standards on goods produced around the world. Developing countries, especially the LDCs, lack scientific equipment and technologies to cope up with such requirements.

27. Article 27.3 (b) of TRIPS relates to patent rights on plants and animals. Similar viewpoints were expressed by Das (1998).

28. Of course, there are other arguments as well, such as concerns for human and labor rights, the plea that there are certain basic labor and human standards that have to be observed—the so-called psychic or moral spillover arguments that would resist gross and large-scale abuses. See Steiner and Alston (1996) and Tay (2002).

29. The United States banned tuna imports from Mexico, alleging that Mexican fishing boats did not use the dolphin-friendly nets required under US regulations. Another famous example of an environmental issue involved in international trade was the shrimp-turtle case. The root of the case lay with the fact that in many countries fishermen caught turtles while catching shrimp as they lacked what is called a turtle exclusion device (TED), designed by the US National Marine Fisheries Services. In 1989 the US Congress prohibited imports of shrimps from countries that did not use TED to reduce the incidence of turtle deaths, but the law excluded several countries with which the United States were negotiating settlements. The law, however, came into full force, to all shrimp-importing countries, in 1995 with the US Court of International Trade ruling to that effect.

Conclusion

Not long ago, Francis Fukuyama (1989) saw "The End of History" with the end of the Cold War that saw the "ultimate triumph of Western liberal democracy" with the twentieth century returning "full circle to where it started," to "an un-abashed victory of economic and political liberalism," defying convergence between capitalism and socialism as many liberals and nonliberals predicted, or possibility of communist utopia as the eventual culmination of deterministic dialectical process that Marxists so feverishly professed and fought for during the best part of the twentieth century. And then came Samuel P. Huntington's (1993) prophetic claims that the fundamental source of conflict in the new world "will not be primarily ideological or primarily economic," that "the dominating force of conflict will [rather] be cultural," that the "principal conflicts of global politics will occur between nations and groups of different civilizations," and that the "fault lines between civilizations will be the battle lines of the future."

With such euphoria sweeping across the world in the immediate aftermath of the long and protracted Cold War, with history coming into full circle with a triumphant liberal democracy, clash of civilizations shifting grounds away from economic and political ideologies to cultural fronts, and the global community effectively moving toward a unipolar world, developing countries were left with no credible alternative but to opt for neoliberal ideals that were aggressively pushed forward by grandiose victors, embracing laissez-faire capitalism and Western democracy as the synonyms of growth and development.

Historically, the neoliberal globalists pushed forward such an ideological agenda through the Bretton Woods institutions, but with the triumphant victory in the Cold War, the WTO was founded to epitomize inflexible imperatives of these nations under the guise of the so-called "Washington Consensus," or "the Golden Straightjacket," or "single-undertaking approach," as the most favored path to growth and prosperity. The WTO, by its design and undertaking, emerged as the banner-carrier free-market multilateral organization that not only called for unprecedented scale of liberalization of economies across the world, but also promised that such liberalizations will bring prosperity to all nations. The ideological baggage that accompanied the emergence of the WTO underpinned the postulations of mainstream economic theory that assured all countries, including scores of institutionally and structurally handicapped economies, that liberalization will bring prosperity to all parts of the world, and that market forces will eventually correct irregularities associated with unequal global-distribution patterns.

Although many developing countries had reservations with the "ideological baggage" of the WTO or the so-called "single-undertaking approach" that came as its hallmark, and were less enthusiastic in signing up for the WTO, which, to many of them, essentially symbolized unabashed commitment to new world order that epitomized unquestioned supremacy of neoliberalism over anything else ever tried or professed anywhere in the world, such was the milieu in the post–Cold War world that they had little option but to go along with the wind. It is not that all developing countries were herded into accepting the new multilateral trade regimes of the WTO; buoyed away with the euphoria of the end of Cold War or the end of history, or the shifting grounds for clash of civilizations, many of them even expected that rising tides will raise all boats—they will also have their legitimate share in the ensuing global prosperity. The member-driven decision making structure of the WTO—as opposed to staff-driven organizations like the World Bank and the IMF—also emboldened beliefs among member countries that despite neoliberal birthmarks strewn across all its agreements, the WTO can be geared to the interests and options of developing countries as well.

Those hopes and promises, however, have not materialized so far. Objective conditions in the contemporary world economy quite convincingly indicate that benefits of economic liberalization or globalization are increasingly accruing to industrialized countries, while most of the developing countries, albeit with the exception of a few newly industrialized economies, and almost all the LDCs, are increasingly being marginalized. The evidence is striking and compelling—no matter whether viewed in terms of flows of finance, trade and technology, trends in economic growth, standard of living, or economic disparity. Worse still, although all WTO rounds since the Marrakech Declaration reiterated commitments to reverse the processes of marginalization and mainstreaming the LDCs in the global economy, the process of marginalization has actually been deepening further, rather than softening, in recent years and decades. The momentum toward globalization seems to be pursued at the expense of the poorest countries, as if the global community is willing to write off one-tenth of the humanity that lives in the LDCs—creating "pockets of persistent poverty in the global economy" (UNCTAD 2000b).

The seemingly inexorable process of marginalization of the LDCs in the contemporary world economy raises serious doubts about the credibility and claims of mainstream economic theory that free trade would benefit all countries irrespective of their level of development, industrial and technological capabilities, and other structural characteristics. At the same time, protectionist trade regimes pursued by developing countries, under the so-called special and differential treatment measures granted by the GATT/WTO trade regimes, have not only failed to promote economic growth and industrialization in many developing countries, but also led to counterdevelopments and dysfunctional consequences in some of those countries. Serious questions have also been raised whether preferential treatments have led to trade retardation rather than trade creation, whether such preferences were guided more by the interests of developed countries, rather than the real concern for eradicating poverty and reducing marginalization of the LDCs. The LDCs are actually caught in a unique dilemma—while fifty years of preferential treatments hardly helped them to move to a track of sustainable growth, they are also least prepared to compete in a liberal global trading system in which all contracting parties must adhere to the same or almost the same set of rules.

At the same time, developing countries in general, and the LDCs in particular, continue to be greatly disserved by the WTO trade regimes, as two of the major sectors of export interest to these countries—agriculture and textiles and clothing—still face formidable trade barriers in developed-country markets. Agriculture is the key sector for income or growth potentials of the LDCs, or reduction of poverty in these countries. Thanks to complicated interpretations of the UR agreement on agriculture, and deeply entrenched and powerful vested interests in industrialized countries, resistance to agricultural trade liberalization has not diminished in developed countries, reduction of governmental support to domestic production as well as exports has not materialized at the scale as was promised or expected, and developing countries are yet to receive the promised benefits from agricultural trade liberalization—the so-called structural transformation in global agricultural production and consumption still remains a pipe dream. With promised growth in agricultural exports in jeopardy, the LDCs are being effectively turned into backwaters of global prosperity.

Similarly, international trade in the textiles and clothing sector, another sector of great export interest to the LDCs, has long been characterized by a high level of protection, almost systematically orchestrated by the developed world. Although the cost of protection had been exorbitant for the consumers in the developed world and bitter for the developing exporting countries as restricted access and discriminatory trade practices under the MFA regimes gravely hindered their growth potential, complete elimination of the MFA regime and full integration of the textiles and clothing sector into GATT 1994 is not likely even after the phasing out of the MFA regime. Trade in textiles and clothing will face high tariffs and tariff peaks in developed countries even after the complete phasing out of the MFA.

But the world is now well into what we called the third wave of globalization, in which, cross-border trade and foreign direct investment, production, and marketing have been increasing in massive scale and magnitude, affecting every corner of every country in the world. And in this new world, as Sachs (1998) points out, poorer nations have been incorporated in the global system, through trade, finance, and production and a growing web of treaties and institutions, "as partners and market participants rather than colonial dependencies." What is needed is to make sure that the world system actually treats the poorer nations as "partners and market participants," that the benefits of globalization are fairly shared with the four-fifths of the world's population who live in developing countries. What needed is to understand that all critics of globalization are not "knee-jerk protectionists who do not understand the principle of comparative advantage and the complexities of trade laws and institutions" (Rodrik 1997), and that contemporary theory of economic development must address "consciousness and culture seriously as the matrix within which economic behavior is formed" (Fukuyama 1989).

What is needed is reinventing of neoliberalism itself—the archetypical foundation of the contemporary momentum toward globalization—by buttressing its logic of capital and profit through injections of concerns for justice and fairness in the access to the wealth created by the world's finite resources. For globalization to succeed, neoliberals must provide modus operandi to turn "have-nots" into "have" nations in the twenty first century (Kennedy 1993), otherwise no defense of globalization will work, rather discontent will grow in leaps and bounds. There is no question that globalization is needed, there is no question of turning back—humankind pays awful prices for turning back, as that means turning back on other nations, reversal of growth and prosperity and peace and security of humankind itself. The central issue is not that humankind does not need institutions for global governance, it is just that such institutions should be freed from the clutches of wicked minds, from mindless profit seekers, shrewd power mongers, and organized vested interests.

For the LDCs, the central question is not how to reverse the processes of liberalization and globalization, but how to make these processes work for the reversal of their marginalization in the contemporary world economy. For them the central problem is that globalization is still largely "about the winners continuing to win and the losers continuing to lose,"[1] while the world community suffers from the "20-year-old credibility problem" over commitments to reverse processes that marginalize them.[2] The problem is further multiplied by the fact that developing countries are being asked to commit further liberalizations, in issues that are clearly in the interest of developed countries, while they have so far hardly reaped benefits from the areas that are already liberalized, and crucial sectors of export interest to them still face severe trade protection in developed country markets. The experience with the GATT/WTO trade regimes clearly indicates that the global trading system has failed to guarantee nondiscrimination in trade policies, or fairness in trade outcomes, when it comes to the interests and concerns of developing countries and the LDCs.

Any attempt to make the globalization process work, or, for that matter, turning the WTO into an effective organization, must address its credibility problem first—the promises made must be kept, the decisions must be transparent, decision makers and enforcers must be accountable, and, above all, the will of a few powerful members cannot be passed on as the will of the WTO itself. Second, objective reality must be reckoned with—that benefits of globalization are largely accruing to a few industrialized countries, while one-tenth of the humanity who live in the LDCs is increasingly being marginalized, must be acknowledged and acted upon. A responsible watchdog institution cannot promote interests of a few, while disserving others. Third, decision-making structures of the WTO need thorough overhauling—not only has the so-called Green Room Process outlived its usefulness, it has become highly counterproductive. Of the five WTO ministerials held so far, two ended in fiasco or failure—that's a 40 percent failure rate. A clear message has to be sent that the WTO decision-making structure is capable of addressing interests of all members, not only the powerful countries or transnational corporations, and that its platform is equipped with mechanisms to address inequalities in bargaining power in multilateral trade negotiations.

Most important, devising a pragmatic and effective package for mainstreaming LDCs in the world economy poses a serious challenge for the global community in general, and for the WTO in particular. One of the prime tasks of the WTO, at this critical juncture of its evolution, has to be undertaking of thoughtful and far-sighted actions to reverse the processes of marginalization of LDCs. Unless WTO can ensure greater market access for goods of export interest to LDCs, and a fair share for the LDCs in the benefits stemming from liberalization of trade, and unless it can thoroughly revamp special and differential treatment (SDT) measures that have disserved the LDCs, the WTO will never succeed in reversing marginalization of the LDCs. Following are some suggestions that could be useful in devising any meaningful strategy for reversing the processes of marginalization of the LDCs, and, thereby, integrating them into the fiercely competitive and rapidly changing global economy.

First, appoint an independent global commission for the LDCs. An independent global commission—composed of leading international trade theorists and practitioners, distinguished global personalities, representatives from both developed and developing countries and key multilateral institutions, and nongovernmental organizations—will examine the GATT/WTO trade regimes from the perspectives of interests, capabilities, and options of the LDCs in the contemporary world economy. The commission, much like the Haberler Commission of the 1950s, will evaluate preferential treatments to identify pitfalls and dysfunctional consequences of those measures, and recommend appropriate measures that can play an effective role in mainstreaming LDCs in the global economy. It will reexamine the so-called "single-undertaking approach" of the WTO to see how that helps or hinders interests of the LDCs. It will also examine the aid policies of developed countries and multilateral institutions to make sure that they are geared to actual growth and development of the LDCs. Experience with aid, notwithstanding claims by the World Bank and IMF, indicates that foreign aid policies are largely geared to the needs and preference of donors, and compromised by powerful nexus between donors and inefficient and corrupt bureaucracies in poorer countries.[3] Above all, the commission will separate the wheat from the chaff, it will prescribe a transparent, predictable, free, and fair international trade regime, which will ensure equitable benefits for developing countries, especially for the LDCs, from the processes of globalization and liberalization.

Second, establish an exclusive think tank for the LDCs. It is obvious that meaningful integration of the LDCs into the global economy would require nothing less than building development capabilities, raising efficiency levels, lowering wastages, and enhancing their trade participation, negotiation, and bargaining capacities. One way to accomplish such a feat would be to establish an exclusive think tank for the LDCs. The LDCs may establish a formal institution—titled the Organization of the Least Developed Countries (OLDC). The think tank will work as its central secretariat, just as the OECD works for the interests of industrially advanced countries. The resources currently going to build trade and development capacities, under the soc-called Integrated Framework, can be pooled together so that all LDCs, under the guidance of centralized institutional capabilities of the OLDC secretariat, may be able to articulate their needs and concerns more rigorously, enabling them to negotiate with their counterparts in multilateral trade negotiations more efficiently. Currently, UNCTAD serves a great purpose in projecting the case of the LDCs, but it works under the UN system. Perhaps UNCTAD can be converted into an exclusive think tank for the proposed OLDC to serve as a catalyst for identifying opportunities and challenges associated with the globalization and liberalization processes for the LDCs.

Third, ensure meaningful market access for LDC goods. Most immediate attention, however, should be concentrated on ensuring market access for the developing countries and the LDCs. It is amazing that the LDCs, which command just about 0.5 percent of world trade, face so many trade restrictions in developed countries. Even if all restrictions were removed, the LDCs would take a long time to double or triple their shares in global trade. And even if they are able to accomplish such a feat, they would still control less than 2 percent of global trade. Unless the walls of protectionism in the developed world is dismantled and the tangled webs of protectionist rules and regimes are tore apart, no attempt to reduce or reverse the processes of marginalization of the LDCs will succeed.

With developed countries taking advantage of the end-loaded transition schedule of textile and clothing, commercially meaningful integration of the sector still remains a far cry. Still, trade in the agricultural sector is conditioned by a plethora of tariff and nontariff barriers, compounded by dominance of multinational businesses, and thanks to resistance from developed countries, market access negotiations in agriculture still remains as acrimonious as ever. It is simply unconscionable to demand further liberalization of trade regimes in developing countries and the LDCS—as is being done under various UR agreements such as GATS and TRIPS and under the so-called new generation issues—without ensuring a proper share of these countries in the benefits stemming from liberalization of trade. No failure of the WTO could be more perilous or more pronounced than the failure to ensure greater market access for goods originating in developing countries and LDCs, and similarly, no success of the WTO will be more magnanimous or more credible than success in this area.

Finally, strengthen authority and participation of the LDCs in multilateral institutions. The goal of reversal of marginalization of the LDCs in the global economy cannot be achieved without providing an effective platform for promoting the interests of developing countries and the LDCs. Such an initiative would require, first, strengthening of authority and participation of the LDCs in the decision-making structures and processes of the Bretton Woods institutions. These institutions exert awful influence and power over domestic and international economic, financial, and trade policies of the LDCs, leaving little scope for these countries to shape their own governance and policy making. There is no doubt that by design or default, these institutions promote primarily the interests of developed countries, and often impose "the same-size-fits-all" kind of off-the-shelf strategies that prolong, rather than shorten, dependence on global businesses and investments, contributing to further marginalization of these countries.

The WTO platform, although much better than the Bretton Woods institutions, needs overhauling too, especially with respect to the so-called Green Room Process. Taken together, efficiency, transparency, and accountability of all three institutions—the World Bank, the IMF, and the WTO—are essential for improving global governance. What is needed is an immediate global initiative to thoroughly revamp all these multilateral institutions, through a watershed event, like the Bretton Woods Conference or the Marrakech Declaration, to make third-wave globalization work for all nations—be they large or small, rich or poor, bastions of global prosperity, in search of prosperity, or in the backwaters of global prosperity.

NOTES

1. Malaysian prime minister Mahathir bin Mohamad's U Thant Memorial Lecture entitled "Globalization, Global Community and the United Nations," presented at the United Nations University, Tokyo, on June 7, 2001.

2. Former Secretary-General of UNCTAD Ruben Ricupero, while launching the Third UN Conference on Least Developed Countries (LDCs) in Brussels in 2001 (*UN Chronicle.* Issue 4. 2000).

3. Bangladesh, the largest of the LDCs, provides a glaring example in this respect. This country is perhaps the largest recipient of foreign aid among the LDCs, and continues to be so, although for the last three consecutive years it has been ranked as the most corrupt country in the world by the Berlin-based Transparency International. Most of this corruption has to do with official transactions; still aid flow to the country is on the rise. Bangladesh, however, is no exception. Numerous studies show that foreign aid has been a primary source of bureaucratic and political corruption in poorer countries.

References

ADB (Asian Development Bank). (2000). *Asian Development Outlook 2000.* Manila: Oxford University Press.

———. (2001). *Asian Development Outlook 2001.* Manila: Oxford University Press.

Adlung, Rudolf, and others. (2002). The GATS: Key Features and Sectors. In *Development, Trade and the WTO: A Handbook,* eds. Barnard Hoekman, Aaditya Matoo, and Philip English. (2002). Washington, DC: World Bank. 259–279.

Agenor, Pierre-Richard. (2002). Does Globalization Hurt the Poor? Washington, DC: World Bank. Draft Paper.

Aggarwal, V. (1985). *Liberal Protectionism: The International Politics of Organized Textile Trade.* Berkeley: University of California Press.

Ajami, Fouad. (1993). The Summoning. Reprinted in *Globalization and the Challenge of a New Century—A Reader,* eds. Patrick O'Meara, Howard Mehlinger, and Mathew Krain (2000). Bloomington: Indiana University Press. 63–70.

Amjadi, Azita, Ulrich Reinke, and Alexander Yeats. (2000). Did External Barriers Cause the Marginalization of Sub-Saharan Africa in World Trade? Washington,, DC: International Trade Division.

Anderson, James E. (1997). The Uruguay Round and welfare in some distorted agricultural economies. Boston College and NBER paper, sponsored by the World Bank.

Anderson, K., and Tyres, R. 1995. How Developing countries could gain from agricultural trade liberalization in the Uruguay Round. In *Agricultural Trade Liberalization: Implications for Developing Countries,* eds. I. Goldin and O. Knudsen (1995). Paris: OECD.

Anderson, K. (1999). Agriculture, Developing Countries and the WTO Millennium Round. Paper presented at the World Bank's Conference on Agriculture and the New Trade Agenda from a Development Perspective. October 1–2.

Anderson, K., B. Hoekman, and A. Strutt. (1999). Agriculture and the WTO: Next Steps. Washington, DC: World Bank

Anderson, K., Erwidodo, and M. Ingco. (1999). Integrating Agriculture into the WTO: the Next Phase. The WTO/World Bank Conference on Developing Countries in a Millennium Round, WTO Secretariat, Geneva, 20-21 September 1999.

Appleyard, Dennis R., and Alfred J. Field. 2001. *International Economics*. Fourth Edition. New York: McGraw-Hill.

Bacchetta, Marc, and Bijit Bora. (2003). Industrial Tariff Liberalization and the Doha Development Agenda. Geneva: World Trade organization, Development and Economic Research Division.

Bairoch, Paul. (1982). International Industrialization levels from 1750 to 1980. Journal of European Economic History 11:268–333.

––––––. (1993). *Economics and World History, Myths and Paradoxes*. London, Harvester.

Bairoch, Paul, and R. Kozul-Wright. (1996). Global Myth: Some Historical Reflections on Integration, Industrialization and Growth in the World Economy. UNCTAD Discussion Paper No 113.

––––––. (1998). Globalization Myths. In *Transnational Corporations and the Global Economy*, eds. Richard Kozul-Wright and Robert Rowthorn (1998). London: Macmillan.

Balassa, B., and Michalopoulous, J. (1985). Liberalizing World Trade. World Bank Discussion Paper. Washington, DC.

Baldwin, Robert E. (1969). The Case against Infant Industry Protection. *Journal of Political Economy* 77:295–305.

––––––. (1996). The Political Economy of Trade Policy: Integrating the Perspectives of Economists and Political Scientists. In *The Political Economy of Trade Policy: Papers in Honor of Jagdish Bhagwati*, eds. Robert Feenstra, Gene Grossman, and Douglas Irwin (1996). Cambridge: MIT Press. 147–173.

Barber, Benjamin R. (1992). Jihad vs. McWorld. Reprinted in *Globalization and the Challenge of a New Century—A Reader*, eds. Patrick O'Meara, Howard Mehlinger, and Mathew Krain (2000). Bloomington: Indiana University Press. 23–33.

Beck, Thorsten. (2000). Financial Dependence and International Trade. Washington, DC: World Bank.

Ben-David, Dan, Hakan Nordstrom and L. Alan Winters. (2001). *Trade, Income Disparity and Poverty*. Geneva: World Trade Organization.

Bergsten, Fred C. (1996). Competitive Liberalization and Global Free Trade: A Vision for the early 21st Century. APEC Working Paper 96–15. Institute for International Economics. Washington, DC.

––––––. (1998). Fifty Years of the GATT/WTO: Lessons from the past for strategies for the future. Presented at the symposium on the World Trading System in Geneva in April 1998, sponsored by the WTO and the Graduate Institute of International Studies in Geneva.

Bhagwati, Jagdish. (1984). Splintering and Disembodiment of Services and Developing Nations. The World Economy, 7:133–144.

––––––. (1988). *Protectionism*. Cambridge: MIT Press.

––––––. (1991). *The World Trading System at Risk*. Princeton: Princeton University Press.

––––––. (2002). *Free Trade Today*. Princeton: Princeton University Press.

––––––. (2004). *In Defense of Globalization*. New York: Oxford University Press.

BIS (Bank of International Settlement). (1996). *International Banking and Financial Market Developments*. Basle: Bank of International Settlement.

Bleaney, N., and D. Greenaway. (1993). Long run trends in the relative prices of primary commodities and in the terms of trade of developing countries. *Oxford Economic Papers* (July).

Bora, Bijit. (2002). Market Access Issues: What's at stake? Geneva: WTO Public Symposium. 29th April. Mimeo.

Brenton, Paul. (2003). Integrating the Least Developed Countries into the World Trading System: The Current Impact of EU Preferences under Everything But Arms. Washington, DC: World Bank. Policy Research Working Paper 3018.

Bridges (Newsletter of the Society for International Development). October 2001, Volume 6, Issue 5.

Bridges (Weekly Trade News Digest). 12 December, 2001; February 19, 2003.

Brittan, Sir Leon. (1996). World Trade and Agriculture: The Challenges Ahead. Address at the Irish Cooperative organization Society (Ireland) on November 4.

Brown, Drusilla K. (1989). Trade and Welfare effects of the European Schemes of the Generalized System of Preferences. *Economic Development and Cultural Change* 37:757–776.

Buffie, Edward. (2001). *Trade Policy in Developing Countries*. Cambridge: Cambridge University Press.

Cable, V. (1987). Textiles and Clothing in a New Round of Trade Negotiations. *World Bank Economic Review*. September.

Chanda, Rupa. (2002). Movement of natural persons and the GATS Major Trade Policy Impediments. In *Development, Trade and the WTO: A Handbook*. Edited by Barnard Hoekman, Aaditya Matoo, and Philip English. Washington, DC: World Bank. 304–314.

Chang, Ha-Joon. (2000). Intellectual Property Rights and Economic Development: Historical Lessons and Emerging Issues. Background paper for UNDP Human Development Report 2001. New York: UNDP.

Clark, Don P., and Simonetta Zarrilli. (1992). Non-Tariff Measures and Industrial Nation Imports of GSP-Covered Products. *Southern Economic Journal* 59 (October): 284–293.

Clark, I. (1999). *Globalization and International Relations*. Oxford: Oxford University Press.

Clark, X., D. Dollar, and A. Kraay. (2001). Decomposing Global Inequality, 1960–99. Washington, DC: World Bank.

Cline, William, R. (1983). *Trade Policies in the 1980s*. Cambridge: MIT Press.

———. (1990). The future of World Trade in Textiles and Apparel. Washington, DC: Institute of International Economics.

Correa, Carlos. (1998). *Implementing the TRIPS Agreement: General Context and Implications for Developing Countries*. Penang, Malaysia: Third World Network.

———. (2000). *Intellectual Property Rights, the WTO and Developing Countries: The TRIPS Agreement and Policy Options*. Penang, Malaysia: Third World Network.

Culpepper, Roy. (2000). Capital Volatility and Long-term Financing For the Poorest Countries. Manila: Asian Development Bank.

Cuyvers, Ludo. (1998). The generalized System of Preferences of the European Union, with special reference to ASEAN and Thailand. Bangkok: Center for ASEAN Studies. March.

DAC Journal—Development Cooperation: 2001 Report, Vol. 3, No. 1 (2002).

Dam, Kenneth. (1970). *The GATT: Law and International Economic Integration.* Chicago and London: University of Chicago Press.

Dan, David, and David H. Papell. (1998). Slowdowns and Meltdowns: Post-war Growth Evidence from 74 countries. *Review of Economics and Statistics* 80:561–571.

Das, Bhagirath Lal. (1998). *Some Suggestions for Improvements in the WTO Agreements.* Penang, Malaysia: Third World Network.

———. 20001. *Negotiations on Agriculture and Services in the WTO: Suggestions for Modalities/Guidelines.* Trade & Development Series No. 10. Penang, Malaysia: Third World Network.

Das, Dilip K. (1999). *The Millennium Round and the Asian Economics.* Manila: Asian Development Bank. Occasional Paper No. 20. November.

———. (2000). Debacle at Seattle: The Way the Cookie Crumbled. *Journal of World Trade.* 34: 181–201.

Dean, J., S. Desai, and J. Reidel. (1994). Trade Policy Reform in Developing Countries since 1985. A review of the evidence. World Bank Discussion Paper No. 267.

Dee, P., and Hanslow, K. (2000). Multilateral Liberalization of Services Trade. Staff Research Paper. Canberra: Productivity Commission. March.

Delich, Valentina. (2002). Developing countries and the WTO Dispute Settlement System. In *Development, Trade and the WTO: A Handbook,* eds. Barnard Hoekman, Aaditya Matoo, and Philip English (2002). Washington, DC: World Bank. 71–80.

Dickerson, Kitty G. (1991). *Textiles and Apparel in the International Economy.* New York: Macmillan Publishing Company.

Dollar, D. (1992). Outward-oriented developing countries really do grow more rapidly—evidence from 95 LDCs, 1976–1985. *Economic Development and Cultural Change* 40:523–44.

Dollar, D., and Aart Kraay. (2001). Trade, Growth and Poverty. Washington, DC: World Bank. Development Research Group.

Dowlah, Caf. (1998). The Agreement on Textile and Clothing under the Uruguay Round: A Mixed Bag for the Developing Countries? *BIISS Journal.* Vol. 19. No. 2.

———. (1999). The Future of the Readymade Clothing Industry of Bangladesh in the Post-Uruguay Round World. *The World Economy.* September.

———. (2001). Agriculture and the New WTO Round: Economic Analysis of Interests and Options for Bangladesh. Presented at the Workshop on A New WTO Round on Agriculture, SPS, and the Environment: Capturing the benefits for South Asia. Jointly organized by the World Bank, the UNCTAD and the SAARC Secretariat. New Delhi. January 11–13.

———. (2002). Dynamics of Food-assisted Development Strategies in Bangladesh. *The International Journal of Social Welfare.* Vol.11. Issue 1.

———. (2003a). Mainstreaming Least Developed Countries into Global Economy—Does Continuation of Special and Differential Treatment Measures Make Sense? Presented at the International Conference on Economic Development and Fair Trade, organized by the Tsinghua University, Beijing, and Oxfam, Hong Kong, on October 24–26, in Beijing.

———. (2003b). Agriculture and the New Trade Agenda in the WTO Negotiations: Economic Analysis of Interests and Options for Bangladesh. In *Direction in Development: Agriculture, Trade, and the WTO in South Asia,* ed. Merlinda D. Ingco (2003). Washington, DC: World Bank.

———. (2004). Multilateral Trade Negotiations under The GATT/WTO: How They contribute to the Marginalization of the Least Developed Countries in the World Economy? Presented at International Conference of New England Business Administration Association, held on May 14–15, 2004 at Southern Connecticut State University, New Haven.

Drahos, Peter. (2003). When the weak bargain with the strong: Negotiations in the WTO. Paper presented at the International Conference Harmonious Development and Fair Trade in Beijing. Organized by the Tsinghua University, Beijing and Oxfam, Hong Kong on October 24–26.

ECOSOC (UN Economic and Social Council). (2003). Report of the fourth session of Committee for Development Policy. *News From ECOSOC.* Volume 2, Number 1.

Edwards, M. (1999). *Future Positive: International Cooperation in the 21st Century.* London: Earthscan.

Edwards, Sebastian. (1993). Openness, trade liberalization and growth in developing countries. *Journal of Economic Literature* 31:1358–393.

Einarsson, Peter. (2000). Agricultural trade policy as if food security and ecological sustainability mattered. Swedish Society for Nature Conservation and the Program of Global Studies. Sweden.

Erzan, R., and Holmes, P. (1990). Phasing Out the Multi-Fiber Arrangement. *The World Economy* 13:191–211.

EU Food Security Network. (1999). Overview of the GATT Agreement on Agriculture. Solagral. April.

European Communities. (1999). The Relevance of Fundamental WTO Principles of National Treatment, Transparency and Most Favored Nation Treatment to Competition Policy and Vice Versa, communication to the WTO, 12 April 1999.

EUROSTAT. 1997. *Internal and External Trade of the European Union (04 #1996).* Brussels: European Union.

FAO (Food and Agricultural Organization). (1998). *Impact of the Uruguay Round on Agriculture.* Rome: FAO.

———. (2000). *Agriculture, Trade and Food Security*, Vol. I. Rome: Food and Agriculture Organization.

———. (2001a). *Agriculture, Trade and Food Security,* Vol. II. Rome: Food and Agriculture Organization.

———. (2001b). The Role of Agriculture in the Development of LDCs and their Integration into the World Economy. Paper prepared for the Third United Nations Conference on LDCs, Brussels, 14–20 May, 001.

FAOSTAT (online FAO Statistical Database—http://apps.fao.org/page/collections?subsd=agriculture) August 2000. Rome: Food and Agriculture Organization.

Finger, Michael J., and Alan L. Winters. (2002). Reciprocity in the WTO. In *Development, Trade, and the WTO—A Reader.* Eds. Bernard Hoekman, Aaditya Mattoo, and Philip English. (2002). Washington, DC: World Bank. 50-61.

Finger, Michael J., and P. Schuler. (1999). Implementation of Uruguay Round Commitments: The Development Challenge. *The World Economy* 23:491–510.

Fitchett, D. 1987. Agriculture. In *The Uruguay Round: A Handbook on the Multilateral Trade Negotiations*, eds. Michael J. Finger and A. Olechoski (1987). Washington, DC: World Bank.

Frankel, J., and D. Romer. (1999). Does Trade Cause Growth? *American Economic Review* 89:379–399.

Fukusaku, Kiichiro. (2000). Special and Differential Treatment for Developing Countries: Does it help those who help themselves? Helsinki: UNU World Institute for Development Economics Research. Working papers No. 197.

Fukuyama, Francis. (1989). The End of History. Reprinted in *Globalization and the Challenge of a New Century—A Reader*, eds. Patrick O'Meara, Howard Mehlinger, and Mathew Krain (2000). Bloomington: Indiana University Press. 161–180.

GATT (General Agreement on Tariffs and Trade). (1958). *Trends in International Trade*. Geneva: GATT.

———. (1954). *Basic Instruments and Documents. Third Supplement*. Geneva: GATT.

———. (1972). *Basic Agreements and Selected Documents*. 18th Supplement. Geneva: GATT

———. (1979). The Tokyo Round of Multilateral Trade Negotiations, Report by the Director-General of GATT. Geneva: GATT.

———. (1984). *Textiles and Clothing in the World Economy. A GATT Analysis of Textile Trade Policies*. Geneva.

———. (1994). A Description of the Provisions Relating to Developing Countries in the Uruguay Round Agreements, Legal Instruments, and Ministerial Decisions. Geneva: COM.TD/510.

Gibbs, M., and M. Mashayekhi. (1998). The Uruguay Round Negotiations on Investment: Lessons for the future. Division on Trade in Goods and Services and Commodities. Geneva: UNCTAD.

Goldin, Ian, Halsey Rogers, and Nicholas Stern. (2001). The Role and Effectiveness of Development Assistance: Lessons from World Bank Experience. Washington, DC: World Bank.

Goldstein, J. (1993). *Ideas, Interests, and American Trade Policy*. Ithaca: Cornell University Press.

Golt, Sidney. (1988). *GATT Negotiations 1986–90: Origins, Issues and Prospects*. London: British-North American Committee.

Grilli, E. R., and M. C. Yang. (1988). Primary product prices, manufactured goods prices, and terms of trade of developing countries: What the long run evidence shows? *World Bank Economic Review*. January.

Griswold, Daniel T. (2001). The Blessings and Challenges of Globalization. Washington, DC: Cato Institute. Center for Trade Policy Studies.

Hamilton, C. (1988). Restrictiveness and International Transmission of the New Protectionism. In *Issues in US-EC Trade Relations*, eds. R. Baldwin, C. Hamilton, and A. Sapir (1988). Chicago: National Bureau of Economic Research and University of Chicago Press.

Harrison, A. (1995). Openness and Growth: A Time Series, Cross Country Analysis for Developing Countries. *NBER Working Paper* no. 5222. August.

Harrison Glenn, et al. (1996). Quantifying the Uruguay Round. In *The Uruguay Round and the Developing Countries*, eds. W. Martin and A. Winters (1996). Washington, DC: World Bank.

Harrison, Glenn, Thomas Rutherford, and David Taylor. (1995). Quantifying the Outcome of the Uruguay Round. *Finance and Development*. December.

Hathaway, Dale E., and Melinda D. Ingco. (1996). Agricultural Liberalization and the Uruguay Round. In *The Uruguay Round and the Developing Countries*, eds. W. Martin and A. Winters (1996). Washington, DC: World Bank.

Healy, Stephen, Richard Pearce, and Michael Stockbridge. (1998). *The Implications of the Uruguay Round Agreement on Agriculture for Developing Countries*. Rome: Food and Agricultural Organization (FAO).

Heckscher, Eli F. (1934). *Mercantilism*, Vols. 1 & 2. London: George Allen and Unwin.

Held, David. (ed). (2000). *A Globalizing World? Culture, Economics, Politics*. London: Routledge.

Helleiner, Gerald K. (2000). Markets, Politics and Globalization: Can the Global Economy Be Civilized? Tenth Raul Prebisch Lecture, Geneva, 11 December.

Heritage Foundation and the *Wall Street Journal*. (2004). The Index of Economic Freedom 2004. Washington, DC: Heritage Foundation.

Hertel, T. W., and W. Martin. (1999). Liberalizing Agriculture and Manufactures in a Millennium Round: Implications for Developing Countries. *The World Economy* 23:455–470.

——— . (2000). Liberalizing agriculture and manufactures in a millennium round: implications for developing countries. *World Economy*: 23–24:455–469.

Hertel, T. W., W. Martin, K. Yanagishima, and B. Dimaranan. (1996). Liberalizing Manufactures Trade in a Changing World Economy. In *The Uruguay Round and the Developing Countries*, eds. W. Martin and A. Winters (1996). Washington, DC: World Bank.

Hirschman, A. (1958). *The Strategies of Economic Development*. New Haven: Yale University Press.

Hirst, P. Q., and G. E. Thompson. (1999). *Globalization in Question: The International Economy and the Possibilities of Governance*. Cambridge: Polity Press.

Hobsbawm, Eric. (1994). *The Age of Empire, 1875–1914*. London: Abacus.

Hodge, James. (2002). Liberalization of Trade in Services in Developing Countries. In *Development, Trade and the WTO: A Handbook*, eds. Barnard Hoekman, Aaditya Matoo, and Philip English. Washington, DC: World Bank.

Hoekman, Barnard. (2002). The WTO: Functions and Basic Principles. In *Development, Trade and the WTO: A Handbook*, eds. Barnard Hoekman, Aaditya Matoo, and Philip English. Washington, DC: World Bank.

Hoekman, Barnard, Aaditya Matoo, and Philip English. (eds.) (2002). *Development, Trade and the WTO: A Handbook*. Washington, DC: World Bank.

Hoekman, Barnard, Francis Ng, and Marcelo Olarreaga. (2002). Eliminating Excessive Tariffs on Exports of Least Developed Countries. Washington, DC: Development Research Group, World Bank.

Hoekman, Barnard, and Kym Anderson. (1999). Developing Countries and the New Trade Agenda. Washington, DC: World Bank. Policy Research Working Paper No. 2125. Development Research Group.

Hoekman, Barnard, and Michael M. Kostecki. (1995). *The Political Economy of the World Trading System: From GATT to WTO*. New York: Oxford University Press.

——— . (2001). *The Political Economy of the World Trading System: The WTO and Beyond*. New York: Oxford University Press.

Howard, Lyall. (1998). Unfinished business—global trade reform in agriculture. *Agribusiness Review*. October.

Hudec, Robert E. (1993). *Enforcing International Trade Law*. Salem, NH: Butterworth.

——— . (1987). *Developing Countries in the GATT Legal System*. London: Trade Policy Research Center.

————. (2002). The Adequacy of WTO Dispute Settlement Remedies: A Developing Country Perspective. In *Development, Trade and the WTO: A Handbook*, eds. Barnard Hoekman, Aaditya Matoo, and Philip English. Washington, DC: World Bank.

Hufbauer, Gary C., and Kimberly A. Elliott. (1994). *Measuring the Costs of Protection in the United States*. Washington, DC: Institute for International Economics.

Huntington, Samuel P. (1993). The Clash of Civilizations? Reprinted in *Globalization and the Challenge of a New Century—A Reader*, eds. Patrick O'Meara, Howard Mehlinger, and Mathew Krain (2000). Bloomington: Indiana University Press.

Hyvarinen, Antero. 2000. Implications of the Implementation of the Agreement of Textiles and Clothing (ATC) on the Developing Countries Producing/Exporting Textiles and Clothing. Brussels: International Trade Center.

IMF (International Monetary Fund) and World Bank. (2002). Market Access for Developing Country Exports—Selected Issues. Washington, DC.

IMF/OECD/UN/World Bank Group (2000). *A better World for All—Progress Towards the International Development Goals*.

Inama, Stefano. (2003). Trade Preferences and the WTO Negotiations on Market Access. Mimeo, United Nations Commission on Trade and Development (UNCTAD). Geneva.

Ingco, Melinda. (1997). Has Agricultural Trade Liberalization Improved Welfare in the Least Developed Countries? Yes. Washington, DC: World Bank. Policy Research Working Paper 1748.

————. (ed). (2003). *Direction in Development: Agriculture, Trade, and the WTO in South Asia*. Washington, DC: World Bank.

Ingco, Melinda, and Tonia Kandiero. (2001). Agriculture and the New WTO Trade Agenda: Experiences, Challenges, Interests and Options for South Asia. Washington, DC. World Bank. Draft Report. May 13.

ITC (International Trade Center). (1996). *Business Guide to the Uruguay Round*. Geneva: ITC and the Commonwealth Secretariat.

————. . 2000. Implications of the Implementation of the Agreement of Textiles and Clothing (ATC) on the Developing Countries Producing/Exporting Textiles and Clothing. Brussels: International Trade Center.

ITCB. (2002). European Union's New GSP Scheme: Final regulation modifies some earlier proposals. Brussels.

Jackson, J. H. (1990). *Restructuring the GATT System*. London: Pinter Publishers.

————. (1992). *The World Trading System*. Cambridge: MIT Press.

————. (1997). *The World Trading System: Law and Policy of International Economic Relations*. Cambridge: MIT Press.

Jenkins, G. P. (1980). *Costs and Consequences of the New Protectionism*. Ottawa: North South Institute.

Jha, Veena. (2002). Environmental Regulation and the WTO. In *Development, Trade and the WTO: A Handbook*, eds. Barnard Hoekman, Aaditya Matoo, and Philip English. Washington, DC: World Bank. 472–484.

Josling, Tim. 1998. International Trade Policy: The TWO Agenda for Agriculture. Paper presented at the Center for Applied Economics and Policy Studies. Massey University, Palmerston North. New Zealand. August 18.

Kaldor, N. (1966). *Causes of the Slow Rate of Economic Growth of the United Kingdom*. Cambridge: Cambridge University Press.

————. (1967). *Strategic Factors in Economic Development*. Ithaca: Cornell University Press.

Kapstein, Ethan B. (1999). *Sharing the Wealth: Workers and the World Economy*. New York: W. W. Norton.

Karsenty, Guy, and Sam Laird. (1987). The Generalized System of Preferences: A Quantitative Assessment of the Direct Trade Effects and of Policy Options. Geneva: UNCTAD Discussion Papers.

Kemper, R. (1980). The Tokyo Round: Results and Implications for Developing Countries. Washington, DC: World Bank Staff Working Paper. No. 372.

Kennedy, Paul. (1993) Preparing for 21st Century: Winners and Losers. Reprinted in *Globalization and the Challenge of a New Century—A Reader*, eds. Patrick O'Meara, Howard Mehlinger, and Mathew Krain (2000). Bloomington: Indiana University Press. 323–354.

Keynes, John Maynard. (1936). *The General Theory of Employment, Interest and Money*. London: Macmillan.

Khor, Martin. 1999. Synergies between Liberalization, Environment and Sustainable Development. Paper presented at the WTO symposium on trade and environment, Geneva, March.

————. (2000). Globalization and the South: Some critical issues. Geneva: UNCTAD Discussion Paper no. 147. April.

————. (2001). Rethinking IPRs and the TRIPS Agreement. Paper presented at the Oxfam seminar on TRIPS, Brussels, March 2001.

Kirmani, N., Molanji, P., and Mayer, T. (1984). Effects of Increased Market Access on Exports of developing Countries. Washington, DC: IMF Staff Paper.

Knappe, Matthias. 2003. Report on the Conference on the Future of Trading in Textiles and Clothing after 2005. Brussels: International Trade Center. 5–6 May.

Konandreas, Panos, and Jim Greenfield. (1996). Uruguay Round commitments on domestic support: their implications for developing countries. *Food Policy* 21:433–446.

Kozul-Wright, R. and Rowthorn, R. E. (eds.) (1998). *Transnational Corporations and the Global Economy*. London: Macmillan.

Krasner, S. (1983). Structural Causes and Regime Consequences: Regimes as Intervening Variables. In *International Regimes*, ed. S. Krasner. Ithaca: Cornell University Press.

Krueger, Anne O. (1974). The Political Economy of the rent seeking society. *American Economic Review*. Vol. 64, No. 3, June.

————. (1978). *Liberalization Attempts and Consequences*. New York: National Bureau of Economic Research.

————. (1999a). Developing Countries and the Next Round of Multilateral Trade Negotiations. Washington, DC: World Bank. Policy Research Paper No. 2118. Development Research Group.

————. (1999b). Trade Creation and Trade Diversion under NAFTA. Cambridge: National Bureau of Economic Research. Working paper 7429.

Krueger, Anne O., M. Schiff, and A. Valdes. (1988). Agricultural Incentives in Developing Countries: Measuring the effects of sectoral and economy-wide policies. *World Bank Economic Review* 2(3):255–271.

Laird, Sam. (2002). Market Access Issues and the WTO: An Overview. In *Development, Trade and the WTO: A Handbook*, eds. Barnard Hoekman, Aaditya Matoo, and Philip English. Washington, DC: World Bank.

Lecomte, Henri-Baerbard. (2000). ACP-EU trade arrangements in a post-Lome World: Towards a successful partnership? *ICTSD Globalization Dialogue—Africa.* May.

Leutwiller, Fritz, et al. (1985). *Trade Policies for a Better Future: Proposals for Action.*
Geneva: GATT.

Lindert, Peter H., and Jeffrey G. Williamson. (2001). Does Globalization Make the World
More Unequal? National Bureau of Economic Research (NBER) Paper 8228. Cambridge, MA.

Lindland, Jostein. (1997). *The Impact of the Uruguay Round on Tariff Escalation in Agricultural Products.* Rome: Food and Agricultural Organization (FAO).

List, Fredrick. (1856). *The National System of Political Economy.* Trans. G. A. Matile, Phil-
adelphia: J. B. Lippincott.

Little, Imd., T. Scitovsky, and M. Scott. (1970). *Industry and Trade in Some Developing
Countries.* Oxford: Oxford University Press.

Lutz, M., and H. W. Singer. (1994). The link between increased trade openness and the
terms of trade: An empirical investigation. *World Development* 22:1697–1709.

MacPhee, Craig R., and Victor I. Oguledo. (1991). The Trade Effects of the US Generalized
System of Preferences, *Atlantic Economic Journal* 19:19–26.

Maddison, A. (1995). *Monitoring the World Economy, 1820–1992.* Paris: OECD.

———. (2001). *The World Economy: A Millennium Perspective.* Paris: OECD.

Martin, R. (1994). Stateless monies, global financial integration, and national economic au-
tonomy: the end of geography. In *Money, Power, and Space,* eds. S. Corbridge et al..
Oxford: Blackwell.

Martin, Will. (2001). Trade Policies and Developing Countries. Washington, DC: World
Bank.

Martin, Will, and Alan Winters. (eds.) (1996). *The Uruguay Round and the Developing
Countries.* Cambridge: Cambridge University Press.

Maskus, Kieth. (1997). The International Regulation of Intellectual Property. Paper presented at IESG Conference, University of Nottingham. October.

———. (2000). *Intellectual Property Rights in the Global Economy.* Washington, DC: Institute for International Economics.

———. (2002). Benefiting from Intellectual Property Protection. In *Development, Trade
and the WTO: A Handbook,* eds. Barnard Hoekman, Aaditya Matoo, and Philip
English. Washington, DC: World Bank.

Mathews, Alan. (2000). Multilateral Trade Reform in Agriculture and the Developing
Countries. Trinity Economic Paper Series. Trinity College. Paper no. 2000/10.

———. (2001). The position of the developing countries in the WTO negotiations on agricultural trade liberalization. Trinity Economic Paper series. Trinity College. Paper
no. 01/01.

Maurer, A., and P. Chauvet. (2002). The Magnitude of Flows of Global Trade in Services.
In *Development, Trade, and the WTO—A Reader.* Eds. Bernard Hoekman, Aaditya
Mattoo, and Philip English (2000). Washington, DC: World Bank. 235–246.

Mayer, Jorg. (2000). Globalization, Technology Transfer and Skill Accumulation in
Low-Income Countries. Helsinki: UN/WIDER.

McCalman, P. (1999). Reaping What you Sow: An Empirical Analysis of International Patent Harmonization. Working Paper in Economics and Econometrics, 374. Canberra:
Australian National University.

McGuire, Dan. (2001). The Structure of World Markets in Wheat, Corn and Rice. Institute
of Agriculture and Trade Policy. Minneapolis.

Mihaelopolous, Constantine. (1999). The Role of Special and Differential Treatment for Developing Countries in GATT and the World Trade Organization. Washington, DC: World Bank Working Paper Series.

———. (2000). Trade and Development in the GATT and WTO: The Role of Special and Differential Treatment for Developing Countries. Washington, DC: World Bank, February 28.

———. (2002). WTO Accession. In *Development, Trade and the WTO: A Handbook*, eds. Barnard Hoekman, Aaditya Matoo, and Philip English. Washington, DC: World Bank.

Mittelhauser, Mark. (1997). Employment Trends in Textiles and Apparel, 1973–2005. *Monthly Labor Review*. August. 24–35

Mukerji, Asoke. (2000). Developing Countries and the WTO: Issues of Implementation. *Journal of World Trade* 34(6):33–34.

Murphy, Sophia. (2002). Managing the Invisible Hand: Markets, Farmers and International Trade. Canada: Institute of Agriculture and Trade Policy.

Myint, H. (1958). The Classical Theory of International Trade and Underdeveloped Countries. *Economic Journal, 68.*

Nayyar, Deepak, and Julius Court. (2002). Governing Globalization: Issues and Institutions. Helsinki: UNU/WIDER. Policy Brief No. 5.

Ng, Francis, and Alexander Yeats. (1996). Open Economies Work Better? Did Africa's Protectionist Policies Cause its Marginalization in World Trade? Washington, DC: World Bank. Policy Research Working Paper No. 1636.

Norgues, Julio J. 2002. Comment to "Trade, Growth, and Poverty—A Selective Survey" by Andrew Berg and Anne Krueger, and "Doha and World Poverty Target," by L. Alan Winters, presented at the Annual World Bank Conference on Development Economics. May.

OECD (Organization for Economic Cooperation and Development). (1997). *The Uruguay Round Agreement on Agriculture and Processed Agricultural Products.* Paris.

———. (1999). Distributional Effect of Agricultural Support in Selected OECD Countries. Paris: Directorate of Food, Agriculture and Fisheries.

———. (2000). *Agricultural Policies in OECD Countries: Monitoring and Evaluation 2000.* Paris: OECD Secretariat.

———. (2002). The Incidence and Income Transfer Efficiency of Farm Support Measures. Paris: Directorate of Food, Agriculture and Fisheries.

Oxfam. (2001). *Patent Injustice: How World Trade Rules Threaten the Health of Poor People.* Oxfam Briefing Paper, London.

Ozden C., and E. Reinhardt, E. (2002a). The Political Economy of US Trade Preferences for Developing Countries, 1976–2000. Manuscript, Emory University.

———. (2002b) The Perversity of Preferences: GSP and Developing Country Trade Policies, 1976–2000. World Bank Policy Research Working Paper. Washington, DC: World Bank.

Pakistan. (2000). Request by Pakistan for an extension of the transition period under the provisions of Article 5.3 of the Agreement on Trade-Related Investment Measures. Submission of Pakistan to the WTO Secretariat. January.

Panic, M. (1988). *National Management of International Economy.* London: Macmillan Press.

Porter, T. (1993). *States, Markets and Regimes in Global Finance.* Basingstoke: Macmillan.

Prebisch, Raul. (1950). *The Economic Development of Latin America and Its Principal Problems.* New York: United Nations.

————. (1959). Commercial Policy in Underdeveloped Economies, *American Economic Review, Papers and Proceedings.* May.

————. (1984). Five Stages in my Thinking on Development. In G. M. Meir and D. Seers. eds. *Pioneers in Development.* New York: Oxford University Press.

Pritchett, Lant. (2000). Understanding Patterns of Economic Growth: Searching for Hills among Plateaus, Mountains, and Plains. Washington, DC: *The World Bank Economic Review.*

Pugel, Thomas A., and Peter H. Lindert. (2000). *International Economics.* New York: Irwin and McGraw-Hill.

Puri, Hardeep, and Philippe Brusick. (1989). Trade-Related Investment Measures: Issues for Developing Countries in the Uruguay Round. In UNCTAD, *Uruguay Round: Papers on Selected Issues.* Geneva: UNCTAD. 203–217.

Raghavan, Chakravarthi. (1993). US, EC Press Others to Fall in Line., *SUNS* #3201, December.

————. (2000). Globalization Policies not Working. London: Third World Network. February.

————. (2001a). Integrated Framework for LDCs and mainstreaming LDCs. London: Third World Network. January.

————. (2001b). Developing Countries Turn Down Guidelines for GATS Talks. *SUNS* #4841, February.

Roberson, D. (2000). Civil Society and the WTO. *The World Economy* 23:1119–1135.

Robertson, R. (1992). *Globalization: Social Theory and Global Culture.* London: Sage.

Robinson, Sherman. (1994). Commentary: GATT Agreement Provides Opportunities for Developing Countries. IFPRI Report. February.

Rodriguez, F., and D. Rodrik. (1999). Trade Policy and Economic Growth: A Skeptic's Guide to the Cross-National Evidence. Discussion Paper No. 2143. Center for Economic Policy Research. May.

Rodrik, Dani. (1997). Has Globalization Gone Too Far? Washington, DC: Institute for International Economics.

————. 1998. Why do more Open Economies have Bigger Governments? *Journal of Political Economy* 106 (5): 997–1032.

————. (2000). Sense and Nonsense in the Globalization Debate. In *Globalization and the Challenge of a New Century—A Reader,* eds. Patrick O'Meara, Howard Mehlinger, and Mathew Krain. Bloomington: Indiana University Press.

————. (ed.) (2003). *In Search of Prosperity: Analytical Narratives on Economic Growth.* Princeton: Princeton University Press.

Rowley, Anthony. (1999). Globalization: A Balance Sheet Approach. Manila: Asian Development Bank.

Ruggie, John. (1992). International regimes, transactions, and change: Embedded Liberalism in the postwar economic order. *International Organization* 36 (2), Spring.

Sachs, Jeffrey. (1998). International Economics: Unlocking the Mysteries of Globalization. Reprinted in *Globalization and the Challenge of a New Century—A Reader,* eds. Patrick O'Meara, Howard Mehlinger and Mathew Krain (2000). Bloomington: Indiana University Press. 217–226.

Sachs, Jeffrey, and Andrew Werner. (1995). Economic Reform and the process of global integration. Brookings Papers on Economic Activity 1:1–118.

Safadi, R., and S. Laird. (1996). The Uruguay Round Agreements: Impact on Developing Countries. *World Development* 24 (7): 1223–1242.

Sally, Razeen. (2003). Whither the WTO? A Progress Report on the Doha Round. Washington, DC: Cato Institute.

Sampson, Gary P. (2000). *Trade, Environment and the WTO: The Post-Seattle Agenda.* Washington, DC: Overseas Development Council.

Sauve, P., and R. Stern. (eds.) (2000). *Services 2000: New Directions in Services Trade Liberalization.* Washington, DC: Brookings Institution.

Schiff, Maurice. (2000). Multilateral trade liberalization, political disintegration, and the choice of free trade agreements versus customs unions. Washington, DC: World Bank, Development Research Department.

Schiff, Maurice, and Alberto Valdes. (1992). The Political Economy of Agricultural Pricing. In *A Synthesis on the Economics of Developing Countries,* World Bank Comparative Study, Vol. 4. Baltimore: Johns Hopkins University Press.

Schmeil, Nadja. (2000). Credibility is issue at May LDC Meeting. The United Nations Chronicle-Online Edition. Volume 37, Number 4.

Schmukler, S., and P. Zoido-Lobaton. (2001). Financial Globalization: Opportunities and Challenges for Developing Counties. Washington, DC: World Bank.

Scholte, Jan A. (2000). *Globalization: A Critical Introduction.* New York: Palgrave.

Scholte, Jan A., and R. O'Brien, and M. Williams. (1999). The World Trade organization and Civil Society. In *Trade Politics,* eds. B. Hocking and S. McGuire. New York: Routledge.

Schott, Jeffrey, J. 1994. *The Uruguay Round: An Assessment.* Washington, DC: Institute for International Economics.

Schott, Jeffrey, J., and J. Watal. (2000). Decision-making in the WTO. *International Economic Policy Briefs* 2000–2002 (March).

Shafaeddin, S. M. (1994). The Impact of Trade Liberalization on Export and GDP Growth in Least Developed Countries. Discussion Paper No. 85. Geneva: UNCTAD.

———. (2000). Free trade or fair trade? Geneva: UNCTAD Discussion Paper No. 153. December.

Shukla, S. P. (2000). From GATT to WTO and Beyond. Helsinki: UNU/WIDER. Working paper no. 195. August.

Shutt, Harry. (1985). *The Myth of Free Trade.* London: Basil Blackwell.

Sinclair, Scott. (2000). *GATS: How the World Trade Organization's New "Services" Negotiations Threaten Democracy.* Ottawa: Canadian Center for Policy Alternatives.

Singer, H. (1950). The distribution of gains between investing and borrowing countries. *American Economic Review,* Papers and Proceedings. 40:473–485.

Smarzynskya, Beata K. (2002). Does Foreign Direct Investment Increase the Productivity of Domestic Firms? In search of spillovers through backward linkages. Washington, DC: World Bank Policy Research Working Paper 2923.

South Center. (2001). LDCs face tightening international poverty trap. Geneva: *The South Bulletin 38.*

———. (2002). Special and Differential Treatment under the WTO. Geneva.

Spraos, J. (1980). The statistical debate on the net barter terms of trade between primary commodities and manufactures , *Economic Journal.* March.

Srinivasan, T. N. (1998). *Developing Countries and the Multilateral Trading System.* Boulder, CO: Westview Press.

Steiner, Henry J., and Philip Alston. (1996). *International Human Rights in Context.* Oxford: Clarendon Press.

Stern, Robert M. (2002). Quantifying Barriers to Trade in Services. In *Development, Trade and the WTO: A Handbook*, eds. Barnard Hoekman, Aaditya Matoo, and Philip English. Washington, DC: World Bank.

Stevens, C. (1999). *The WTO Agreement on Agriculture and Food Security.* London: Commonwealth Secretariat.

Stiglitz, Joseph E. (2000). Globalization and the Logic of International Collective Action: Re-examining the Bretton Woods Institutions. Helsinki: UNU/WIDER.

——— . (2002). *Globalization and Its Discontent.* New York: W. W. Norton.

Subramanium, Arvind. (1994). 'The case for low uniform tariffs. *Finance and Development.* April.

Supper, Erich. (2000). The Post-Uruguay Round Tariff Environment for Developing Country Exports: Tariff Peaks and Tariff Escalation. In *Positive Agenda and Future Trade Negotiations.* Geneva: UNCTAD. 89–123.

Sutherland, Peter, and John Sewell. (2000). Challenge facing the WTO and policies to address global governance. Washington, DC: Overseas Development Council.

Tangermann, Stefan. (1994). An Assessment of the Uruguay Round Agreement on Agriculture. Institute of Agricultural Economics, University of Gottingen, June 1994.

——— . 2002. The future of preferential trading arrangements for developing countries and the current round of WTO negotiations on agriculture. Rome: FAO.

Tangermann, Stefan, and T. Jostling. (1999). The Interests of Developing Countries in the Next Round of WTO Agricultural Negotiations. Paper presented at the UNCTAD Workshop on Developing a proactive and coherent trade agenda for African countries. Pretoria. June 29–July 2.

Tay, Simon. 2002. Trade and Labor: Text, Institutions and Context. In *Development, Trade and the WTO: A Handbook*, eds. Barnard Hoekman, Aaditya Matoo, and Philip English. Washington, DC: World Bank.

Third World Network. (1998). *Options for Implementing the TRIPS Agreement in Developing Countries.* Penang, Malaysia: Third World Network.

——— . (2001). The Multilateral Trading System: A Development Perspective. UNDP.

Thirlwall, A. P. (2003). *Growth and Development: With Special Reference to Developing Economies.* New York: Palgrave.

Thurow, L. 1992. *Head to Head: The Coming Economic Battle among Japan, Europe and America.* New York: Allen and Unwin.

Todaro, M. (1994). *Economic Development.* New York: Longman.

Trela, I., and J. Whalley. (1990a). Unraveling the Threads of the MFA. In *Textile Trade and the Developing Countries: Eliminating the Multifiber Arrangement in the 1990s*, ed. In C. Hamilton. Washington, DC: World Bank.

——— . (1990b). Global Effects of Developed Country Trade Restrictions on Textile and Apparel. *Economic Journal.* December.

——— . 1993. Internal Quota Allocation Schemes and the Costs of the MFA. Center for the Study of International Economic Relations. University of Western Ontario. London.

Tussie, Diana. (1987). *The Less Developed Countries and the World Trading System: A Challenge to the GATT.* London: Pinter Press.

Tussie, Diana, and Miguel F. Lengyel. (2002). Developing Countries: Turning Participation into Influence. In *Development, Trade, and the WTO—A Reader,* eds., Bernard Hoekman, Aaditya Mattoo, and Philip English. Washington, DC: World Bank.

UNCTAD (United Nations Conference on Trade and Development). (1986). *Protectionism and Structural Adjustment.* New York: United Nations.

———. (1994). *The Outcome of the Uruguay Round: Supporting Papers to the Trade and Development Report, 1994.* Geneva: United Nations.

———. (1996). *The TRIPS Agreement and Developing Countries.* Geneva: UNCTAD.

———. (1997). *Trade and Development Report, 1997.* Geneva: United Nations.

———. (1998). *Statistical Year Book 1997.* Geneva: United Nations.

———. (1999a). *The Lest Developed Countries 1999 Report.* Geneva: United Nations.

———. (1999b). Integrating Least Developed Countries into the Global Economy: Proposals for a Comprehensive New Plan of Action in the Context of the Third WTO Ministerial Conference. Geneva: UNCTAD/LDC/106. October 6.

———. (1999c). *Trade and Development Report, 1999.* New York: United Nations.

———. (2000a). *Statistical Profiles of the Least Developed Countries.* Geneva: United Nations.

———. (2000b). *The Lest Developed Countries 2000 Report.* Geneva: United Nations.

———. (2000c). *Positive Agenda and Future Trade Negotiations,* Geneva: UNCTAD

———. (2002). *The Least Developed Countries Report 2002: Escaping the Poverty Trap.* Geneva: United Nations.

———. (2003). *World Investment Report 2003. FDI Policies for Development: National and International Perspectives.* Geneva: United Nations.

UNDP (United Nations Development Program). (1996). *Human Development Report 1996.* New York: United Nations.

———. 1999. *Globalization with a human face—UN Human Development Report 1999.* New York: Oxford University Press.

———. (2000). *Human Development Report 2000.* New York: Oxford University Press.

———. (2003). Human Development Report 2003. New York: Oxford University Press.

———. (2004). Human Development Report 2004. New York: Oxford University Press.

UNIDO (United Nations Industrial Development Organization). (2000). UNIDO Round Table: Marginalization versus Prosperity. Geneva: UNIDO Office For Policy Issues and Strategic Research. Report of Panel 3: Fighting Marginalization through Sustainable Industrial Development.

Unnevehr, Laurian J. (2001). Food Safety and Food Quality. Washington, DC: International Food Policy Research Institute.

USITC (United States International Trade Commission). (1989). *The Economic Effects of Significant US Import Restraints.* Washington, DC: ITC Publication # 2222. October.

Valdes, Alberto. (1999). Overview of the Global Impact of the Uruguay Round and Lessons from Early Reformers. In *Implications of the Uruguay Round Agreement for South Asia: The Case of Agriculture,* eds. Beniot Blarel, Garry Pursell and Alberto Valdes. New Delhi: World Bank.

Valdes, Alberto, and Alex F. McCalla. (1996). The Uruguay Round and agricultural policies in developing countries and economies in transition. *Food Policy* 21:419–431.

Valdes, Alberto, and Joachim Zietz. (1995). Distortions in World Food Markets in the Wake of GATT: Evidence and Policy Implications. *World Development* 23:6:913–926.

Watal, Jayashree. (2002). Implementing the TRIPs Agreement. In *Development, Trade and the WTO: A Handbook*, eds. Barnard Hoekman, Aaditya Matoo, and Philip English. Washington, DC: World Bank.

Watkins, Kevin. (2003). Northern Agricultural Policies and World Poverty: Will the Doha Development Round Make a Difference? *Annual World Bank Conference on Development Economics*. Paris. May 15–16.

Whalley, John. (1990). Non-discriminatory discrimination: Special and Differential Treatments under the GATT for Developing Countries. *Economic Journal* 100:1318–1328.

——— . (1994). Agreement on Textiles and Clothing. In *OECD Documents: The New World Trading System*. Paris: OECD. 73–81.

——— . (1999). Special and Differential Treatment in the Millennium Round. *World Economy*.

Whalley, John, and Colleen Hamilton. (1996). *The Trading System after the Uruguay Round*. Washington, DC: Institute for International Economics.

Wiemann, Jurgen. (2002). Developing countries and the WTO Round: Winners or losers? Or: Winners and Losers? Paper presented at the conference organized by the Research Institute of the DGAP. January 28.

Wolf, Martin. (1990). How to Cut the Textile Knot: Alternative Modalities for Integration into GATT. In *Textiles Trade and the Developing Countries: Eliminating the Multi-fiber Arrangement in the 1990s*, ed. Carl Hamilton. Washington, DC: World Bank.

Woods, Ngaire, and Amrita Narlikar. (2001). Governance and the Limits of Accountability: The WTO, the IMF and the World Bank. *International Journal of Social Science*. November.

World Bank. (1993). *The East Asian Miracle*. New York: Oxford University Press.

——— . (1997) *World Development Report 1997. The State in a Changing World*. New York: Oxford University Press.

——— . (1999). *World Development Indicators*. Washington, DC: World Bank.

——— . (2000). *World Development Report 2000/01: Attacking Poverty*. New York: Oxford University Press.

——— . (2002). *Globalization, Growth, and Poverty*. Washington, DC: World Bank and Oxford University Press.

——— . (2003a). *Global Economic Prospects: Realizing the Development Promise of the Doha Agenda, 2004*. Washington, DC: World Bank.

——— . (2003b). *World Development Report 2004*. New York: Oxford University Press.

WTO (World Trade Organization). (1998a). Major Review of the Implementation of the Agreement on Textiles and Clothing in the First Stage of the Integration Process. WTO Document G/C/W/105, February 4.

——— . (1998b). *Annual Report (Globalization and Trade)*. Geneva: WTO.

——— . (1999). Proposals for Addressing Concerns of Marginalization of Certain Small Economies. WT/CC/W/361. Geneva. October.

——— . (2000a). Agricultural Trade Performance by Developing Countries, 1990–1998, Background Paper by the WTO Secretariat, Geneva, May 23.

——— . (2000b). Integrated Framework for Trade-related assistance to LDCs: The process to date, concerns and suggested improvements. Geneva: WT/Comtd/LDC/W/18.

——— . (2001a). Ministerial Declaration. Doha: WTO Ministerial Conference. 9–14 November.

———. (2001b). Preparation for the Fourth Session of the Ministerial Conference: Draft Ministerial Declaration Revision. October.

———. (2001c). Declaration on the TRIPS Agreement and Public Health, adopted 14 November.

———. (2001d). GATS—Fact and Fiction. Geneva: WTO.

———. (2002). *World Trade Development in 2001 and Prospects for 2002.* Geneva: WTO.

———. (2003a). *Trade Policy Trends in WTO Members.* Geneva: WTO.

———. (2003b). *World Trade Report 2003.* Geneva: WTO.

Yang, Y. (1993). The impact of the Phasing out on World Clothing and Textile Markets. National Center for Development Studies, Australian National University, Canberra, Australia.

Zakaria, Fareed. (1997). The Rise of Illiberal Democracy. Reprinted in *Globalization and the Challenge of a New Century—A Reader*, eds. Patrick O'Meara, Howard Mehlinger, and Mathew Krain (2000). Bloomington: Indiana University Press.

Zanzibar Declaration. (2001). The Least Developed Countries Trade Ministers' Meeting. Zanzibar, United Republic of Tanzania. July.

Zysman, J. (1983). *Governments, markets and growth: Financial systems and the politics of Industrial Change.* Ithaca: Cornell University Press.

Index

About the Author

CAF DOWLAH is Professor of Economics, and Director, Center of Economics Education at the City University of New York, Queensborough College. He also heads the Division of Economic Analysis and Global Cooperation of the City University of New York International Center for Environmental Resources and Development (ICERD). Previous publications of the author include *The Life and Times of Soviet Socialism* (Praeger, 1997) and *Soviet Political Economy in Transition: From Lenin to Gorbachev* (Greenwood, 1992).